# U•X•L Encyclopedia of World Mythology

**VOLUME 5:** Q–Z

# U•X•L Encyclopedia of World Mythology

VOLUME 5: Q–Z

**U·X·L**
*A part of Gale, Cengage Learning*

Detroit • New York • San Francisco • New Haven, Conn • Waterville, Maine • London

**U·X·L Encyclopedia of World Mythology**

Product manager: Meggin Condino

Project editor: Rebecca Parks

Editorial: Jennifer Stock, Kim Hunt

Rights Acquisition and Management: Kelly A. Quin, Scott Bragg, Aja Perales

Composition: Evi Abou-El-Seoud

Manufacturing: Rita Wimberley

Imaging: Lezlie Light

Product Design: Jennifer Wahi



Cover photographs reproduced by permission of Purestock/Getty Images (picture of Statue of Poseidon); Voon Poh Le/Dreamstime.com (drawing of paper cut dragon); Werner Forman/Art Resource, NY (picture of an incense burner of a sun god); Charles Walker/Topfoto/The Image Works (photo of a papyrus drawing of Anubis weighing the heart); and The Art Archive/Richard Wagner/Museum Bayreuth/Gianni Dagli Orti (photo of a drawing of a valkyrie).



LIBRARY OF CONGRESS CATALOGING-IN-PUBLICATION DATA

U*X*L encyclopedia of world mythology
p. cm.
Includes bibliographical references and index.
ISBN 978-1-4144-3030-0 (set) -- ISBN 978-1-4144-3036-2 (vol. 1) -- ISBN 978-1-4144-3037-9 (vol. 2) -- ISBN 978-1-4144-3038-6 (vol. 3) -- ISBN 978-1-4144-3039-3 (vol. 4) -- ISBN 978-1-4144-3040-9 (vol. 5)
1. Mythology—Encyclopedias, Juvenile. I. Title: UXL encyclopedia of world mythology. II. Title: Encyclopedia of world mythology.

BL303.U95 2009
201'.303—dc22 2008012696

Gale
27500 Drake
Farmington Hills, MI 48331-3535

ISBN-13: 978-1-4144-3030-0 (set) ISBN-10: 1-4144-3030-2 (set)
ISBN-13: 978-1-4144-3036-2 (Vol. 1) ISBN-10: 1-4144-3036-1 (Vol. 1)
ISBN-13: 978-1-4144-3037-9 (Vol. 2) ISBN-10: 1-4144-3037-X (Vol. 2)
ISBN-13: 978-1-4144-3038-6 (Vol. 3) ISBN-10: 1-4144-3038-8 (Vol. 3)
ISBN-13: 978-1-4144-3039-3 (Vol. 4) ISBN-10: 1-4144-3039-6 (Vol. 4)
ISBN-13: 978-1-4144-3040-9 (Vol. 5) ISBN-10: 1-4144-3040-X (Vol. 5)

This title is also available as an e-book.
ISBN-13: 978-1-4144-3846-7 ISBN-10: 1-4144-3846-X
Contact your Gale, a part of Cengage Learning sales representative for ordering information.

Printed in the United States of America
1 2 3 4 5 6 7 12 11 10 09 08

# *Table of Contents*

# *Table of Contents by Culture*

**BUDDHIST**



**CANAANITE**



**CELTIC**



**CHINESE/TAOIST**



**CHRISTIAN**

## CROSS-CULTURAL



## EGYPTIAN



## FINNISH



## FRENCH



## GERMAN



## GREEK AND ROMAN

# *Reader's Guide*

The *U•X•L Encyclopedia of World Mythology* examines the major characters, stories, and themes of mythologies from cultures around the globe, from African to Zoroastrian. Arranged alphabetically in an A–Z format, each entry provides the reader with an overview of the topic as well as contextual analysis to explain the topic's importance to the culture from which it came. In addition, each entry explains the topic's influence on modern life, and prompts the reader with a discussion question or reading/writing suggestion to inspire further analysis. There are five different types of entries: Character, Deity, Myth, Theme, and Culture. The entry types are designated by icons that are shown in a legend that appears on each page starting a new letter grouping so that you can easily tell which type of entry you are reading.

## Types of Entries Found in This Book

*Character* entries generally focus on a single mythical character, such as a hero. In some cases, character entries deal with groups of similar or related beings—for example, Trolls or Valkyries. Deities (gods) are found in their own unique type of entry.

*Deity* entries contain information about a god or goddess. An example would be Zeus (pronounced ZOOS), the leader of the ancient Greek gods. Deities are very similar to other mythical characters, except that they often appear in many different myths; each Deity entry provides a summary of the most important myths related to that deity.

*Myth* entries focus on a specific story as opposed to a certain character. One example is the entry on the Holy Grail, which tells the legend of the vessel's origins as well as the many people who sought to locate it. In some cases, the myth is primarily concerned with a single character; the entry on the Golden Fleece, for example, features Jason as the main character. Like the Holy Grail entry, however, this entry focuses on the legends surrounding the object in question rather than the character involved.

*Theme* entries examine how one single theme, idea, or motif is addressed in the mythologies of different cultures. An example would be the Reincarnation entry that examines different cultural depictions of this eternal cycle of death and rebirth.

*Culture* entries contain a survey of the myths and beliefs of a particular culture. Each entry also provides historical and cultural context for understanding how the culture helped to shape, or was shaped by, the beliefs of other cultures.

## Types of Rubrics Found in This Book

Each entry type is organized in specific rubrics to allow for ease of comparison across entries. The rubrics that appear in these entries are: *Character/Myth/Theme Overview*; *Core Deities and Characters*; *Major Myths*; *[Subject] in Context*; *Key Themes and Symbols*; *[Subject] in Art, Literature, and Everyday Life*; and *Read, Write, Think, Discuss.* In addition, the character, deity, and myth entries all have key facts sections in the margins that provide basic information about the entry, including the country or culture of origin, a pronunciation guide where necessary, alternate names for the character (when applicable), written or other sources in which the subject appears, and information on the character's family (when applicable).

*Character Overview* offers detailed information about the character's place within the mythology of its given culture. This may include information about the character's personality, summaries of notable feats, and relationships with other mythological characters. *Myth Overview* includes a summary of the myth being discussed. *Theme Overview* provides a brief description of the theme being discussed, as well as a rundown of the major points common when examining that theme in different mythologies.

*Core Deities and Characters* includes brief descriptions of the main deities and other characters that figure prominently in the given culture's mythology. This is not a comprehensive list of all the gods or characters mentioned in a particular culture.

*Major Myths* features a brief summary of all the most important or best-known myths related to the subject of the entry. For example, the entry on Odin (pronounced OH-din), chief god of Norse mythology, includes the tale describing how he gave up one of his eyes in order to be able to see the future.

*[Subject] in Context* provides additional cultural and historical information that helps you understand the subject by seeing through the eyes of the people who made it part of their culture. The entry on the weaver Arachne (pronounced uh-RAK-nee), for instance, includes information on the importance of weaving as a domestic duty in ancient Greece.

*Key Themes and Symbols* outlines the most important themes in the tales related to the subject. This section also includes explanations of symbols associated with the subject of the entry, or which appear in myths related to the subject. For example, this section may explain the meaning of certain objects a god is usually shown carrying.

*[Subject] in Art, Literature, and Everyday Life* includes references to the subject in well-known works of art, literature, film, and other media. This section may also mention other ways in which the subject appears in popular culture. For example, the fact that a leprechaun (pronounced LEP-ruh-kawn) appears as the mascot for Lucky Charms cereal is mentioned in this section of the Leprechauns entry.

*Read, Write, Think, Discuss* uses the material in the entry as a springboard for further discussion and learning. This section may include suggestions for further reading that are related to the subject of the entry, discussion questions regarding topics touched upon in the entry, writing prompts that explore related issues and themes, or research prompts that encourage you to delve deeper into the topics presented.

Most of the entries end with cross-references that point you to related entries in the encyclopedia. In addition, words that appear in bold within the entry are also related entries, making it easy to find additional information that will enhance your understanding of the topic.

## Other Sections in This Book

This encyclopedia also contains other sections that you may find useful when studying world mythology. One of these is a "Timeline of World Mythology," which provides important dates from many cultures that are important to the development of their respective mythologies. A glossary in the front matter supplements the definitions that are included within the entries. Teachers will find the section on "Research and Activity Ideas" helpful in coming up with classroom activities related to the topic of mythology to engage students further in the subject. A section titled "Where to Learn More" provides you with other sources to learn more about the topic of mythology, organized by culture. You will also encounter sidebars in many of the entries; these sections offer interesting information that is related to, but not essential to, your understanding of the subject of the entry.

## Comments and Suggestions

We welcome your comments on the *U•X•L Encyclopedia of World Mythology* and suggestions for other topics to consider. Please write to Editors, *U•X•L Encyclopedia of World Mythology,* Gale, 27500 Drake Rd., Farmington Hills, Michigan, 48331-3535.

# *Introduction*

On the surface, myths are stories of gods, heroes, and monsters that can include fanciful tales about the creation and destruction of worlds, or awe-inspiring adventures of brave explorers in exotic or supernatural places. However, myths are not just random imaginings; they are cultivated and shaped by the cultures in which they arise. For this reason, a myth can function as a mirror for the culture that created it, reflecting the values, geographic location, natural resources, technological state, and social organization of the people who believe in it.

## Values

The values of a culture are often revealed through that culture's myths and legends. For example, a myth common in Micronesian culture tells of a porpoise girl who married a human and had children; after living many years as a human, she decided to return to the sea. Before she left, she warned her children against eating porpoise, since they might unknowingly eat some of their own family members by doing so. Myths such as these are often used to provide colorful reasons for taboos, or rules against certain behaviors. In this case, the myth explains a taboo among the Micronesian peoples against hunting and eating porpoises.

## Geography

Myths often reflect a culture's geographic circumstances. For example, the people of the Norse culture live in a region that has harsh, icy winters. It is no coincidence that, according to their myths, the being whose death led to the creation of the world was a giant made of frost. By contrast, the people of ancient Egypt lived in an dry, sunny land; their most important gods, such as Ra, were closely associated with the sun. Geographic features are also often part of a culture's myths, or used as inspiration for mythological tales. Spider Rock, a tall peak located at Canyon de Chelly National Monument in Arizona, is said by the Hopi people to be the home of the creation goddess Spider Woman. The Atlas mountains in northern Africa took their name from the myth that the Titan Atlas (pronounced AT-luhs) had once stood there holding up the heavens, but had been transformed to stone in order to make his task easier.

## Natural Resources

Myths can also reflect the natural resources available to a culture, or the resources most prized by a certain group. In Mesoamerican and American Indian myths, maize (commonly referred to as corn) often appears as a food offered directly from gods or goddesses, or grown from the body of a deity. This reflects not only the importance of maize in the diets of early North and Central American cultures, but also the ready availability of maize, which does not appear as a native plant anywhere else in the world. Similarly, the olive tree, which is native to the coastal areas along the Mediterranean Sea, is one of the most important trees in ancient Greek myth. The city of Athens, it is said, was named for the goddess Athena (pronounced uh-THEE-nuh) after she gave its citizens the very first domesticated olive tree.

Sometimes, myths can reflect the importance of natural resources to an outside culture. For example, the Muisca people of what is now Colombia engaged in a ceremony in which their king covered himself in gold dust and took a raft out to the middle of a local lake; there he threw gold trinkets into the water as offerings to the gods. Gold was not commonly available, and was prized for its ceremonial significance; however, when Spanish explorers arrived in the New World and heard of this practice, they interpreted this to mean that gold must be commonplace in the area. This led to the myth of El Dorado, an entire city made of gold that many Spanish explorers believed to exist and spent decades trying to locate.

## Technology

A culture's state of technological development can also be reflected in its myths. The earliest ancient Greek myths of Uranus (pronounced

YOOR-uh-nuhs) state that his son Cronus (pronounced KROH-nuhs) attacked him with a sickle made of obsidian. Obsidian is a stone that can be chipped to create a sharp edge, and was used by cultures older than the ancient Greeks, who relied on metals such as bronze and steel for their weapons. This might suggest that the myth arose from an earlier age; at the very least, it reflects the idea that, from the perspective of the Greeks, the myth took place in the distant past.

## Social Order

Myths can also offer a snapshot of a culture's social organization. The Old Testament tale of the Tower of Babel offers an explanation for the many tribes found in the ancient Near East: they had once been united, and sought to build a tower that would reach all the way to heaven. In order to stop this act of self-importance, God caused the people to speak in different languages. Unable to understand each other, they abandoned the ambitious project and scattered into groups across the region.

Besides offering social order, myths can reinforce cultural views on the roles different types of individuals should assume in a society. The myth of Arachne (pronounced uh-RAK-nee) illustrates a fact known from other historical sources: weaving and fabric-making was the domestic duty of wives and daughters, and it was a skill highly prized in the homes of ancient Greece. Tales of characters such as Danaë (pronounced DAN-uh-ee), who was imprisoned in a tower by her father in order to prevent her from having a child, indicate the relative powerlessness of many women in ancient Greek society.

## Different Cultures, Different Perspectives

To see how cultures reflect their own unique characteristics through myth, one can examine how a single theme—such as fertility—is treated in a variety of different cultures. Fertility is the ability to produce life, growth, or offspring, and is therefore common in most, if not all, mythologies. For many cultures, fertility is a key element in the creation of the world. The egg, one of the most common symbols of fertility, appears in Chinese mythology as the first object to form from the disorder that previously existed in place of the world. In many cultures, including ancient Greece, the main gods are born from a single mother;

in the case of the Greeks, the mother is Gaia (pronounced GAY-uh), also known as Earth.

For cultures that relied upon agriculture, fertility was an important element of the changing seasons and the growth of crops. In these cases, fertility was seen as a gift from nature that could be revoked by cruel weather or the actions of the gods. Such is the case in the ancient Greek myth of Persephone (pronounced per-SEF-uh-nee); when the goddess is taken to the underworld by Hades (pronounced HAY-deez), her mother—the fertility goddess Demeter (pronounced di-MEE-ter)—became sad, which caused all vegetation to wither and die.

For the ancient Egyptians, fertility represented not just crop growth and human birth, but also rebirth into the afterlife through death. This explains why Hathor (pronounced HATH-or), the mother goddess of fertility who supported all life, was also the maintainer of the dead. It was believed that Hathor provided food for the dead to help them make the long journey to the realm of the afterlife.

For early Semitic cultures, the notion of fertility was not always positive. In the story of Lilith, the little-known first wife of Adam (the first man), the independent-minded woman left her husband and went to live by the Red Sea, where she gave birth to many demons each day. The myth seems to suggest that fertility is a power that can be used for good or evil, and that the key to using this power positively is for wives to dutifully respect the wishes of their husbands. This same theme is found in the earlier Babylonian myth of Tiamat (pronounced TYAH-maht), who gave birth to not only the gods but also to an army of monsters that fought to defend her from her son, the hero Marduk (pronounced MAHR-dook).

These are just a few of the many ways in which different cultures can take a single idea and interpret it through their own tales. Rest assured that the myths discussed in this book are wondrous legends that capture the imagination of the reader. They are also mirrors in which we can see not only ourselves, but the reflections of cultures old and new, far and near—allowing us to celebrate their unique differences, and at the same time recognize those common elements that make these enchanting stories universally beloved and appreciated by readers and students around the world.

# *Timeline of World Mythology*

**c. 3400 BCE** Early Sumerian writing is first developed.

**c. 3100 BCE** Egyptian writing, commonly known as hieroglyphics, is first developed.

**c. 2852–2205 BCE** During this time period, China is supposedly ruled by the Three Sovereigns and Five Emperors, mythical figures that may have been based on actual historical leaders.

**c. 2100 BCE** Earliest known version of the *Epic of Gilgamesh* is recorded in Sumerian.

**c. 1553–1536 BCE** Egyptian pharaoh Akhenaten establishes official worship of Aten, a single supreme god, instead of the usual group of gods recognized by ancient Egyptians.

**c. 1250 BCE** The Trojan War supposedly occurs around this time period. Despite the war's importance to Greek and Roman mythology, modern scholars are not sure whether the war was an actual historical event or just a myth.

**c. 1100 BCE** The Babylonian creation epic *Enuma Elish* is documented on clay tablets discovered nearly three thousand years later in the ruined library of Ashurbanipal, located in modern-day Iraq.

**c. 800 BCE** The Greek alphabet is invented, leading to a flowering of Greek literature based on myth.

**c. 750 BCE** The Greek epics known as the *Iliad* and the *Odyssey* are written by the poet Homer. Based on the events surrounding the

Trojan War, these two stories are the source of many myths and characters in Greek and Roman mythology.

**c. 750 BCE** The Greek poet Hesiod writes his *Theogony*, which details the origins of the Greek gods.

**c. 563–480 BCE** According to tradition, Gautama Buddha, the founder of Buddhism, is believed to have lived in ancient India and Nepal during this time.

**525–456 BCE** The Greek dramatist Aeschylus writes tragedies detailing the lives of mythical characters, including *Seven Against Thebes*, *Agamemnon*, and *The Eumenides*.

**c. 500–100 BCE** The oldest version of the *Ramayana*, the Hindu epic about the incarnation of the god Vishnu named Rama, is written.

**c. 496–406 BCE** Ancient Greek playwright Sophocles creates classic plays such as *Antigone* and *Oedipus the King*.

**c. 450 BCE** The Book of Genesis, containing stories fundamental to early Christianity, Judaism, and Islam, is collected and organized into its modern form.

**c. 431 BCE** Greek builders complete work on the temple of Athena known as the Parthenon, one of the few ancient Greek structures to survive to modern times.

**c. 150–50 BCE** The Gundestrup cauldron, a silver bowl depicting various Celtic deities and rituals, is created. The bowl is later recovered from a peat bog in Denmark in 1891.

**c. 29–19 BCE** Roman poet Virgil creates his mythical epic, the *Aeneid*, detailing the founding of Rome.

**c. 4 BCE–33 CE** Jesus, believed by Christians to be the son of God, supposedly lives during this time period.

**c. 8 CE** Roman poet Ovid completes his epic work *Metamorphoses*. It is one of the best existing sources for tales of ancient Greek and Roman mythology.

**c. 100 CE** The *Mahabharata*, a massive epic recognized as one of the most important pieces of literature in Hinduism, is organized into its modern form from source material dating back as far as the ninth century BCE.

**c. 570–632 CE** The prophet Muhammad, founder of Islam, supposedly lives during this time.

**c. 800–840 CE** The oldest surviving remnants of *The Book of One Thousand and One Nights*, a collection of Near Eastern folktales and legends, are written in Syrian.

**c. 1000 CE** The Ramsund carving, a stone artifact bearing an illustration of the tale of Sigurd, is created in Sweden. The tale is documented in the *Volsunga* saga.

**c. 1010 CE** The oldest surviving manuscript of the Old English epic *Beowulf* is written. It is recognized as the first significant work of English literature.

**c. 1100** Monks at the Clonmacnoise monastery compile the *Book of the Dun Cow*, the earliest written collection of Irish myths and legends still in existence.

**c. 1138** Geoffrey of Monmouth's *History of the Kings of Britain* is published, featuring the first well-known tales of the legendary King Arthur.

**c. 1180–1210** The *Nibelungenlied*, a German epic based largely on earlier German and Norse legends such as the *Volsunga* saga, is written by an unknown poet.

**c. 1220** Icelandic scholar Snorri Sturluson writes the Prose Edda, a comprehensive collection of Norse myths and legends gathered from older sources.

**c. 1350** The *White Book of Rhydderch*, containing most of the Welsh myths and legends later gathered in the *Mabinogion*, first appears.

**1485** Thomas Malory publishes *Le Morte D'Arthur*, widely considered to be the most authoritative version of the legend of King Arthur.

**c. 1489** *A Lytell Geste of Robin Hode*, one of the most comprehensive versions of the life of the legendary British character of Robin Hood, is published.

**c. 1550** The *Popol Vuh*, a codex containing Mayan creation myths and legends, is written. The book, written in the Quiché language but using Latin characters, was likely based on an older book written in Mayan hieroglyphics that has since been lost.

**1835** Elias Lonnrot publishes the *Kalevala*, an epic made up of Finnish songs and oral myths gathered during years of field research.

**1849** Archeologist Henry Layard discovers clay tablets containing the Babylonian creation epic *Enuma Elish* in Iraq. The epic, lost for centuries, is unknown to modern scholars before this discovery.

**1880** Journalist Joel Chandler Harris publishes *Uncle Remus, His Songs and Sayings: the Folk-Lore of the Old Plantation*, a collection of myths and folktales gathered from African American slaves working in the South. Many of the tales are derived from older stories from African myth. Although the book is successful and spawns three sequels, Harris is accused by some of taking cultural myths and passing them off as his own works.

# *Words to Know*

**benevolent:** Helpful or well-meaning.

**caste:** A social level in India's complex social class system.

**cauldron:** Kettle.

**chaos:** Disorder.

**chivalry:** A moral code popularized in Europe in the Middle Ages that stressed such traits as generosity, bravery, courtesy, and respect toward women.

**constellation:** Group of stars.

**cosmogony:** The study of, or a theory about, the origin of the universe.

**deity:** God or goddess.

**demigod:** Person with one parent who was human and one parent who was a god.

**destiny:** Predetermined future.

**divination:** Predicting the future.

**dualistic:** Having two sides or a double nature.

**epic:** A long, grand-scale poem.

**fertility:** The ability to reproduce; can refer to human ability to produce children or the ability of the earth to sustain plant life.

**hierarchy:** Ranked order of importance.

**hubris:** Too much self-confidence.

**immortal:** Living forever.

**imperial:** Royal, or related to an empire.

**indigenous:** Native to a given area.

**Judeo-Christian:** Related to the religious tradition shared by Judaism and Christianity. The faiths share a holy book, many fundamental principles, and a belief in a single, all-powerful god.

**matriarchal:** Female-dominated. Often refers to societies in which a family's name and property are passed down through the mother's side of the family.

**mediator:** A go-between.

**monotheism:** The belief in a single god as opposed to many gods.

**mummification:** The drying and preserving of a body to keep it from rotting after death.

**nymph:** A female nature deity.

**omen:** A mystical sign of an event to come.

**oracle:** Person through whom the gods communicated with humans.

**pagan:** Someone who worships pre-Christian gods.

**pantheon:** The entire collection of gods recognized by a group of people.

**patriarchal:** Male-dominated. Often refers to societies in which the family name and wealth are passed through the father.

**patron:** A protector or supporter.

**pharaoh:** A king of ancient Egypt.

**polytheism:** Belief in many gods.

**primal:** Fundamental; existing since the beginning.

**prophet:** A person able to see the plans of the gods or foretell future events.

**pyre:** A large pile of burning wood used in some cultures to cremate a dead body.

**resurrected:** Brought back to life.

**revelation:** The communication of divine truth or divine will to human beings.

**rune:** A character from an ancient and magical alphabet.

**seer:** A person who can see the future.

**shaman:** A person who uses magic to heal or look after the members of his tribe.

**sorcerer:** Wizard.

**syncretism:** The blending or fusion of different religions or belief systems.

**tradition:** A time-honored practice, or set of such practices.

**underworld:** Land of the dead.

**utopia:** A place of social, economic and political perfection.

# *Research and Activity Ideas*

Teachers wishing to enrich their students' understanding of world mythologies might try some of the following group activities. Each uses art, music, drama, speech, research, or scientific experimentation to put the students in closer contact with the cultures, myths, and figures they are studying.

## Greek Mythology: A Pageant of Gods

In this activity, students get to be gods and goddesses for a day during the classroom "Pageant of the Gods," an event modeled after a beauty pageant. Each student selects (with teacher approval) a deity from Greek mythology. Students then research their deity, write a 250-word description of the deity, and create costumes so they can dress as their deity. On the day of the pageant, the teacher collects the students' descriptions and reads them aloud as each student models his or her costume for the class.

### Materials required for the students:

Common household materials for costume

### Materials required for the teacher:

None

***Optional extension:*** The class throws a post-pageant potluck of Greek food.

## Anglo-Saxon Mythology: Old English Translation

Students are often surprised to learn that *Beowulf* is written in English. The original Old English text looks almost unrecognizable to them. In this activity (which students may work on in the classroom, in the library, or at home), the teacher begins by discussing the history of the English language and its evolution over the past one thousand years (since the writing of *Beowulf*). The teacher then models how a linguist would go about translating something written in Old English or Middle English (using an accessible text such as *The Canterbury Tales* as an example), and makes various resources for translation available to the students (see below). The class as a whole works on translating the first two lines of *Beowulf.* The teacher then assigns small groups of students a couple lines each of the opening section of *Beowulf* to translate and gloss. When each group is ready with their translations, the students assemble the modern English version of the opening of *Beowulf* and discuss what they learned about the various Old English words they studied.

### Materials required for the students:

None

### Materials required for the teacher:

Copies of an Old English version of the first part of *Beowulf* for distribution to students.

There are multiple Old English dictionaries available online, so student groups could work on this activity in the classroom if a sufficient number of computer workstations with Internet access are available. There are also many Old English dictionaries in print form. If none is available in the school library, some can be checked out from the public library.

## Egyptian Mythology: Mummify a Chicken

The ancient Egyptians believed preserving a person's body ensured their safe passage into the afterlife. The process of Egyptian mummification was a secret for many centuries until ancient Greek historian Herodotus recorded some information about the process in the fifth century BCE. Archaeologists have recently refined their understanding of Egyptian mummification practices. In this activity, students conduct their own mummification experiment on chickens.

The teacher contextualizes the activity by showing students a video on mummies and asking them to read both Herodotus's account of mummification and more recent articles about mummification that center on the research of Egyptologist Bob Brier.

Once students understand the basics of mummification, groups of five or six students can begin their science experiment, outlined below. The teacher should preface the experiment with safety guidelines for handling raw chicken.

### Materials required for students:

Scale

One fresh chicken per group (bone-in chicken breast or leg may substitute)

Disposable plastic gloves (available at drugstores)

Carton of salt per group per week

Spice mixture (any strong powdered spices will do; powdered cloves, cinnamon, and ginger are good choices)

Extra-large (gallon size) air-tight freezer bags

Roll of gauze per group (available at drugstore)

Disposable aluminum trays for holding chickens

Cooking oil

Notebook for each group

### Materials required for the teacher:

Video on mummies. A good option is: *Mummies: Secrets of the Pharaohs* (2007), available on DVD.

Reading material on mummies, including Herodotus's account. See: http://discovermagazine.com/2007/oct/mummification-is-back-from-the-dead; http://www.nationalgeographic.com/tv/mummy/; http://www.mummytombs.com/egypt/herodotus.htm

Plenty of paper towels and hand soap.

### Procedure

1. All students put on plastic gloves.

2. Weigh each chicken (unnecessary if weight printed on packaging) and record the weight in a notebook. Record details of the chicken's appearance in the notebook.
3. Remove chicken organs and dispose of them. Rinse the chicken thoroughly in a sink.
4. Pat the chicken dry with paper towels. Make sure the chicken is completely dry, or the mummification process might not work.
5. Rub the spices all over the chicken, both inside and outside, then salt the entire chicken and fill the chicken cavity with salt.
6. Seal the chicken in the air-tight bag and place it in the aluminum tray.
7. Remove gloves and wash hands thoroughly with soap and water.
8. Once a week, put on plastic gloves, remove the chicken from the bag, dispose of the bag and accumulated liquid, and weigh the chicken. Record the weight in a notebook and make notes on changes in the chicken's appearance. Respice and resalt the chicken, fill the chicken cavity with salt, and seal it in a new bag. Remove gloves and wash hands. Repeat this step until no more liquid drains from the chicken.
9. When liquid no longer drains from the chicken, the mummy is done! Wipe off all the salt and rub a light coat of cooking oil on the mummy. Wrap it tightly in gauze.

***Optional extension:*** Students can decorate their mummies using hieroglyphics and build shoebox sarcophagi for them.

## Near Eastern Mythology: Gilgamesh and the Cedar Forest

The story of Gilgamesh's heroics against the demon Humbaba of the Cedar Forest is one of the most exciting parts of the *Epic of Gilgamesh*. In this activity, students write, stage, and perform a three-act play based on this part of the epic. Necessary tasks will include writing, costume design, set design, and acting. The teacher can divide tasks among students as necessary.

### Materials required for the students:

Household items for costumes

Cardboard, paint, tape, and other materials for sets

Copy of the *Epic of Gilgamesh*

**Materials required for the teacher:**

None

## Hindu Mythology: Salute the Sun

The practice of yoga, an ancient mental and physical discipline designed to promote spiritual perfection, is mentioned in most of the Hindu holy texts. Today, the physical aspects of yoga have become a widely popular form of exercise around the world. In this activity, the students and teacher will make yoga poses part of their own daily routine.

The teacher introduces the activity by discussing the history of yoga from ancient to modern times, by showing a video on the history of yoga, and by distributing readings from ancient Hindu texts dealing with the practice of yoga. After a class discussion on the video and texts, the teacher leads students through a basic "sun salutation" series of poses with the aid of an instructional yoga video (students may wish to bring a towel or mat from home, as some parts of the sun salutation involve getting on the floor). Students and the teacher will perform the sun salutation every day, preferably at the beginning of class, either for the duration of the semester or for another set period of time. Students will conclude the activity by writing a summary of their feelings about their yoga "experiment."

**Materials required for the students:**

Towel or mat to put on floor during sun salutations.

**Materials required for teacher:**

A DVD on the history of yoga. Recommended: *Yoga Unveiled* (2004), an excellent documentary series on the history of yoga.

An instructional yoga video that includes the "sun salutation" sequence (many available).

Handouts of ancient Indian writings on yoga. See *The Shambhala Encyclopedia of Yoga* (2000) and *The Yoga and the Bhagavad Gita* (2007).

## African Mythology: Storytelling

Anansi the Spider was a trickster god of West African origin who was known as a master storyteller. In this activity, students work on their own storytelling skills while learning about the spread of Anansi stories from Africa to the Americas.

The teacher begins this activity by discussing the ways that oral traditions have helped the African American community preserve some part of their West African cultural heritage. The spread of stories about Anansi around Caribbean and American slave communities is an example, with the Uncle Remus stories of Joel Chandler Harris being a good demonstration of how the Anansi tales have evolved. The class then conducts a preliminary discussion about what the elements of a good spoken story might be, then watches or listens to models of storytelling. After listening to the stories, the class discusses common elements in the stories and techniques the storytellers used to keep the audience's attention and build interest.

Students then read a variety of Anansi and Uncle Remus stories on their own. With teacher approval, they select one story and prepare it for oral presentation in class (several students may select the same story). After the presentations, students can discuss their reactions to the various oral presentations, pointing out what was effective and ineffective.

#### Materials required for the students:

Optional: props for story presentation

#### Materials required for the teacher:

Background reading on West African oral traditions.

Recordings or videos of skilled storytellers. See *The American Storyteller Series* or the CD recording *Tell Me a Story: Timeless Folktales from Around the World* (which includes an Anansi story).

***Optional extension:*** The teacher may arrange for students with especially strong oral presentations to share their stories at a school assembly or as visiting speakers in another classroom.

### Micronesian and Melanesian Mythology: Island Hopping

The many islands that make up Micronesia and Melanesia are largely unfamiliar to most students. In this activity, students learn more about these faraway places.

The teacher introduces this activity by hanging up a large map of the South Pacific, with detail of Micronesian and Melanesian islands. The teacher explains that, during every class session, the class will learn the location of and key facts about a particular island. Each day, one student is given the name of an island. It is that student's homework assignment that night to learn the location of the island, its population, and its key industries. The student must also learn two interesting facts about the island. The next day, the student places a push pin (or other marker) on the map showing the location of his or her island. The student presents the information to the class, writes it down on an index card, and files the index card in the class "island" box. In this way, the students learn about a new Micronesian or Melanesian island every day and build a ready resource of information about the islands.

**Materials required for the students:**

None

**Materials required for the teacher:**

Large wall map with sufficient detail of Micronesia and Melanesia

Index cards

Box for island index cards

Push pins, stickers, or other markers for islands

## Northern European Mythology: The Scroll of the Nibelungen

The *Nibelungenlied* is an epic poem set in pre-Christian Germany. The tale contains many adventures, fights, and triumphs. In this activity, students prepare a graphic-novel version of the *Nibelungenlied.*

To introduce this activity, the teacher gives students a synopsis of the *Nibelungenlied* and describes the various interpretations of the saga (including Richard Wagner's opera and J. R. R. Tolkien's *Lord of the Rings* triology). The teacher then explains that the class will create a graphic novel of the *Nibelungenlied* on a continuous scroll of paper. The teacher shows models of various graphic novels and discusses the conventions of graphic novel representations.

Students are divided into groups of three or four, and each group receives one chapter or section of the *Nibelungenlied* as its assignment.

After reading their sections, the groups meet to discuss possible graphical representations of the action in their chapters and present their ideas to the teacher for approval. After gaining approval, student groups work, one group at a time, to draw and color their chapters on the scroll. When the scroll is finished, each group makes a short presentation explaining what happens in their chapter and how they chose to represent the action. The final scroll can be displayed around the classroom walls or along a school hallway.

**Materials required by the students:**

None

**Materials required by the teacher:**

Easel paper roll (200 feet)

Markers, colored pencils, and crayons

Copies of *Nibelungenlied* chapters for students (or refer students to http://omacl.org/Nibelungenlied/)

## Inca Mythology: Make a Siku

A siku is an Andean pan pipe. Pipes such as these were important in Inca culture, and remain a prominent feature in Andean music. In this activity, students will make their own sikus.

The teacher begins this activity by playing some Andean pan pipe music, showing students the Andes on a map, and discussing the ways in which Inca culture remains part of the lives of Native Americans in countries like Peru. The teacher shows a picture of a pan pipe (or, ideally, an actual pan pipe) to the students and explains they will build their own.

Students need ten drinking straws each (they can bring them from home, or the teacher can provide them) and a pair of scissors. To make the pipe:

1. Set aside two of the straws. Cut the remaining straws so that each is one-half inch shorter than the next. The first straw is uncut. The second straw is one-half inch shorter than the first. The third is one inch shorter than the first, and so on.
2. Cut the remaining straws into equal pieces. These pieces will be used as spacers between pipe pieces.

3. Arrange the straws from longest to shortest (left to right) with the tops of the straws lined up.
4. Put spacer pieces between each part of the pipe so they are an equal distance apart.
5. Tape the pipe in position, making sure the tops of the straws stay in alignment.
6. The pipe is finished. Cover in paper and decorate if desired. Blow across the tops of straws to play.

**Materials required by the students:**

Ten drinking straws

Scissors

Tape

**Materials required by the teacher:**

Andean pipe music

Pictures of a pan pipe or an actual pan pipe

Picture of the Andes on a map

# U•X•L Encyclopedia of World Mythology

VOLUME 5: Q–Z

# QR

## Quetzalcoatl

### Character Overview

For thousands of years, Quetzalcoatl was one of the most important figures in the traditional mythologies of Mesoamerica, an area roughly corresponding to modern Central America. As a god, culture hero, or legendary ruler, Quetzalcoatl appeared in some of the region's most powerful and enduring stories. He represented life, health, and the arts and crafts of civilization, such as farming, cooking, and music.

The name *Quetzalcoatl* means "Feathered Serpent." It brings together the magnificent green-plumed quetzal bird, symbolizing the heavens and the wind, and the snake, symbolizing the earth and fertility. Quetzalcoatl's name can also be translated as "precious twin." In some myths, he had a twin brother named Xolotl (pronounced shoh-LOHT-l), who had a human body and the head of a dog or an ocelot, a spotted wildcat.

**Nationality/Culture**
Aztec, Toltec, and Mayan

**Pronunciation**
keht-sahl-koh-AHT-l

**Alternate Names**
Kukulcan (Mayan)

**Appears In**
Mesoamerican oral myths, the Florentine Codex

**Lineage**
Son of Coatlicue

### Major Myths

According to some accounts, Quetzalcoatl was the son of the earth goddess **Coatlicue** (pronounced koh-aht-LEE-kway). He and three brother gods created the **sun**, the heavens, and the earth. In the Aztec creation myth, Quetzalcoatl's conflicts with the god **Tezcatlipoca** (pronounced tehs-cah-tlee-POH-cah) brought about the creation and destruction of

*Quetzalcoatl as he bursts from the serpent's jaws of the earth in his form as Morning Star.* WERNER FORMAN/ART RESOURCE, NY.

a series of four suns and earths, leading to the fifth sun and today's earth.

At first there were no people under the fifth sun. The inhabitants of the earlier worlds had died, and their bones littered Mictlan (pronounced MEEKT-lahn), the **underworld** or land of the dead. Quetzalcoatl and his twin, Xolotl, journeyed to Mictlan to find the bones, arousing the fury of the Death Lord. As he fled from the underworld, Quetzalcoatl dropped the bones, and they broke into pieces. He gathered up the pieces and took them to the earth goddess Cihuacoatl (pronounced shee-wah-koh-AHT-l), who ground them into flour. Quetzalcoatl moistened the flour with his own blood, which gave it life. Then he and Xolotl shaped the mixture into human forms and taught the new creatures how to reproduce themselves.

Besides creating humans, Quetzalcoatl also protected and helped them. Some myths say that he introduced the cultivation of maize, or

**corn**, the staple food of Mexico. He did this by disguising himself as a black ant and stealing the precious grain from the red ants. He also taught people astronomy, calendar making, and various crafts, and was the favored god of merchants.

Quetzalcoatl's departure from his people was the work of his old enemy, Tezcatlipoca, who wanted people to make bloodier sacrifices than the flowers, jade, and butterflies they offered to Quetzalcoatl. Tezcatlipoca tricked Quetzalcoatl by getting him drunk and then holding up a mirror that showed Tezcatlipoca's cruel face. Believing that he was looking at his own imperfect image, Quetzalcoatl decided to leave the world and threw himself onto a funeral pyre, a large pile of burning wood used in some cultures to cremate a dead body. As his body burned, birds flew forth from the flames, and his heart went up into the heavens to become the morning and evening star known in modern times as the planet Venus. Another version of the myth states that Quetzalcoatl sailed east into the sea on a raft of serpents. Many Aztecs believed that he would come back to his people at the end of a fifty-two-year cycle. In the early 1500s, the Spanish conqueror Hernán Cortés took advantage of this belief by encouraging the people of Mexico to view him as the return of the hero-god Quetzalcoatl. According to some reports, this may have allowed Cortés to more easily subdue and conquer the local people.

## Quetzalcoatl in Context

Quetzalcoatl occupied a central place in the pantheon (collection of recognized gods) of the Aztec people of central Mexico, but he dates back to a time long before the Aztecs. Images of the Feathered Serpent appear on a temple building in Teotihuacán, a Mexican archaeological site from the third century CE. These images are found together with images of rain and water, suggesting close ties between Quetzalcoatl and the god of rain and vegetation.

To the Toltecs, who flourished in the region from the 800s to the 1100s, Quetzalcoatl was the deity of the morning and evening stars and the wind. When the Aztecs rose to power in the 1400s, they brought Quetzalcoatl into their pantheon and made him a culture hero, a bringer not just of life but also of civilization. These old myths merged with legends about a priest-king named Quetzalcoatl, possibly a real historical figure. Stories about a Toltec king named Topiltzin Quetzalcoatl, famed as an enlightened and good ruler, may have contributed to the image of

Quetzalcoatl as a culture hero. Later, as groups from central Mexico migrated into southern Mexico and the Yucatán peninsula and blended with the local Maya population, the Feathered Serpent took his place in the Mayan pantheon under the name Kukulcan (pronounced koo-kool-KAHN).

## Key Themes and Symbols

One of the most important themes in the myth of Quetzalcoatl is the idea of a god as a friend and helper to humans. Aside from giving humans life, Quetzalcoatl taught humans all the basic skills they needed to function as a civilization, such as growing crops and learning the cycles of nature and the stars. He even stole corn from the ants so that humans could grow and eat it. Another theme common to Central American mythology is the idea of blood as life. Quetzalcoatl creates humans by mixing bone flour with his own blood, thereby giving them life. This theme is also seen in the idea of human **sacrifice**, which, according to myth, Quetzalcoatl does not condone.

## Quetzalcoatl in Art, Literature, and Everyday Life

Quetzalcoatl was portrayed in two ways. As the Feathered Serpent, he was a snake with wings or covered with feathers. He could also appear in human form as a warrior wearing a tall, cone-shaped crown or cap made of ocelot skin and a pendant fashioned of jade or a conch shell. The pendant, known as the "wind jewel," symbolized one of Quetzalcoatl's other roles, that of Ehecatl, god of wind and movement. Buildings dedicated to this god were circular or cylindrical in shape to minimize their resistance to the wind.

In modern culture, Quetzalcoatl has appeared as a character in some form on television shows, such as *Star Trek* and *The X-Files*. The god has also appeared—with varying degrees of faithfulness to the myth—in several video games, including *Final Fantasy VIII* and *Castlevania: Dawn of Sorrow*. The god also lent his name to a type of flying dinosaur called a pterosaur, which was officially named *Quetzalcoatlus*.

## Read, Write, Think, Discuss

Carlos Fuentes, one of modern Mexico's leading writers, compares Quetzalcoatl with the mythic figures **Prometheus**, **Odysseus**, and Moses. All three had to leave their cultures, but obtained gifts or wisdom that renewed those cultures. Using your library, the Internet, or other available resources, research these important figures. What similarities do you see between them and Quetzalcoatl? What are the main differences?

**SEE ALSO** Aztec Mythology; Coatlicue; Huitzilopochtli; Mayan Mythology; Tezcatlipoca

# Ra

**Nationality/Culture**
Egyptian

**Pronunciation**
RAH or RAY

**Alternate Names**
Re

**Appears In**
Ancient Egyptian myths and prayers

**Lineage**
None

## Character Overview

One of the most important gods in **Egyptian mythology**, the **sun** god Ra (also known as Re) was the supreme power in the universe. The giver of life, he was often merged with the god **Amun** as Amun-Ra. Some myths present Ra as the head of the Egyptian pantheon and ruler of all the gods. Others say that he was the only god, and that all other deities were merely aspects of Ra.

In some creation myths, Ra emerged from either an ancient mound or waters as Ra-Atum, and created Tefnut (pronounced TEF-noot, meaning "moisture") and Shu (pronounced SHOO, meaning "air"). From this first divine pair sprang the sky goddess **Nut** (pronounced NOOT) and earth god Geb, who created the universe and gave birth to the gods **Osiris** (pronounced oh-SYE-ris), **Isis** (pronounced EYE-sis), **Set**, Nephthys (pronounced NEF-this), and **Horus** the Elder (pronounced HOHR-uhs).

## Major Myths

Ra appeared in many myths and legends. As the sun god, he rode across the sky in a golden ship, bringing light and warmth to all creatures living on earth. When the sun set in the evening, he descended to the **underworld**, or land of the dead, and brought light and air to the people who dwelled there. Each evening Ra's servants helped him battle his eternal enemy, the mighty snake Apophis (pronounced uh-POH-fis), who tried to swallow Ra and all his creations. Some stories said that Ra sailed along the body of Nut, the sky goddess, during the day and then traveled through her body at night, being born anew each morning.

According to one series of myths, Ra first ruled during a golden age. Everything he saw was perfect, and the sight of such wonders brought tears to his eyes. The tears fell to earth and grew into human beings. In time, however, Ra became angry with the humans because of their actions. He summoned his divine eye, the beautiful goddess **Hathor** (pronounced HATH-or), and transformed her into Sekhmet (pronounced SEK-met), a savage lioness. Ra sent the lioness to earth to kill humans, but after she had caused massive bloodshed, he decided to save the humans that remained. He played a trick on Sekhmet, getting her so drunk on beer that she forgot to continue killing. Nevertheless, death had now been introduced into the world.

In another myth, the goddess Isis wished to learn the secret name of Ra. The name contained great power, which Isis planned to use to make her magical spells stronger. By this time, Ra had become quite old. Isis collected some of the spit that drooled down his chin, mixed it with clay, and made a poisonous snake. One day as Ra was out walking, the snake bit him. Tormented by terrible pain, Ra summoned the other gods to help him. Isis promised to relieve his suffering, but only if he revealed his powerful secret name. He finally agreed, and Isis used the name in a magical spell to remove the poison and heal the sun god.

## Ra in Context

The chief center for Ra's worship in ancient Egypt was the city of Heliopolis (pronounced hee-lee-OP-uh-luhs). As worship of Ra grew, it challenged the supremacy of all other local religions and eventually became a part of them. Ra remained the principal god throughout the history of ancient Egypt, and Egyptian pharaohs, or rulers, claimed to be the sons of Ra in order to link themselves to him.

## Key Themes and Symbols

Because ancient Egyptian deities were so often combined with other gods in different regions and during different periods, Ra symbolized many different things. However, two elements of Ra's character were fairly constant. First, Ra was directly linked to the sun, which meant he also embodied light and life-giving warmth. Second, Ra was associated with the leaders of Egypt, and was seen as the symbolic leader of Egyptian culture.

### Ra in Art, Literature, and Everyday Life

In ancient art, the god Ra is commonly shown with the head of a falcon wearing a shining solar disk on its head. In modern times, Ra has been referenced in many books, television shows, and films. Ra appeared as a main character in the 1994 science fiction film *Stargate*, which suggested that Ra was actually an alien who came to be worshipped by the ancient Egyptians for his advanced technological powers.

### Read, Write, Think, Discuss

Using your library, the Internet, or other available resources, research the gods known as Amun-Ra, Atum-Ra, and Ra-Horakhty. How are these gods related to Ra? Why do you think the identities of other gods became linked to Ra? Does seeing how religious beliefs change throughout history challenge the idea that religion and myth are based on eternal, unchanging truths?

**SEE ALSO** Amun; Creation Stories; Egyptian Mythology; Hathor; Isis; Nut; Osiris; Set; Thoth; Underworld

# Ragnarok

**Nationality/Culture**
Norse

**Pronunciation**
RAHG-nuh-rok

**Alternate Names**
None

**Appears In**
The Eddas

### Myth Overview

According to **Norse mythology**, the world will end at Ragnarok, a time of great destruction when the gods will wage a final battle with the **giants** and other evil forces. Ragnarok has not yet arrived, but the events leading to it have already been set in motion.

Before Ragnarok begins, the world will suffer a terrible winter lasting three years. During this period the **sun** will grow dim, evil forces will be released, and wars will rage among humans. The trickster **Loki** (pronounced LOH-kee) will gather the frost giants and sail to Asgard (pronounced AHS-gahrd), the home of the gods. The wolf **Fenrir** (pronounced FEN-reer), the serpent Jormungand (pronounced YAWR-moon-gahnd), and **Hel**, the goddess of the dead, will break free and join Loki and other evil characters in a battle against the gods.

On the morning of Ragnarok, the god **Heimdall** (pronounced HAYM-dahl) will sound his mighty horn, summoning the gods to battle. During the terrible struggle that follows, all the great gods—including **Odin** (pronounced OH-din) and **Thor**—will be killed. Loki and the monsters, giants, and other evil beings will also perish. The earth will be set on **fire**, the sun and moon will be destroyed, the sky will fall, and the world will finally sink beneath the sea and vanish.

Ragnarok will not be the end of everything, however. The World Tree **Yggdrasill** (pronounced IG-druh-sil) will survive, and two humans—Lif and Lifthrasir—and some animals will be sheltered among its branches. New land will rise from the oceans, and a fresh green earth will emerge. Lif and Lifthrasir will repopulate the world. Some of the gods—including the once-dead **Balder** (pronounced BAWL-der)—will also return and rebuild Asgard, ushering in a new golden age. Giants and other evil beings will not reappear but will fade as a distant memory.

## Ragnarok in Context

Nearly all cultures have a mythology related to the end of the world, or at least the end of humankind. The way in which the people of a culture view this end-time is a reflection of the values and beliefs found in that culture. In Norse mythology, the myth of Ragnarok reflects the cycle of death and rebirth seen in nature, but on a far grander scale.

## Key Themes and Symbols

One theme found in the myth of Ragnarok is the physical death of the gods. Nearly all the Norse gods are said to be slain during the battle at Ragnarok. All of these deaths occur in very physical ways; Odin, for example, is eaten by the giant wolf Fenrir. One of the few gods spared at Ragnarok is Balder, who has already died and is reborn after the conflict.

Another important theme is the rebellion of the natural world. This is shown in the continuous winter that lasts for three years, and in the disappearance of the sun, moon, and stars. The myth also contains references to grand-scale earthquakes and **floods**. After the great destruction, however, the idea of renewal and rebirth remains a core element of the myth of Ragnarok.

*According to Norse mythology, the world will end at Ragnarok, a time of great destruction when the gods will wage a final battle with the giants.* © NATIONALMUSEUM, STOCKHOLM, SWEDEN/THE BRIDGEMAN ART LIBRARY.

## Ragnarok in Art, Literature, and Everyday Life

The myth of Ragnarok has captured the imagination of people around the world. Most notably, the myth was used as inspiration for the fourth and final opera of Richard Wagner's *The Ring of the Nibelung* cycle, first

## The End of the World

*Most cultures have some vision of how the world will end.*

| Event | Culture | Description |
|---|---|---|
| Judgment Day or the Apocalypse | Christian | Though there is some disagreement over the order and duration of events, the Christian view of the end of the world involves the return of Jesus Christ to Earth, a Last Judgment in which the saved are separated from the damned, one thousand years of peace, and the loosing of Satan's forces on Earth. |
| Qiyamah | Islam | As in Christianity, in Islam there is a day of judgment. God rewards the good and punishes the bad, and the world is destroyed. |
| Ragnarok | Norse | A giant battle of the gods, giants, and forces of evil will destroy the earth. |
| The end of the Kali Yuga | Hindu | The Hindu belief system is cyclical, with time broken into long ages called kalpas, each consisting of four periods. We are now said to be in the Kali Yuga, the final, darkest period of the current age. At the end of the Kali Yuga, Shiva will destroy the earth in preparation for a new kalpa. |

ILLUSTRATION BY ANAXOS, INC./CENGAGE LEARNING, GALE.

performed in its entirety in 1876. The opera, known as *The Twilight of the Gods*—a literal translation of "Ragnarok"—differs substantially from the Norse version of the myth.

*Ragnarok* has been used as the name of a popular Korean comic series, an animated television series, and a multiplayer online role-playing game series. The world depicted in these only loosely resembles the realms of Norse mythology, though many characters are modeled after the Norse gods and other mythical beings.

## Read, Write, Think, Discuss

Multiple times throughout recorded history, large groups of people have become convinced that the world was about the end. Throughout Europe, people were convinced that the year 1000 would be the end. When the next millennium arrived, dire predictions of global disaster resurfaced. Using your library, the Internet, or other available sources, research failed "end of the world" predictions. Pick one, then write a paper about the social environment surrounding the predication, who made the prediction, what evidence that person used, and whether any part of the prediction came true.

**SEE ALSO** Fenrir; Giants; Heimdall; Hel; Loki; Norse Mythology; Odin; Serpents and Snakes; Thor; Yggdrasill

# *Ramayana, The*

**Nationality/Culture**
Hindu

**Pronunciation**
rah-MAY-yah-nuh

**Alternate Names**
None

**Appears In**
The *Ramayana*

## Myth Overview

One of the most famous epics in Hindu literature, the *Ramayana* tells of the life and adventures of Rama, a legendary hero who is worshipped as a god in many parts of India. Probably written in the 200s BCE, the *Ramayana* is attributed to Valmiki, a wise man who also appears as a character in the work. Based on numerous legends, the *Ramayana* also incorporates sacred material from the Vedas, a collection of ancient Hindu religious texts.

**Early Life of Rama** According to the *Ramayana*, Rama (pronounced RAH-muh) was the seventh incarnation—or bodily form—of the god **Vishnu** (pronounced VISH-noo). Born as the eldest son of King Dasaratha of Ayodhya (pronounced ah-YOH-dee-uh), he was conceived when Vishnu gave three of the king's wives a special potion to drink. Dasaratha's senior wife, Kausalya (pronounced kow-SAHL-yuh), gave birth to Rama. The other wives gave birth to Rama's brothers—Bharata (pronounced

BAH-rah-tah), and the **twins** Lakshmana (pronounced LAHK-shmah-nah) and Satrughna (pronounced shah-TROO-gnuh). Rama inherited half of Vishnu's supernatural power, while his brothers shared the rest.

The four brothers grew up as close friends, particularly Rama and Lakshmana. One day a wise man named Vishvamitra (pronounced vish-VAH-mi-truh) asked Rama and his brothers to help defeat Taraka (pronounced TAH-rah-kah), queen of a race of demons called the Rakshasas (pronounced RAHK-shah-sahs). Rama and Lakshmana agreed to help, and Rama killed Taraka. Vishvamitra then took the brothers to the court of King Janaka (pronounced JAH-nah-kah), where Rama entered a contest for the hand of Sita (pronounced SEE-tah), the king's daughter. By bending and breaking a sacred bow given to the king by the god **Shiva** (pronounced SHEE-vuh), Rama won the contest.

Soon after the marriage of Rama and Sita, King Dasaratha decided to turn over his throne to Rama. However, his wife Kaikeyi (pronounced kye-KEE-yee), the mother of Bharata, reminded Dasaratha that he had once promised to grant her two wishes. Reluctantly, the king granted Kaikeyi her wishes—to banish Rama and place Bharata on the throne.

A dutiful son, Rama accepted his banishment and went to the Dandaka (pronounced DAHN-duh-kuh) Forest with Sita and Lakshmana. King Dasaratha died of grief soon after they departed. Bharata had been away during these earlier events. When called back to take the throne, he agreed to rule only during his brother's absence and acknowledged Rama as the rightful king.

**Battling the Rakshasas** During his exile in the forest, Rama helped defend the wise men living there against the evil Rakshasas. One of these demons, the hideous giantess Surpanakha (pronounced shur-PAH-nah-kah), offered to marry both Rama and Lakshmana. When they refused, the giantess attacked Sita, but the brothers cut off Surpanakha's ears and nose and drove her away. Surpanakha sent her younger brother Khara (pronounced KAH-ruh) and an army of demons to avenge her, but Rama and Lakshmana defeated and killed them all.

Furious at this defeat, Surpanakha went to her older brother Ravana (pronounced RAH-vuh-nuh), the demon king of Sri Lanka, and plotted revenge. When the giantess told Ravana about the beautiful Sita, he went to Dandaka Forest. Disguised as a beggar, the demon king kidnapped Sita and carried her back to his kingdom. He then tried to get Sita to marry him, but she rejected all his advances—even when he threatened to kill and eat her.

Meanwhile, Rama and Lakshmana set off in search of Sita. Along the way they met the monkey king Sugriva (pronounced soo-GREE-vuh), son of the god **Surya** (pronounced SOOR-yuh), and formed an alliance. They helped him win back his throne from his wicked half-brother Vali (pronounced VAH-lee). In return, the brothers received help from the monkey armies. After the monkey god Hanuman (pronounced HAH-noo-mahn) discovered where Sita had been taken, the monkey armies marched to Sri Lanka and defeated the Rakshasas in a series of battles. During the fighting, Rama killed Ravana and was reunited with Sita.

**Rama and Sita** After their reunion, Rama wondered whether Sita had remained faithful while held captive by Ravana. Sita proclaimed her innocence and proved it by passing through a **fire** unharmed. The fire god Agni (pronounced AG-nee) also spoke on her behalf, and Rama accepted her innocence.

The couple returned to Ayodhya, and Rama began a long reign of peace and prosperity. But the people still questioned Sita's faithfulness. In time, Rama began to doubt her innocence as well, and he banished her. While in exile, Sita found refuge with an old wise man named Valmiki (pronounced vahl-MEE-kee), and she gave birth to Rama's twin sons, Kusa and Lava.

After many years, the two boys visited Ayodhya. When Rama saw them, he recognized them as his sons and called Sita back from exile. Sita returned, and exhausted from having to continually protest her innocence, she called on Bhumidevi, the Earth Goddess, to release her from this world. Bhumidevi granted her wish, and the earth opened up beneath Sita and swallowed her.

Grief stricken by the loss of Sita, Rama asked the gods to end his sorrow. The gods told Rama that he must either enter **heaven** or stay on earth. Rama chose to follow Sita to eternity, so he walked into the river Sarayu and drowned. Upon Rama's death, the god **Brahma** (pronounced BRAH-muh) welcomed the hero into heaven.

## The *Ramayana* in Context

The *Ramayana* has been extremely influential in India and Southeast Asia since the early Middle Ages. Its stamp can be seen in visual arts, architecture, dance, and poetry throughout the region. Like the Greek epics the ***Iliad*** and the ***Odyssey***, the *Ramayana* is significant on both an artistic and cultural level, as the story of Rama has become inextricably linked to Indians' sense of national identity. The *Ramayana* presents, in allegorical form, many Hindu concepts, including the idea of *dharma* (pronounced DAR-muh) or duty, and Indian cultural values such as loyalty and respect for the family. Despite India's rapid modernization, the *Ramayana* remains extremely popular. The Indian film and television industry frequently draws on the tale in its productions.

## Key Themes and Symbols

One of the main themes in the *Ramayana* is the importance of faithfulness and keeping one's word: Dasaratha wanted to place Rama on the throne, but his wife insisted that he keep his word to her; Rama accepted and understood that Dasaratha had to fulfill his promise, and accepted his banishment without bitterness; and Sita proved over and over that she was a faithful wife.

Another theme at the core of the *Ramayana* is that of a rightful heir returning to his throne. Rama is considered by King Dasaratha to be the best choice for ruling the kingdom, but is banished due to the influence of one of the king's jealous wives. The bulk of the tale involves his banishment and ultimate claiming of the throne. The story of the monkey king Sugriva also mirrors Rama's tale: he also must win back his rightful throne from his half-brother.

## The *Ramayana* in Art, Literature, and Everyday Life

Not only is the *Ramayana* one of the most popular tales of India, it has also been embraced by other cultures from Tibet to the Philippines. The Chinese epic *Journey to the West* may also be inspired by the *Ramayana*. The epic was used as the basis for the wildly popular Indian television series *Ramayan* (1987), which earned over 100 million viewers and caused a virtual shutdown in businesses and public services throughout India during its time slot. The comic book series *Ramayan 3392 A.D.* (2006), conceived by doctor and author Deepak Chopra, is a futuristic retelling of the legend that aims to popularize the tale among English-speaking readers.

### Read, Write, Think, Discuss

The predicament faced by Rama—jealousy and resentment at his status as first-born son by his father's later wife—is not unlike some of the complicated dynamics found in modern families. Do you think Rama's situation is similar to that of a child whose parent remarries and has additional children with the new spouse? What issues do you think are shared by both Rama and modern children from split-parent households? In what ways are the issues facing modern families different from Rama and his clan?

**SEE ALSO** Brahma; Devils and Demons; Hinduism and Mythology; Indra; Vishnu

# Rangi and Papa

**Nationality/Culture**
Polynesian

**Pronunciation**
RANG-gee and PAH-pah

**Alternate Names**
None

**Appears In**
Polynesian creation myths

**Lineage**
Children of Te Po and Te Kore

## Character Overview

In **Polynesian mythology**, Rangi (Father Sky) and Papa (Mother Earth) were the two supreme creator deities (gods and goddesses). They were the source from which all things in the universe originated, including other gods, humans, and the various creatures and features of the earth. Rangi and Papa played an especially important role in the mythology of the Maori (pronounced MAH-aw-ree) people of New Zealand.

## Major Myths

According to Maori mythology, Rangi and Papa were created from two ancient beings—Te Po (night) and Te Kore (emptiness)—who existed in darkness before the creation of the universe. From the beginning, Rangi and Papa were locked together in a tight and continuing embrace. Into the darkness between their bodies sprang many offspring, including numerous gods.

Trapped between the bodies of their parents, the deities had little space to move around and no light to see. Weary of this situation, the offspring discussed how they could escape the confines of their existence. Tu, the god of war, suggested that they kill Rangi and Papa, but Tane (pronounced TAH-nee), the god of the forests, had a different solution.

*In Polynesian mythology, Rangi and Papa were two creator deities locked in a continuous embrace. When other gods finally separated them, the gods, humans, and other creatures who had been trapped between them scattered into the world.* WERNER FORMAN/ART RESOURCE, NY.

Tane suggested that they make space for themselves by separating their parents. The other gods agreed with this plan, except for the wind god Tawhiri (pronounced tah-WEE-ree), who roared his disapproval.

Several of the gods attempted to separate Rangi and Papa. The first to try was Rongo, the god of cultivated plants. Although he pushed with all his might, he was unable to separate the couple. Next to try was Tangaroa, the god of the sea. He also failed, as did Haumia (pronounced how-MEE-uh), the god of wild plants and vegetables, and Tu, the war god. Finally, it was time for Tane to try. The god of the forests placed his head on his mother Papa, raised his feet in the air, and pushed upward against his father Rangi. Using all his might, Tane finally separated Rangi and Papa, pushing Rangi up into the sky and pressing Papa to the earth.

With Rangi and Papa separated, the space between them became flooded with light. The various deities, humans, and other offspring who had been trapped there scattered into the world. Freed at last, the children of Rangi and Papa began to quarrel among themselves, especially Tane and the sea god Tangaroa. Polynesians believe that the conflicts between the gods cause such things as the growth of weeds in fields, the differences between humans and animals, and the storms that threaten boats at sea.

Heartbroken at being separated from his beloved Papa, Rangi cried. His tears rained down upon the earth from the sky, causing great flooding. At the same time, the wind god Tawhiri showed his anger with his brothers by sending storms and winds to batter the earth, causing great destruction to the forests, seas, and fields. Only the war god Tu could resist his brother, but their struggle flooded the earth, leaving only the islands of Polynesia.

Over time the offspring of Rangi and Papa multiplied and filled the earth with life. But Rangi still cries from time to time when he misses Papa, and his tears fall as rain or as drops of morning dew.

## Rangi and Papa in Context

The creator gods Rangi and Papa reflect an understanding among the Maori people of the process of human reproduction, and show how the Maori view themselves as a part of the natural world. Rangi and Papa are locked in an embrace that resembles the closeness of two people making love. When they are separated, all things in the world are "born" between them. To the Maori, the human process of creation is a model for the mythical process of the creation of the world. The myth also reflects how important a mother's nurturing care is to the Maoris: when the gods decide to separate the pair, they send their father Rangi far away into the sky, but keep their nurturing mother Papa directly beneath their feet so she can continue to provide for them.

## Key Themes and Symbols

Like many mythologies around the world, the myth of Rangi and Papa views nature as comprised of two halves: the sky and the earth. Each is a distinct being, and both are necessary for life. The themes of unity, separation, and grief are also at the center of the myth of Rangi and Papa. When the couple is united, they create all the gods and elements of the earth. These elements, however, are trapped between Rangi and Papa and have no space or light. When Rangi and Papa separate, both good and bad things happen: all plants and animals on earth flourish, but great storms and **floods** cover most of the land. The Maori people still view rain and storms as symbols of the anger and tears of the gods.

### Rangi and Papa in Art, Literature, and Everyday Life

The tale of Rangi and Papa, like most Maori myths, has been passed orally from one generation to the next. Though many of these myths have been written down over the past two centuries, the oral tradition continues among the Maori. The myths of the Maori are also expressed in art, primarily through wood carvings of the mythical figures in the tales.

### Read, Write, Think, Discuss

The Maori view the sky as a father figure and the earth as a mother figure. This is a common theme in creation myths. What is it about the sky that made people associate it with a "father"? And what about the earth suggests a "mother"?

**SEE ALSO** Creation Stories; Polynesian Mythology

## Re

*See* **Ra.**

## Reincarnation

### Theme Overview

Many cultures have myths and legends that tell of **heroes** or other characters who die and then come back to life. When they reappear, though, it is not as their former selves but as other people, as animals, or even as plants. The concept of reincarnation—the reappearance of a spirit or soul in earthly form—is based on the belief that a person's soul continues to exist after death and can be reborn in another body.

## Major Myths

Many world myths and legends feature some form of reincarnation. Ancient Norse kings were regarded as reincarnations of the god **Freyr** (pronounced FRAY). After the introduction of Christianity to Norway, some people believed the Christian saint Olaf was the reincarnation of an earlier pre-Christian king, also named Olaf.

In the Arctic regions, where animals are critical to survival, the Inuit people believe that animals as well as humans have souls that are reborn. Hunters must perform ceremonies for the creatures they kill so the animal spirits can be reborn and hunted in the future. When a person dies, part of his or her soul will be incarnated in the next baby born into the community. Giving the newborn the dead person's name ensures that the child will have some of the ancestor's qualities.

Buddhist tradition includes a set of tales called the *Jatakas* (pronounced JAH-tuh-kuhz) that are based on reincarnation. They tell of Gautama Buddha (pronounced BOO-duh) and his various lives, in which he grew wiser and holier as his soul moved from life to life. In one life, Buddha was a hare who sought spiritual growth through fasting. He realized that if a beggar appeared he would have no food to offer, so he decided that he would offer his own flesh. One of the gods came down from **heaven** and visited the hare in the form of a beggar. The hare willingly hurled himself into a **fire** to provide a meal for his guest, but the god then saved the hare and painted his image on the moon to honor his spirit of self-sacrifice. On his way to becoming Buddha, Gautama passed through more than five hundred lives that included incarnations as an elephant, a priest, a prince, and a hermit.

The Japanese legend of O-Tei (pronounced OH-TAY) illustrates the haunting appeal of the idea of reincarnation. O-Tei was a young girl engaged to be married. She fell ill, and as she lay dying, she promised her future husband that she would come back in a healthier body. She died, and the young man wrote a promise to marry her if she ever returned. Time passed and eventually he married another woman and had a child.

## A Very Long Journey

The Greek historian Herodotus (pronounced heh-ROD-uh-tuhs) recorded ancient Egyptian ideas about reincarnation. The Egyptians, he wrote, believed that the soul passed through a variety of species—animals, marine life, and birds—before once again becoming a human. The entire journey, from the death of a human to rebirth as a human again, took three thousand years. One ancient Egyptian source, the *Book of Going Forth by Day*, partly supports Herodotus's account. It states that the souls of important individuals can return to earth in the form of creatures, such as the heron or crocodile.

But his wife and child also died. Hoping to heal his grief, the man went on a journey. In a village he had never visited, he stayed in an inn where a girl who looked much like O-Tei waited on him. He asked her name, and speaking in the voice of his first love, she told him that her name was O-Tei. She said that she knew of his promise and had returned to him. Then she fainted. When the girl awoke, she had no memory of her former life or what she had said to the man. The two were married and lived happily together.

## Reincarnation in Context

Belief in reincarnation has been shared by a wide variety of peoples, including the ancient Egyptians and Greeks and the Aboriginal people of central Australia. The most complex and influential ideas about reincarnation are found in Asian religions, particularly Hinduism and Buddhism. Cultural groups that believe in reincarnation have different ideas about the way it takes place. Some say that human souls come from a general source of life-giving energy. Others claim that particular individuals are repeatedly reborn in their descendants.

In Australia, most Aborigines believe that human souls come from spirits left behind by ancestral beings who roamed the earth during a mythical period called the **Dreamtime**. The birth of a child is caused by an ancestral spirit entering a woman's body. The spirit waits in a sacred place for the woman to pass by. After death, the person's spirit returns to the ancestral powers.

According to traditional African belief, the souls or spirits of recently dead people linger near the grave for a time, seeking other bodies—reptile, mammal, bird, or human—to inhabit. Many African traditions link reincarnation to the worship of ancestors, who may be reborn as their own descendants or as animals associated with their clans or groups. The Zulu people of southern Africa believe that a person's soul is reborn many times in the bodies of different animals, ranging in size from tiny insects to large elephants, before being born as a human again. The Yoruba (pronounced YAWR-uh-buh) and Edo of western Africa share the widely held notion that people are the reincarnations of their ancestors. They call boys "Father Has Returned" and girls "Mother Has Returned."

Reincarnation plays a central role in Buddhism and Hinduism. It also appears in Jainism (pronounced JYE-niz-uhm) and Sikhism (pronounced SEE-kiz-uhm), two faiths that grew out of Hinduism and are still practiced in India. Jainism shares with Hinduism a belief in many gods. Sikhism is a monotheistic religion that emphasizes the belief in only one god. It combines some elements of Islam with Hinduism.

Hinduism, Buddhism, Jainism, and Sikhism all began in India, where the idea of rebirth first appears in texts dating from about 700 BCE. They share a belief in *samsara*—the wheel of birth and rebirth—and *karma*—the idea that an individual's actions in their current life will determine how they are reborn in their future life. People who have done good deeds and led moral lives are reborn into higher social classes; those who have not are doomed to return as members of the lower classes or as animals. Only by achieving the highest state of spiritual development can a person escape samsara altogether and enter into the state of *nirvana*, total union with the supreme spirit.

## Reincarnation in Art, Literature, and Everyday Life

Reincarnation is still a popular theme in art and literature. Many movies have dealt with the idea of returning to life in a different body, encompassing all genres from horror to comedy. Some notable films that use reincarnation as a central premise include *Audrey Rose* (1977), *Chances Are* (1989), and *Down to Earth* (2001). However, even in modern times, reincarnation is hardly limited to the realm of myth: according to polls conducted in Europe and the United States, about one in five people believe in reincarnation.

## Read, Write, Think, Discuss

Few organized religions include the idea of reincarnation as an official part of recognized beliefs, and some even condemn the notion. However, belief in reincarnation is found across members of many different religious groups—even those that dismiss it as contrary to their religious teachings. Why do you think so many people believe in an idea that does not necessarily fit with the official views of their religion? What might be so appealing about reincarnation? Compare the notion of reincarnation with the belief that humans have only one life and one death. What are some of the positives and negatives of each belief?

**SEE ALSO** Afterlife; Australian Mythology; Buddhism and Mythology; Hinduism and Mythology

# Remus

*See* **Romulus and Remus.**

# Robin Hood

**Nationality/Culture**
British

**Pronunciation**
ROB-in hood

**Alternate Names**
None

**Appears In**
British folk ballads, *A Lytell Geste of Robin Hode*

**Lineage**
Unknown

## Character Overview

Robin Hood was the legendary bandit of England who stole from the rich to help the poor. The stories about Robin Hood appealed to common folk because he stood up against—and frequently outwitted—people in power. Furthermore, his life in the forest—hunting and feasting with his fellow outlaws, coming to the assistance of those in need—seemed like a great and noble adventure.

The earliest known mention of Robin Hood is in William Langland's 1377 work called *Piers Plowman*, in which a character mentions that he knows "rimes of Robin Hood." This and other references from the late 1300s suggest that Robin Hood was well established as a popular legend by that time. One source of the legend may lie in the old French custom of celebrating May Day. A character called Robin des Bois, or Robin of the Woods, was associated with this spring festival and may have been transplanted to England—with a slight name change. May Day celebrations in England in the 1400s featured a festival "king" called Robin Hood.

*A Lytell Geste of Robin Hode*, a collection of ballads, or songs, about the outlaw Robin Hood, was published in England around 1489. From it and other medieval sources, scholars know that Robin Hood was originally associated with several locations in England. One was Barnsdale, in the northern district called Yorkshire. The other was Sherwood Forest in Nottinghamshire, where his principal opponent was the vicious and oppressive Sheriff of Nottingham. Robin's companions included Little John, Alan-a-Dale, Much, and Will Scarlett.

By the 1500s, more elaborate versions of the legend had begun to appear. Some of these suggested that Robin was a nobleman who had fallen into disgrace and had taken to the woods to live with other outlaws. Robin also acquired a girlfriend named Maid Marian and a new companion, a monk called Friar Tuck. His adventures were then definitely linked to Sherwood Forest.

Beginning in the 1700s, various scholars attempted to link Robin Hood with a real-life figure—either a nobleman or an outlaw—but none of their theories has stood up to close examination. Robin was most likely an imaginary character, although some of the tales may have been associated with a real outlaw. Also at about this time, Robin began to be linked with the reigns of King Richard I, "The Lionhearted," who died in 1189, and King John, who died in 1216. The original medieval ballads, however, contain no references to these kings, or to a particular time in which Robin was supposed to have lived. Later versions of the Robin Hood legend placed more emphasis on his nobility and his romance with Marian than on the cruelty and social tensions that appear in the early ballads.

One of the medieval ballads about Robin Hood involved Sir Guy of Gisborne. Robin and his friend Little John had an argument and parted. While Little John was on his own, the Sheriff of Nottingham captured him and tied him to a tree. Robin ran into Sir Guy, who had sworn to slay the outlaw leader. When they each discovered the other's identity, they drew their swords and fought. Robin killed Sir Guy and put on his fallen opponent's clothes. Disguised as Sir Guy, Robin persuaded the sheriff to let him kill Little John, who was still tied to the tree. But instead of slaying Little John, Robin freed him, and the two outlaws drove away the sheriff's men.

Another old story, known as "Robin Hood and the Monk," also began with a quarrel between Robin and John. Robin went into Nottingham to attend church, but a monk recognized him and raised the alarm. Robin killed twelve people before he was captured. When word of his capture reached Robin's comrades in the forest, they planned a rescue. As the monk passed them on his way to tell the king of Robin's capture, Little John and Much seized and beheaded him. John and Much, in disguise, visited the king in London and then returned to Nottingham bearing documents sealed with the royal seal. The sheriff, not recognizing them, welcomed the two men and treated them to a feast. That night Little John and Much killed Robin's jailer and set Robin free. By the time the sheriff realized what had happened, the three outlaws were safe in Sherwood Forest.

Robin Hood's role as the enemy of powerful people and the protector of the poor was clearly illustrated in lines from *A Lytell Geste of Robin Hode*. Robin instructed his followers to do no harm to farmers or countrymen, but to "beat and bind" the bishops and archbishops and never to forget the chief villain, the high sheriff of Nottingham. Some ballads ended with the sheriff's death; in others, the outlaws merely embarrassed the sheriff and stole his riches. In one ballad, the sheriff was robbed and then forced to dress in outlaw green and dine with Robin and his comrades in the forest. Over time, the image of Robin as a clever, lighthearted prankster gained strength. The tales in which he appeared as a highway robber and murderer were forgotten or rewritten.

Legend says that Robin Hood was wounded in a fight and fled to a convent. The head of the nuns was his cousin, and he begged her for help. She made a cut so that blood could flow from his vein, a common medical practice of the time. Unknown to Robin, however, she was his enemy. She left him without tying up the vein, and he lay bleeding in a locked room. Severely weakened, he sounded three faint blasts on his horn. His friends in the forest heard his cry for help and came to the convent, but they were too late to save him. He shot one last arrow, and they buried him where it landed.

## Robin Hood in Context

The Robin Hood ballads reflect the discontent of ordinary people with political conditions in medieval England. The bulk of the population was made up of peasants, poor people who gave up much of what they earned in taxes to the rulers of the land. At the time these tales became popular, peasants were especially upset about new laws that kept them from hunting freely in forests that were now claimed as the property of kings and nobles. Social unrest and rebellion swirled throughout England, and this is reflected in the anti-noble, anti-law themes found in the Robin Hood tales. This unrest between peasants and nobles erupted in an event called the Peasants' Revolt of 1381.

## Key Themes and Symbols

To audiences the original tales and ballads were aimed at, Robin Hood represents economic justice and fairness. While he is depicted as a thief, he is usually shown to be stealing something that was thought to be unfairly taken in the first place, such as tax money. Robin Hood functions much like a trickster in other mythologies: he is a friend to the downtrodden and often antagonizes or fights against those in authority—in this case, sheriffs and the clergy instead of gods. Robin Hood is usually associated with forests and the color green—known as the color of outlaws—and his ever-present bow and arrow.

*The character of Robin Hood, a legendary English bandit, has appeared in many movies over the years, including the 1938 movie* **The Adventures of Robin Hood** *in which Errol Flynn played the title character.* WARNER BROS/THE KOBAL COLLECTION/THE PICTURE DESK, INC.

## Robin Hood in Art, Literature, and Everyday Life

In addition to inspiring many books and poems over the centuries, Robin Hood became the subject of several operas, and in modern times, numerous movies. Some notable retellings of the legends of Robin Hood include the 1938 film *The Adventures of Robin Hood*, starring Errol Flynn in the title role; the 1973 animated Disney adaptation *Robin Hood*; the 1976 film *Robin and Marian*, starring Sean Connery and Audrey Hepburn; and the 1991 film *Robin Hood: Prince of Thieves*, starring Kevin Costner. The character of Robin Hood also made notable appearances in the 1819 Sir Walter Scott novel

*Ivanhoe*, the 1949 Bugs Bunny cartoon *Rabbit Hood*, and the 1981 Terry Gilliam film *Time Bandits*.

### Read, Write, Think, Discuss

Robin Hood was a thief, yet was considered a hero in the many ballads and stories dedicated to him. In modern books, films, and television shows, criminals—especially thieves—often appear as **heroes**, or at least as characters with which the audience is meant to sympathize. Examples of stories with criminals as heroes include the films *Ocean's Eleven* (1960, remade in 2001), *Catch Me If You Can* (2002), and the *Pirates of the Caribbean* series. Why do you think criminals are so often portrayed as heroes? What qualities do hero criminals have that real criminals do not? To which social group do hero criminals generally appeal, and why?

# Roman Mythology

### Roman Mythology in Context

From the founding of the Roman empire to its fall in 476 CE, Rome dominated Europe and much of North Africa, the Near East, and Asia Minor. Although this sprawling empire encompassed many cultures with their own myths and legends, the mythology of the Romans themselves revolved around the founding, history, and **heroes** of the city of Rome. The Romans had developed their own pantheon, or collection of recognized gods and goddesses. After they conquered Greece, however, their deities (gods and goddesses) became increasingly associated with the figures of **Greek mythology**.

Although Rome's early history is difficult to separate from the legends that formed around it, the city appears to have begun as a community of central Italian peoples known as Latins. The Latins merged with the Etruscans, who probably came to Italy from Asia Minor before 800 BCE.

Until 510 BCE, Rome was ruled by kings. Then it became a republic governed by elected officials. The Roman republic eventually dominated most of Italy and conquered the North African coast and Greece. By 31

BCE, Rome governed all the lands around the Mediterranean Sea as well as northwest Europe.

The principal sources of information about Roman mythology appeared during the early years of the empire, between about 20 BCE and 20 CE. The poet Virgil produced Rome's national epic, the ***Aeneid***, which drew on myths that linked the city's founding with Greek deities and legends. Another poet, Ovid, wrote the *Metamorphoses*, a collection of Near Eastern and Greek myths that the Romans had adopted. Ovid's *Fasti* describes Roman myths about the gods according to the festivals in their calendar. In his history of Rome, Livy portrayed legends about the city's founding as though they were historical events. These and other writers worked to create an "official" Roman mythology, one that gave Rome an ancient, distinguished, and glorious heritage.

## Core Deities and Characters

In their early years, the Romans had many deities and spirits called *numina*, or powers, that were believed to inhabit all of nature. Unlike the Greek deities, the numina did not have distinctive, well-defined personalities and characteristics. Few stories about them existed. They were simply the forces that oversaw the activities of daily life. Examples include **Janus** (pronounced JAY-nuhs), god of doorways and archways, and Terminus (pronounced TUR-muh-nuhs), god of boundaries. Many early Roman deities were associated with farming, crops, or the land. Sylvanus (pronounced sil-VAY-nuhs), for example, was the protector of woodcutters and plowmen. Other early deities represented virtues or qualities, such as Concordia (pronounced kon-KOR-dee-uh), goddess of agreement; Fides (pronounced FEE-des), goddess of honesty; and Fortuna (pronounced for-TOO-nuh), goddess of fate or luck.

Captivated by the elaborate and entertaining myths the Greeks had woven around their gods and goddesses, the Romans gradually changed some of their numina into Roman versions of the major Greek deities. The ancient Roman god Saturn, guardian of seeds and planting, became identified with the Titan **Cronus** (pronounced KROH-nuhs), who appeared in Greek mythology as the ancestor of the gods. **Aphrodite** (pronounced af-ro-DYE-tee) became Venus, the Roman goddess of love. **Zeus** (pronounced ZOOS) and **Hera** (pronounced HAIR-uh), the king and queen of the Greek gods, became the Roman Jupiter (pronounced JOO-pi-tur) and Juno (pronounced JOO-noh).

## Raising the Sun

One of Rome's most worshipped goddesses received little literary attention. According to legend, Angerona (pronounced an-juh-ROH-nuh) knew a magical spell to raise the sun in midwinter. Her festival occurred on December 21, the shortest day of the year, when she was believed to say the words that would cause the days to lengthen and spring to return. Even more important, Angerona guarded the secret name of the city of Rome. The gods knew this name, but Rome would be doomed if people ever learned it. Statues of Angerona showed her mouth covered with her hands or a gag so that the secret name could not slip out.

Mars, a Roman deity first associated with agriculture, took on the characteristics of **Ares** (pronounced AIR-eez), the Greek god of war, which explains why the Roman version of this god is concerned with both war and farming. Diana, a traditional Roman goddess of the forests, was identified with **Artemis** (pronounced AHR-tuh-miss), the Greek goddess of the hunt. Minerva (pronounced mi-NUR-vuh) was the Roman version of **Athena** (pronounced uh-THEE-nuh), Neptune of **Poseidon** (pronounced poh-SYE-dun), Vulcan of **Hephaestus** (pronounced hi-FES-tuhs), Mercury (pronounced MUR-kyoo-ree) of **Hermes** (pronounced HUR-meez), Ceres (pronounced SEER-eez) of **Demeter** (pronounced di-MEE-ter), and Bacchus (pronounced BAHK-us) of **Dionysus** (pronounced dye-uh-NYE-suhs). **Apollo** (pronounced uh-POL-oh), too, was brought into the Roman pantheon, where he was known as both Apollo and Phoebus (pronounced FEE-buhs).

The Romans gave their deities some of the characteristics and even some of the stories associated with the Greek gods and goddesses. They also imported other foreign deities, such as **Cybele** (pronounced SIB-uh-lee) from near Troy in Asia Minor, and the Persian god **Mithras** (pronounced MITH-rahs). At the same time, in their own homes they continued to worship their traditional household gods, known as the Lares (pronounced LAIR-eez) and Penates (pronounced puh-NAY-teez).

Roman mythology also includes human heroes. Sometimes these mortals became deities. Romulus (pronounced ROM-yuh-luhs), the legendary founder of the city of Rome, was thought to have become the god Quirinus (pronounced kwi-RYE-nuhs). Many emperors were declared gods by the Roman senate after their deaths, and people worshipped them in temples. The most honored heroes, however, were **Aeneas** (pronounced i-NEE-uhs), **Romulus and Remus**, and others from myths about Rome's beginnings and early history.

## Major Myths

Romans cherished myths about their city's founding. A myth that probably dates from around 400 BCE told of the **twins** Romulus and Remus, offspring of a Latin princess and the god Mars. Although their uncle tried to drown them, they survived under the care of a she-wolf and a woodpecker. Eventually, the twins overthrew their uncle and decided to found a new city on the spot where they had been rescued by the she-wolf. After receiving an omen—a sign from the gods—about the new city, Romulus killed Remus and became the leader as the gods had intended. Rome took its name from him.

The ditch that Romulus dug to mark the boundary of Rome was called the *pomerium* (pronounced poh-MEHR-ee-uhm). Everything within the pomerium was considered to be part of the original, authentic, sacred Rome. Throughout Rome's long history, the Romans preserved landmarks within the pomerium that they associated with the legend of Romulus and Remus. These included a cave on the Palatine Hill where the wolf was said to have nursed the twins, and a nearby hut where Romulus was said to have lived.

According to legend, Romulus made the new city a refuge for criminals, poor people, and runaway slaves to attract citizens. Because this population lacked women, Romulus invited a neighboring people called the Sabines (pronounced SAY-bines) to a religious festival, and the Romans then kidnapped the Sabine women. Titus Tatius (pronounced TAY-shuhs), king of the Sabines, brought an army to wage war on Rome. By that time, however, the Sabine women had married their Roman captors. At their urging, the men made peace, and until his death, Titus ruled at the side of Romulus.

One myth connected with the war between the Romans and the Sabines reveals that a high-ranking Roman woman named Tarpeia (pronounced tahr-PEE-uh) caught sight of Tatius and fell in love with him. Tarpeia betrayed Rome to the Sabine army, but Tatius slew her for her treachery. The myth became part of the city's geography; a rocky outcropping from which the Romans cast murderers and traitors to their

*This ceiling fresco shows a gathering of the gods of Roman mythology.* ALINARI/ART RESOURCE, NY.

deaths was called the Tarpeian Hill. Other legendary figures from Rome's early history include the virtuous wife Lucretia (pronounced loo-KREE-shuh) and the brave soldier Horatius (pronounced hoh-RAY-shuhs), both of whom appear in tales about the downfall of the monarchy and the founding of the Roman Republic.

By the late years of the Republic, Romans had adopted a powerful new myth about their state's origins. This account is most fully told in the *Aeneid*. It revolves around Aeneas, a Trojan prince who fled from his ruined homeland because the gods told him that he was fated to establish a "new Troy." After wandering around the Mediterranean, Aeneas landed in Italy with some Trojan followers. There he married the daughter of the local Latin king. Aeneas's son Ascanius (pronounced ass-KAN-ee-us) founded a settlement called Alba Longa. This version of Roman history emphasized the idea that the gods had always meant for Rome to rule the world. Romulus and Remus were the sons of Rhea Silvia, a princess of Alba Longa, and descendants of Aeneas—a perfect example of Roman willingness and ability to piece together different myths.

Myths arose linking many deities with key events in Roman history. The twin wind gods Castor (pronounced KAS-ter) and Pollux (pronounced POL-uhks), together called the *Dioscuri* (pronounced dye-uh-SKYOO-rye), appear in both Greek and Roman mythology as inseparable brothers who form the constellation Gemini (pronounced JEM-uh-nye). In the Roman version, the Dioscuri fought on the side of the Roman army in a battle in the 490s BCE and brought word of the Roman victory back to the city.

## Key Themes and Symbols

The myths and legends about Roman history celebrate the virtues that Romans especially prized: duty, self-sacrifice, honor, bravery, and piety. Roman deities, too, tended to represent virtues, without the all-too-human weaknesses and vices of the Greek gods. A Greek historian named Dionysius of Halicarnassus recognized this difference when he wrote that the Roman deities were more moral than the Greek deities because the Romans had taken only what was good from the old stories and left out all the disgraceful parts.

## Roman Mythology in Art, Literature, and Everyday Life

The influence of Roman mythology extended farther and lasted longer than the Roman empire. Statues, temples, and other structures associated with Roman deities and myths can be found far from the ancient capital. An old mosaic—a picture made from small pieces of rock or tile—found in Britain shows the she-wolf feeding Romulus and Remus. It is a reminder of the days when Rome ruled Britain and a mark of how far Roman mythology spread.

The Renaissance began with a new interest in ancient Greece and Rome. The mythology of these cultures became part of the store of knowledge of well-educated Europeans. Since that time, hundreds of artists, writers, and musical composers have found inspiration in the *Aeneid* and in Rome's heavily mythologized version of its history.

## Read, Write, Think, Discuss

Although many of the deities in Roman mythology are based on Greek gods and goddesses, they are often better known in modern times by their Roman names. For example, the goddess of love is more easily recognized by the name Venus (Roman) than by Aphrodite (Greek). Even Romanized spellings of Greek names are often more popular, such as Hercules (Roman) instead of **Heracles** (Greek). What reasons can you think of to explain this widespread acceptance of Roman names over the original Greek names?

**SEE ALSO** Aeneas; *Aeneid, The*; Aphrodite; Apollo; Ares; Artemis; Castor and Pollux; Cybele; Greek Mythology; Janus; Lares and Penates; Poseidon; Romulus and Remus

# Romulus and Remus

**Nationality/Culture**
Roman

**Pronunciation**
ROM-yuh-luhs and REE-muhs

**Alternate Names**
None

**Appears In**
Ovid's *Metamorphoses*

**Lineage**
Sons of Mars and Rhea Silvia

## Character Overview

In **Roman mythology**, Romulus and Remus were the twin sons of the god Mars, and were the founders of the city of Rome. Their mother, Rhea Silvia, was the only daughter of King Numitor (pronounced NOO-muh-tor) of Alba Longa. Numitor's brother Amulius (pronounced uh-MYOO-lee-uhs) seized the throne and kept Rhea Silvia from marrying, since any sons she had would be the rightful heirs to the throne. However, Mars, the god of war, made love to her, and she gave birth to Romulus and Remus.

When Amulius found out about the **twins**, he ordered that they be thrown into the Tiber River to drown. The boys floated downstream, coming ashore near a sacred fig tree. A she-wolf and a woodpecker—creatures sacred to Mars—fed the twins and kept them alive until a shepherd found them. Faustulus (pronounced FAW-stoo-luhs), the shepherd, and his wife raised the boys. They grew up to be brave and bold.

The twins became involved in local conflicts and led a group of youths on raids, including a raid on a herd of cattle that belonged to Numitor. Remus was caught and brought before Numitor. In questioning the young man, Numitor realized that Remus was his grandson. Shortly afterward, the twins led a revolt against Amulius. They killed him and put Numitor back on the throne.

Afterward, Romulus and Remus wanted to found a city of their own, so they returned to the place where Faustulus had discovered them. A sign from the gods indicated that Romulus was to be the founder of the new city. He marked out the city boundaries and began to build a city wall. When Remus jumped over the unfinished wall, mocking his brother for thinking that it could keep anyone out of the city, Romulus killed him. Romulus became the sole leader of the new city, named Rome.

To populate Rome, Romulus invited people who had fled from nearby areas to live there. However, most of these settlers were men. The city needed women. Romulus invited the Sabine (pronounced SAY-bye-n) people, who lived in neighboring towns, to come to Rome for a great festival. While the Sabine men were enjoying themselves, the Romans seized the Sabine maidens, drove the men from the city, and married their women. The event became known as the "rape of the Sabine women."

The Sabine men planned revenge and staged several small but unsuccessful raids. Then Titus Tatius (pronounced TAY-shuhs), the Sabine king, led an army against Rome. The Romans were losing the battle when Romulus prayed to Jupiter (pronounced JOO-pi-tur), the king of the gods, for help. At that point, the Sabine women stepped in. They pleaded with the warring men to stop, for they could not bear to see their fathers and husbands killing one another. The two sides agreed to a peace in which the Sabines and Romans formed a union, with Rome as the capital.

Romulus ruled Rome for forty years. He disappeared mysteriously while reviewing his army on the Campus Martius (Field of Mars) in a thunderstorm. Some legends indicate he ascended into the heavens, where he became the god Quirinus (pronounced kwi-RYE-nuhs) and sat alongside Jupiter, the king of the gods.

## Romulus and Remus in Context

The myth of Romulus and Remus reflects the Roman view of their empire as destined by the gods, and the Roman desire to establish a unique cultural identity based on their own origin myths. The transformation

*According to Roman mythology, Romulus and Remus, twin brothers and the legendary founders of Rome, were kept alive as infants by a mother wolf after their uncle ordered them to be abandoned in the wild.* THE LIBRARY OF CONGRESS.

of Romulus from a mortal man to a god would be repeated later in Roman history when the Romans declared other human leaders such as Julius Caesar and Caesar Augustus to be gods after their deaths. This cultural transformation from "man" to "god" is known as *divination* and strengthened the Roman claims to greatness through the glorification of its leaders.

The myth was also meant to strike fear into the hearts of those who might rebel against the Romans. When Romulus kills Remus after he leaps over the wall, he states that anyone attempting to breach the walls of Rome will suffer the same fate. This is a clear message meant not only to stir up Roman pride, but to warn outsiders against ever attempting to take control of the city.

## Key Themes and Symbols

One of the central themes in the myth of Romulus and Remus is the unavoidable nature of destiny. Amulius tries to keep Rhea Silvia from having sons, but the god Mars intervenes. Amulius then tries to keep Romulus and Remus away from his kingdom, but fate keeps them alive, and ultimately they lead a revolt against their wicked uncle. Later, Romulus receives a sign from the gods that he alone is to be the founder of a new city. After his brother insults Romulus by leaping over the wall he builds, Romulus kills his brother and founds the city by himself.

Some scholars have pointed to the killing of Remus by Romulus as being similar to stories in other cultures about twins in which one twin kills the other and creates something from the body of the dead twin. Although Romulus did not actually use the body of Remus in the founding of Rome, it is significant that he killed Remus as Rome is being built, and that the killing involves the city walls. In this way, Remus becomes a sort of **sacrifice** that makes the founding of Rome possible, echoing the theme of sacrifice as being necessary for the advancement of society that is found in other cultures.

## Romulus and Remus in Art, Literature, and Everyday Life

Romulus and Remus were a popular subject in ancient Roman art, and were often depicted suckling from the she-wolf that raised them for a time. Another subject popular with later painters, including Peter Paul Rubens, Jacques-Louis David, and Pablo Picasso, was the abduction of the Sabine women.

In modern times, the legend of the abduction of the Sabines served as the inspiration for a short story by Stephen Vincent Benét titled "The Sobbin' Women," with the setting updated to rural America. This in turn inspired the successful 1954 musical *Seven Brides for Seven Brothers*. Romulus appears as a mysterious enemy of the superhero Wolverine in the Marvel Comics Universe. Remus and Romulus were also the names given to two planets in the *Star Trek* universe, home to the race of aliens known as Romulans.

## Read, Write, Think, Discuss

The myth of Romulus and Remus embraced by ancient Romans as a proud part of their founding history, is a tale of murder, kidnapping, and war. What do you think this says about ancient Roman culture that they created and embraced such a myth as a fundamental part of Roman identity?

**SEE ALSO** Roman Mythology; Sacrifice; Twins

# S

## Sacrifice

### Theme Overview

Many religious ceremonies have included sacrifice, the act of giving up something of value and offering it to a deity or god. Worshippers may make a sacrifice to win the favor of the deity, to give thanks, or to maintain a good relationship with the god. Myths from around the world contain many examples of sacrifices in which animals, humans, and even gods shed blood or die. Sometimes the sacrifice is linked with creation or with the continuation of life on earth. People also make offerings of precious items, such as flowers, wine, and incense, or a portion of the fruit or grain collected during a harvest.

### Major Myths

Many creation myths involve self-sacrifice by gods or ancient beings. In an early Hindu myth, Purusha (pronounced POOR-uh-shuh) is the primal being who allows himself to be dismembered so that creation can take place. His eye becomes the **sun**, his head the sky, his breath the wind, and so on. Purusha became a symbol of the acts of sacrifice that kept the heavens stable. The mythology of the Aztecs of central Mexico told how two of the gods formed the universe by splitting a goddess in half, so that one part of her became the sky and the other part became the earth. The Aztecs performed large-scale rites of human sacrifice as a way of repaying the goddess and the other deities for the violence and sacrifice of creation. In **Norse mythology**, **Odin** (pronounced OH-din), the chief of the gods, made a kind of self-sacrifice by hanging on the World Tree **Yggdrasill** (pronounced IG-druh-sil) for nine days to gain magical knowledge. For this reason, the Norse sometimes sacrificed war captives to Odin by hanging them, and Odin became known as the god of the hanged.

Sacrifice is often an act of worship or obedience. In the book of Genesis in the Bible, God tells Abraham to take his son Isaac to the top of a mountain and sacrifice him. Abraham builds an altar and prepares to sacrifice his son when a voice from **heaven** tells him to stop, saying, "Now I know that you fear God, because you have not withheld from me your son, your only son." Turning around, Abraham notices a ram caught by its horns in a bush. He releases Isaac and sacrifices the ram instead.

Some myths present sacrifice as a way of setting right the relationship between people and gods. The Kikuyu (pronounced kee-KOO-yoo) people of Kenya in eastern Africa tell of a time when no rain fell for three years. The crops dried up, and the people asked their magician what they should do. After performing a magical ceremony, he told them to bring goats to buy a maiden named Wanjiru. The next day everyone gathered around Wanjiru, who began to sink into the ground. When her family tried to help her, those around gave them goats, so the family let her sink. As Wanjiru sank inch by inch into the ground, rain began to fall. By the time she disappeared into the ground, the rain was pouring down. Afterwards, a young warrior who loved Wanjiru went to the place where she had disappeared. Letting himself sink into the **underworld**, he found Wanjiru, brought her back to the surface, and married her.

Sacrifice may be linked to divination, or foretelling the future. The Druids of ancient Britain sacrificed both animals and humans in the belief that they could read the future in the victims' dying movements or in the patterns of their intestines. In the story of **Sunjata** (pronounced soon-JAH-tuh), told by the Mandingo people of Mali in West Africa, a king sacrificed a bull in order to fulfill a prophecy, or prediction. A hunter predicted that if the king agreed to marry a hideous young woman, their child would become a great ruler. In Central America, the Mayan Vision Serpent ceremony—held to consult with the dead and determine the future—included offerings of blood drawn from the king.

## Sacrifice in Context

One type of sacrifice involves the offering of blood or life. According to one theory, the practice of blood sacrifice was based on the belief that life is precious, and therefore valuable to the gods. When freed from an earthly body, it was believed, life returned to its sacred source. In ancient Rome, a person performing a sacrifice said to the god, "Be thou increased by this offering." The idea behind this type of sacrifice was not pain, suffering, or death. Rather, life was being returned to the divine world so that the gods, in turn, would continue to give life to the human world.

Other theories provide different explanations for blood sacrifice. One suggests that it began as a form of magic. Another says that sacrifice may have been viewed as a symbolic meal that the community shared with its deity, or as a reenactment of creation myths. Still another theory claims that sacrifice may have been seen as a way of focusing and controlling aggression within the community.

Hunting peoples generally sacrificed game animals, while herding and farming peoples used domestic animals, such as sheep, goats, chickens, and cattle. Certain types of animals were regarded as the most appropriate sacrifices for particular purposes or for particular deities. Dark-colored animals, for example, might be offered to deities of the underworld (land of the dead), while an all-white animal might be seen as the best gift for a sky god.

The sacrifice of humans has occurred in many parts of the world. There is also evidence that in some communities animals were eventually substituted for human victims. The method of slaughter generally involved either blood (flowing freely or offered in a ceremonial vessel), **fire** (to carry the sacrifice to the god), or both. Sometimes, however, the person to be sacrificed was strangled, hanged, or drowned.

A special person, such as a ruler, priest, head of household, or older member of the community, usually supervised or carried out the sacrifice. The sacrifice was made in front of a group—it was too important an act to be performed privately. Special rituals, such as ceremonial bathing or fasting, often accompanied the sacrifice. The sacrificial offering might be placed on an altar or before a statue of a deity or burned in a sacred fire so that the smoke would carry its scent to the heavens.

## Sacrifice in Art, Literature, and Everyday Life

The theme of sacrifice is found throughout the art and literature of many cultures. The actual physical sacrifice of another living thing, however, is somewhat less common in modern art and literature. The short story "The Lottery" (1948) by Shirley Jackson is perhaps one of the best modern examples of mythic sacrifice in literature. Another example is the sacrifice of Aslan, the lion lord in the C. S. Lewis novel *The Lion, The Witch, and the Wardrobe* (1950); this was also featured in the 2005 film adaptation of the novel. Mayan sacrifice is depicted in the 2006 Darren Aronofsky film *The Fountain*, starring Hugh Jackman as a Spanish conquistador.

## Read, Write, Think, Discuss

The idea of human sacrifice is based on the notion that the death of one—or a few—will result in better conditions for the rest of those living. In other words, the tragedy of the death(s) is outweighed by the greater good accomplished for society. Do you think this is a valid reason? Why or why not? What about those who willingly risk their lives for the good of society, such as police officers and soldiers?

**SEE ALSO** Aztec Mythology; Odin; Sunjata; Yggdrasill

# Santa Claus

*See* **Nicholas, St.**

**Nationality/Culture**
Judeo-Christian

**Pronunciation**
SAYT-n

**Alternate Names**
Shaitan, Iblis (Islamic), Lucifer, Beelzebub, the Devil

**Appears In**
The Old Testament

**Lineage**
None

# Satan

## Character Overview

The Jewish, Christian, and Islamic religions are monotheistic faiths, which means their followers believe in the existence of only one god. That god has a powerful opponent known as Satan, or the Devil. As the three religions developed, Satan's role changed over time. At first, he was a creature under God's control with the task of testing people's faith. In time, however, Satan came to be seen as the prince of darkness, ruler of all evil spirits, enemy of both God and humankind, and source of treachery and wickedness.

Jewish and Christian traditions both offer similar explanations for the Devil's origin. Because God would not create a being of pure evil, Satan was originally an archangel, one of God's most divine or blessed creations. His name is given sometimes as Samael but more often as Lucifer (pronounced LOOS-i-fur), a bright angel called "son of the morning."

Some accounts say that God cast the archangel out of **heaven** because he would not honor Adam, the first man created by God. When the jealous archangel refused to acknowledge "a lowly thing made of dirt," God punished his pride by throwing him down into **hell**. There, as Satan, the fallen archangel ruled over a kingdom of devils, former **angels** who had followed him in his fall.

In Islamic tradition, Satan is known as Shaitan or Iblis (pronounced IB-liss). Like the Jewish and Christian Satan, he is a fallen angel who was punished for refusing to bow down before Adam. But Allah permits Iblis to tempt humans to test their faith.

Other versions of the archangel's fall say that he was thrown out of heaven because of his pride—he dared to compete with God's glory. According to a Hebrew myth, on the third day of creation, Lucifer walked in the Garden of **Eden** covered with brilliant, glittering jewels set in gold. He had become so filled with pride that he planned to rise above the heavens and become God's equal. God cast Satan down, and his glory turned to darkness and ashes.

Christian legends frequently depict Satan as a tempter who tries to lure the faithful into abandoning their faith. Stories such as the legend of Faust show people making bargains with the Devil. They generally give their souls—for which he is always hungry—in exchange for a gift, such as wealth, love, or power. Such bargains always end in terror and despair, unless God steps in to save the poor sinner's soul from Satan.

## Satan in Context

The name *Satan* comes from a Hebrew word meaning "adversary." It first appears in the Hebrew Bible, or Old Testament. In the book of **Job**, God allows this adversary—sometimes called Samael (pronounced SAH-mah-el) in Jewish literature—to heap misfortunes on Job (pronounced

JOHB) to see whether Job will turn against God. Judaism was influenced by earlier Persian religion, in which good and evil struggle with each other for control of the universe and for power over human hearts and minds. The Jewish Satan took on some characteristics of **Ahriman** (pronounced AH-ri-muhn), the Persian god of evil and ruler of demons.

After about 300 BCE, Satan came to be seen as God's enemy, the source and center of all evil in the world. The serpent that tempted **Adam and Eve** in Genesis, the first book of the Bible, was identified with Satan. Since that time, artists and writers have often portrayed Satan as a snake or dragon, or as a monstrous combination of man and dragon. By the time the books of the Bible known as the New Testament were written, Satan's role as the Devil was well established among Christians.

Satan as a mythological character reflects a tendency among many cultures to view the living world as a battleground between the forces of good and the forces of evil. For cultures where belief in a single, all-powerful and loving God prevails, the character of Satan provides an explanation for the existence of death, disease, and misfortune. The idea of Satan has also been used to silence arguments against church doctrine, or accepted teachings. Those who disagree or fail to worship properly were often accused of being agents of Satan, and were punished as heretics (those who believe differently) for their betrayal of God.

## Key Themes and Symbols

As the ruler of Hell, an **underworld** kingdom of darkness and **fire** in which sinners are tormented, Satan is sometimes called the "prince of darkness." The Bible describes him as a "roaring lion" but he is also associated with several other animals, including frogs, **dragons**, and goats. Popular culture frequently portrays him as looking similar to a mythological satyr, with the lower body of a goat, and the upper body resembling that of a human, except for a pair of horns that come out of his head. The animal with which Satan is most often linked is the snake, an association that stems from the belief that Satan was the snake in the Garden of Eden that first tempted mankind to sin. The snake represents the cunning of Satan, who uses the thoughts of humans to tempt them away from serving God rather than attempt to overtake them by force.

The myth of Satan, in its various forms, usually focuses on the idea of temptation as a way to lure people from righteousness. This is

*Satan, also known as the Devil, is the powerful enemy of God in the Jewish, Christian, and Muslim religions. His domain is hell, where he tortures the souls of the damned.* PUBLIC DOMAIN.

illustrated in the myth of the Garden of Eden when Satan, disguised as a snake, tempts Eve to violate the rules God has imposed. It can also be seen in the many myths involving a "deal with the devil," in which a person is enticed into giving up their soul for something they desire.

## Satan in Art, Literature, and Everyday Life

One of the best-known and most influential literary portraits of Satan can be found in *Paradise Lost*, an epic by the English poet John Milton published in 1667. Satan also appears in Dante's *Inferno* (1321), frozen in the bottom circle of Hell. Other popular depictions of Satan can be found in Christopher Marlowe's *Doctor Faustus* (1604), the best-known version of the "make a deal with the devil" story, and the short story "The Devil and Daniel Webster" (1937) by Stephen Vincent Benét.

In modern times, Satan has also appeared as a character in numerous films and television shows. Notable examples include the 1967 comedy *Bedazzled*, and its 2000 remake in which Satan is played by model-turned-actress Elizabeth Hurley. Other notable supporting appearances by Satan include the 2000 Adam Sandler comedy *Little Nicky*, in which the demon is portrayed by Harvey Keitel, and the 2007 television series *Reaper*, in which Ray Wise assumes the role of Satan as he looks to reclaim souls that have escaped from hell.

## Read, Write, Think, Discuss

The United States was first referred to as "the Great Satan" in 1979 by the Ayatollah Ruhollah Khomeini, the leader of the Islamic government of Iran. Since then, the term has been used by many groups and leaders throughout the Middle East to describe the United States. Why do you think so many people believe the United States deserves this label?

SEE ALSO Adam and Eve; Ahriman; Angels; Devils and Demons; Heaven; Hell; Job; Persian Mythology; Semitic Mythology; Serpents and Snakes

# Satyrs

**Nationality/Culture**
Greek

**Pronunciation**
SAY-turz

**Alternate Names**
Panes, Seilenoi, Tityroi, Fauns (Roman)

**Appears In**
Ovid's *Metamorphoses*, Nonnus's *Dionysiaca*

**Lineage**
Sons of the Hekaterides

## Character Overview

In **Greek mythology**, satyrs were half-man, half-beast creatures that lived in forests and hills. Usually pictured as human above the waist and as horse or goat below the waist, satyrs had pointed ears or horns on their heads.

According to some sources, satyrs were the children of goats and mountain **nymphs**, or female nature deities who lived in the mountains. They were sometimes described as the sons of the Hekaterides (pronounced hek-uh-tee-RYE-deez), five nymphs associated with a dance popular in rural areas. However, the Greek poet Hesiod identifies satyrs as brothers of the nymphs, while also calling them "good-for-nothing" and "mischievous." Followers of **Dionysus** (pronounced dye-uh-NYE-suhs), the god of wine and ecstasy, satyrs had a reputation for drunkenness and bad behavior.

*Satyrs were half-man, half-beast creatures that were symbols of fertility and known for being mischievous.* PRIVATE COLLECTION/THE STAPLETON COLLECTION/ THE BRIDGEMAN ART LIBRARY.

There are different categories of satyrs. Panes (pronounced PAN-eez) are satyrs with the legs of goats and are usually considered to be embodiments of the god **Pan**. Though they do not differ dramatically in appearance from satyrs, they are sometimes considered to be separate from satyrs. The Seilenoi (pronounced SAY-luh-noy) are elderly satyrs with white hair and fat bellies, usually found in the company of Dionysus and skilled in the art of winemaking. The Tityroi (pronounced TI-tuh-roy) are satyrs who play a musical instrument called a shepherd's pipe. They may have been local to the island of Crete (pronounced KREET).

## Satyrs in Context

Satyrs reflect two ideal views of life in ancient Greek tradition. The life of a satyr—with its constant drunkenness, passion, and pursuit of women—would be considered Dionysian (named after Dionysus), while a life of restraint, logic, and law would be considered Apollonian (named after Apollo). The Greeks did not view these as separate philosophies, but as equally necessary parts of a fulfilling life. A life lived solely according to one ideal and not the other was not considered successful, at least for humans.

## Key Themes and Symbols

Satyrs were considered symbols of fertility, and were frequently portrayed chasing nymphs. Just as nymphs represented the most feminine qualities of women, satyrs represented the rough-edged, crude, and boisterous aspect of men, especially those from rural areas. Their animal characteristics—horns, furry ears, hoofed legs—symbolize both their closeness with nature and their basest animal desires for food and sex.

## Satyrs in Art, Literature, and Everyday Life

Satyrs were popular figures in ancient Greece, especially among people in rural areas. During the festival of Dionysus in ancient Athens, plays featuring a chorus of boisterous satyrs were performed along with the usual tragedies. More recently, fauns and satyrs have appeared in many works of literature and films. The character of Tumnus in C. S. Lewis's *The Lion, the Witch, and the Wardrobe* (1950) is described as being a faun, and Grover Underwood, from the series *Percy Jackson and the Olympians* by Rick Riordan, is a satyr. In film, satyrs appear in the Disney animated film *Hercules* (1997). Even today, satyrs are still remembered for their lewd antics: the medical condition defined as excessive sexual thoughts or behavior in men is known as satyriasis (pronounced say-tur-EYE-uh-sis).

## Read, Write, Think, Discuss

Satyrs in ancient times were associated with sex, wine, and music—the ancient equivalent of "sex, drugs, and rock and roll." In what ways do satyrs resemble modern "party people"? Is the other ideal in Greek society—the restrained intellectual life—also represented in contemporary society? On which ideal do you think modern society places more value?

**SEE ALSO** Dionysus; Pan

# Sedna

**Nationality/Culture**
Inuit

**Pronunciation**
SAYD-nuh

**Alternate Names**
Sea Woman

**Appears In**
Inuit oral mythology

**Lineage**
Daughter of Anguta

## Character Overview

The Inuit (pronounced IN-yoo-it) are the indigenous, or native, people of northern Canada, Alaska, and Greenland. In Inuit mythology, the goddess Sedna rules the **underworld**, or land of the dead, and the creatures of the sea. Myths about Sedna explain the origin of sea creatures and reflect the harsh environment of the Arctic. Because she provides the animals used for food, Sedna is the most important Inuit deity (god or goddess). Sedna is the daughter of the Inuit creator god Anguta.

## Major Myths

According to one myth, Sedna was a child with an enormous appetite who tried to eat her father Anguta's arm while he was asleep. When he awoke, her father put Sedna in a boat and took her out to sea. He tried to throw her overboard, but she clung tightly to the side of the boat. Her father then chopped off her fingers one joint at a time. As the pieces of Sedna's fingers fell into the water, they turned into whales, seals, and sea lions. When all her fingers were gone, she sank to the bottom of the sea, where she guards the spirits of the dead.

In another version of the story, Sedna was a young woman who refused all the suitors who sought her hand. Then, a seabird disguised as a handsome man visited her and promised that if she married him she would live in luxury for the rest of her days. Against her father's wishes, Sedna married the bird. She soon found out, however, that the bird's promises had been lies. She led an unhappy existence in a flimsy shelter with only raw fish to eat.

When her father came to visit, Sedna asked him to take her home. Her father killed her husband and set off in his boat with Sedna.

However, the other birds stirred up a raging storm on the water. To calm the sea, Sedna's father threw her overboard as an offering to the birds. As in the other tale, she hung on until he cut off her fingers. In some versions of the story, Sedna's father hauled her back into the boat. Angered by her father's cruelty, she had her dogs try to eat him while he slept. When her father awoke, he cursed himself, Sedna, and her dogs. The ground opened up and swallowed them all, and Sedna became goddess of the underworld.

## Sedna in Context

The stories of Sedna reflect the harsh way of life of the Inuit people. Because the Inuit live in the Arctic, an area that is nearly always covered with ice, snow, or frozen soil, they cannot grow crops. Likewise, wild vegetation is scarce, which means the Inuit rely almost entirely on fishing and hunting to provide everything they need to live, including food, clothing, heat, and material for tools or weapons. Because of this, killing animals is an everyday task for the Inuit. It makes sense that these acts would also appear as paths to creation in Inuit mythology.

The Inuit believed that Sedna caused the animals to go away as a sign of her displeasure when social rules regarding birth, death, or hunting were broken. The return of the animals required the intervention of the shaman, or religious leader of the group, who had the ability to communicate with Sedna. The connection between good hunting and good behavior ensured that social order was maintained in Inuit society.

## Key Themes and Symbols

A central theme in the myths of Sedna is disrespect for parents or elders. In the first tale, Sedna was disrespectful to her father when she tried to eat his arm to satisfy her overwhelming hunger. In the second, Sedna again showed disrespect for her father by going against his wishes and marrying the deceitful bird. The theme of **sacrifice** is also present, as when Sedna's father threw her overboard in an attempt to appease the bird-gods. Sedna can also be seen as a sacrifice for the good of the people, since her severed fingers provided the sea animals they needed for food and clothing.

## Sedna in Art, Literature, and Everyday Life

Though Sedna plays an important part in daily Inuit life, she is not well known outside Inuit culture. She did appear in the Canadian children's cartoon series *Inuk* (2001) as the enemy of an Inuit boy who gains the ability to talk to animals. The goddess has also lent her name to the planetoid 90377 Sedna, one of the largest objects in our solar system, found beyond the orbit of the planet Neptune.

## Read, Write, Think, Discuss

Using your library, the Internet, or other available resources, research the habitat and culture of the Inuit people. How does their culture help them to survive in their environment? How and why have their living conditions changed over the centuries? Do you think their myths reflect their history and daily life? If so, how?

**SEE ALSO** Native American Mythology; Underworld

# Seers

## Theme Overview

People who claimed special knowledge of the divine or supernatural realms have appeared in many myths, legends, folktales, and religious traditions. Those known as seers could see things hidden from others. They had the ability to predict the future or speak for the gods. Others with similar magical gifts have been called diviners, oracles, prophets, and shamans. They are said to have received special wisdom, power, or understanding from gods or spirits, and they have generally had a significant role in religion.

## Major Myths

Several seers mentioned in Greek myths were associated with **Apollo**. Mopsus (pronounced MOP-sus), a seer who took part in the quest for the **Golden Fleece**, was sometimes said to be a son of Apollo. The seer **Laocoön** (pronounced lay-OK-oh-ahn) was a priest of Apollo until he broke his vow by fathering children. He tried to warn the Trojans against accepting a gift—a giant wooden horse—given to them by their enemies, the Greeks, but the Trojans refused to listen to him. They brought the horse inside the city walls, and during the night, Greek soldiers hidden inside it overtook the city. Another Trojan, the princess **Cassandra** (pronounced kuh-SAN-druh), was given the ability to see the future by Apollo, who loved her; however, when she rejected the god, she was cursed so that no one would ever believe her prophecies. Although she predicted all the tragic events of the Trojan War, her family and friends believed her to be insane.

The best-known seer of **Greek mythology** was the blind prophet Tiresias (pronounced ty-REE-see-uhs). Several tales account for his blindness. One claims that he was struck blind as a boy when he saw the goddess **Athena** (pronounced uh-THEE-nuh) bathing. Later, Athena felt sorry for Tiresias but could not restore his sight. Instead, she gave him the gift of prophecy and the ability to understand the language of the birds. In another myth, Tiresias came across two snakes mating. He killed the female snake and was transformed into a woman. Seven years later, he again saw two mating snakes; this time he killed the male snake and became a man. Because he had been both a man and a woman, **Zeus** (pronounced ZOOS), the king of the gods, and his wife **Hera** (pronounced HAIR-uh) asked him to settle an argument: Which of the sexes enjoys love more? When Tiresias replied that man gives more pleasure than he receives, Hera struck him blind. To make up for this deed, Zeus gave Tiresias the ability to foresee the future and allowed him to live an extraordinarily long life.

The Druids, priests of an ancient Celtic religion, were said to be seers and magicians. Like the prophets of the ancient Near East, they sometimes held political power as advisers to rulers. The Druid Cathbad (pronounced KAH-bah), who advised King Conchobhar (pronounced KON-kvar) of Ulster in Ireland, foresaw the destruction of the kingdom. Druidic ceremonies of divination included human and animal **sacrifice**.

In **Norse mythology**, the seer **Mimir** (pronounced MEE-mir) guarded a sacred spring located at one of the three roots of the World Tree, **Yggdrasill** (pronounced IG-druh-sil). **Odin** (pronounced OH-din) gained magical knowledge by drinking from the spring, but he had to pay for it by giving one of his eyes to Mimir. The Norse goddess **Freyja** (pronounced FRAY-uh) was also a seer. She introduced the gods to the type of divination called *seid*, which involved going into a trance and answering questions about the future.

The ceremonies described in Norse myths are similar to some of the rituals performed by traditional Siberian and Native American shamans.

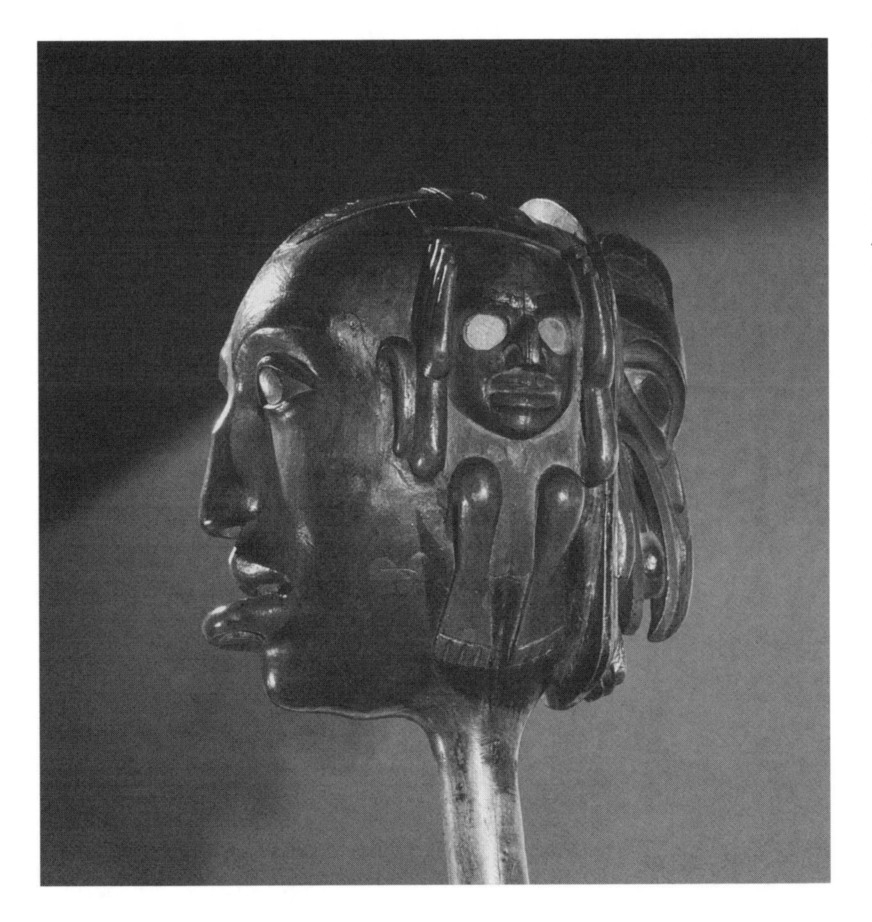

*A shaman's rattle. Native American shamans had magical powers similar to those of seers, only shamans used their powers primarily for healing rather than for predicting the future.* WERNER FORMAN/ ART RESOURCE, NY.

Shamans were believed to have the power to communicate with or travel to the spirit world. Generally, they did so for the purpose of healing rather than for predicting the future. Sometimes spirits spoke through shamans. According to the Haida (pronounced HYE-duh) of the Pacific Northwest, the spirit known as Lagua spoke through a shaman and taught the Haida how to use iron.

Hindu mythology includes many wise and holy men called seers or sages. They possess great spiritual power as a result of living pure and simple lives. A few seers are considered demigods—half human, half god—born from the thoughts of the god **Brahma** (pronounced BRAH-muh). Often, Hindu wise men are the teachers of kings or **heroes**. Although generally virtuous, some display pride or anger. One myth tells of Vishvamitra (pronounced vish-VAH-mi-truh), a proud seer whose standards were so high and whose demands were so great that he destroyed his king.

## Seers in Context

Seers have used various techniques of divination, or trying to foretell the future. In the ancient world, Babylonian, Egyptian, and Greek seers often relied on the interpretation of dreams to predict the future, believing dreams to be messages or warnings from the gods. Seers and diviners also explained the significance of events thought to be omens, or messages from the gods. Oracles, such as the famous oracle of Apollo (pronounced uh-POL-oh) at **Delphi** (pronounced DEL-fye) in ancient Greece, were often associated with a particular temple or shrine. They asked questions of the gods on behalf of worshippers or pilgrims and then gave the gods' answers.

Some seers, claiming to be divinely inspired, spoke on a wide range of issues. In the ancient Near East, prophets and diviners frequently became involved in politics. Hebrew prophets such as Samuel, **Elijah**, and Amos did not merely foretell the future, they also criticized religious practices and social conditions they believed were wrong.

## Seers in Art, Literature, and Everyday Life

Seers have endured as characters in myths and stories in nearly every culture around the world. Perhaps the most well-known seer in modern times remains Nostradamus, a real-life chemist who published books filled with predictions in the sixteenth century. Seers usually appear in popular culture as fortune-tellers: In the 1985 film *Pee Wee's Big Adventure*, for example, the main character embarks on a journey to find a stolen bicycle using the words of a fortune-teller as his only guide. Several self-proclaimed modern seers and psychics have gained fame by touting their abilities to speak with the dead; they claim to use this supernatural connection to gain secret information and predict future events.

## Read, Write, Think, Discuss

Seers were popular before the rise of science. In modern societies, has science eclipsed the role of seers totally, or do you think there are still areas of the unknown that justify the role of seers? What might those areas be, and why would a seer, rather than a scientist, be able to access them?

**SEE ALSO** Cassandra; Delphi; Freyja; Laocoön; Mimir

# Semitic Mythology

## Semitic Mythology in Context

Semitic mythology arose among several cultures that flourished in the ancient Near East, a region that extended from Mesopotamia (pronounced mess-uh-puh-TAY-mee-uh) in modern Iraq to the eastern coast of the Mediterranean Sea. These groups of people spoke Semitic languages, had similar religions, and worshipped related deities (gods and goddesses). Three major religions—Judaism, Christianity, and Islam—grew out of Semitic traditions. Semitic peoples shared many of the same myths and legends. Among their major gods and goddesses were those responsible for creation, fertility, death, and the **afterlife**. The names of the deities varied slightly from culture to culture.

Between about 3000 and 300 BCE, ancient Mesopotamia was home to a series of civilizations, beginning with the Sumerians, who built the first city-states. The Sumerians lived in the southern part of the region between the Tigris and Euphrates rivers. They were followed by the Akkadians (pronounced uh-KAY-dee-uhnz), who settled to the north, the Babylonians (pronounced bab-uh-LOH-nee-uhnz), and the Assyrians (pronounced uh-SEER-ee-uhnz). Later, Sumer and Akkad became known as Babylonia. The Assyrians settled even farther north along the Tigris.

The Sumerians did not speak a Semitic language. However, the Akkadians and other Semitic peoples who later rose to power in Mesopotamia adopted many parts of Sumerian culture, mythology, and religion. This Sumerian influence shaped thinking and storytelling in the region for thousands of years.

The Canaanites were Semitic peoples who occupied the lands along the eastern coast of the Mediterranean Sea. Canaanite culture flourished in the city of Ugarit, on the Syrian coast, between 1500 and 1200 BCE. Their culture was continued by the Phoenicians, who settled south of Ugarit and later established a colony at Carthage, in what is now Tunisia.

The ancient Israelites were a Semitic people who settled in Canaan. In time, they established the kingdoms of Israel and Judah, where the modern nation of Israel is today. In 722 BCE, the Assyrians gained control of the kingdom of Israel. The Babylonians conquered Judah in 586 BCE, destroying the city of Jerusalem and removing its inhabitants to Babylon for some years. Eventually the people of Judah came to be known as Jews.

## Core Deities and Characters

Many of the gods found in Semitic mythology are known by several names. Over time, the Sumerian goddess Inanna (pronounced ee-NAH-nah) became known by her Akkadian name, **Ishtar** (pronounced ISH-tahr). Dumuzi (pronounced DOO-moo-zee), Inanna's husband, also acquired other names; the people of early Israel called him Tammuz (pronounced TAH-mooz). Although there was significant overlap with main figures such as these, different Semitic cultures also had unique gods and goddesses.

**Mesopotamian Deities** All Mesopotamian peoples honored a fertility goddess, such as Inanna or Ishtar. They also recognized three creator gods, called An, Enlil (pronounced EN-lil), and Enki (pronounced EN-kee) by the Sumerians, and Anu (pronounced AH-noo), Enlil, and Ea (pronounced AY-ah) by the Akkadians, Babylonians, and Assyrians. An was the chief of the gods. Enlil was a god of wind and land who could be destructive, and Enki was usually associated with water, wisdom, and the arts of civilization. The moon god, known as Sin or Nanna, appeared in a myth in which demons tried to devour him. The powerful god **Marduk** (pronounced MAHR-dook) stopped the demons before they could finish the job. The moon god grew to his former size and repeated that growth every month, marking the passage of time.

Mythology was closely interwoven with political power in ancient Mesopotamia. Monarchs were believed to rule by the will of the gods and were responsible for maintaining good relations between the heavenly world and their kingdoms. Each of the early city-states had one of the deities of the pantheon—the collection of recognized gods and goddesses—as its patron, who was worshipped by the people and viewed as a protector. The importance of the deity rose and fell with the fortunes of its city. A main theme of ***Enuma Elish***, the Babylonian creation epic, is the rise of Marduk, the god associated with Babylon. Marduk became a leader of the gods, just as Babylon rose to power in the region.

**Canaanite Deities** The chief of the Ugaritic pantheon was **El**, the father of the gods, who was generally portrayed as a wise old man. **Baal**

(pronounced BAY-uhl), an active and powerful deity, was associated with fertility and sometimes identified with the storm god Adad. Asherah (pronounced ASH-er-ah), the mother of the gods, was the wife of El.

**Jewish Deities and Characters** Over the years the Jews produced sacred books, some of which form the Tanach (pronounced tah-NAHK), a set of documents known to Christians as the Old Testament of the Bible. These books include myths and legends about the history of the early Israelites, as well as information about their religious beliefs. Traditional Jewish stories were influenced by ancient Semitic mythology. Connections are clearly seen in such stories as the fight between **Cain and Abel** and the great flood survived by **Noah** in his ark. In the same way, the story of creation in the book of Genesis in the Old Testament contains parallels to Mesopotamian myths about how Marduk organized the universe. One major difference between Jewish tradition and earlier Semitic mythology, however, is that Judaism was and is monotheistic: instead of a pantheon of deities, it referred to a single, all-powerful deity, sometimes called Yahweh.

## Major Myths

Since so many different cultural traditions are grouped together under the banner of Semitic mythology, the various myths are best presented in groups according to their cultural origins.

**Sumerian Myths** One of the central Sumerian myths, the story of Inanna and Dumuzi, shows how part of the ancient mythology survived in later cultures. Inanna, goddess of light, life, and fertility, was ready to choose a husband. Two men wanted to marry her—Enkimdu (pronounced EHN-keem-doo), a farmer, and Dumuzi, a shepherd. Inanna leaned toward Enkimdu, but Dumuzi told her that his flocks and herds of livestock could produce more wealth than could Enkimdu's fields. The rivals competed for Inanna's hand until Enkimdu withdrew. Enkimdu then allowed Dumuzi to graze his flocks on his land, and in turn Dumuzi invited Enkimdu to attend his wedding to the goddess. The rivalry between the farmer and the herder in this myth is echoed in the Jewish story of Cain and Abel. Some historians of mythology believe that such tales grew out of ancient social tensions between settled agricultural communities and roving groups of livestock herders.

*Ishtar was the Akkadian name for the Sumerian goddess Inanna, a central figure in Semitic mythology.* ASSYRIAN SCHOOL/THE BRIDGEMAN ART LIBRARY/GETTY IMAGES.

One widespread story about Inanna and Dumuzi says that Inanna descended into the **underworld**, or land of the dead, and became a corpse there. The gods managed to restore her to life, but Dumuzi had to go to the underworld as her substitute. He came to be seen as a god of vegetation who had to die and be reborn each year. Many later myths about dying gods, including that of **Adonis** (pronounced uh-DON-is) in **Greek mythology**, resemble the story of Inanna and Dumuzi.

Another basic Semitic myth that came from Sumer is the story of a flood that covered the earth after humans angered the gods. Warned by the gods (or God) to build a boat, one righteous man—such as Noah—and his family survived the flood to give humankind a new start.

**Mesopotamian Myths** The myths of the Akkadians, Babylonians, and Assyrians depicted a world full of mysterious spiritual powers that could threaten humans. People dreaded demons and ghosts and used magical spells for protection against them. They worshipped a pantheon of a dozen or so major deities and many other minor gods.

The best-known Mesopotamian myth is the Babylonian epic of **Gilgamesh** (pronounced GIL-guh-mesh). It is the story of a hero king's search for immortality, or the ability to live forever. A bold and brave warrior, Gilgamesh performed many extraordinary feats during his journey. Although he failed to obtain his goal—the secret of eternal life—he gained greater wisdom about how to make his life meaningful.

Another legend that deals with the question of why humans die is the myth of Adapa, the first human being. The water god Ea formed Adapa out of mud. Although Adapa was mortal, Ea's touch gave him divine strength and wisdom. One day, when Adapa was fishing, the wind overturned his boat. Adapa cursed the wind. According to one version of the story, the wind was in the form of a bird, and Adapa tore off its wings. The high god Anu called Adapa to **heaven** to explain his actions. Adapa asked his father, Ea, for advice on how to act in heaven. Ea told him to wear mourning clothes, to be humble, and to refuse food and drink because they would kill him. So when Anu offered food, Adapa declined it. Unfortunately, Ea's advice had been mistaken. The food Adapa rejected was the food of immortality that would have allowed human beings to live forever. Adapa's choice meant that all men and women must die.

Marduk appears in a Babylonian myth about Zu, a bird god from the underworld. A frequent enemy of the other gods, Zu stole the tablets that gave Enlil control over the universe. When the high god Anu asked for a volunteer to attack Zu, several gods refused because of Zu's new power. Finally, Marduk took on Zu, defeated him, and recovered the tablets. This restored the universe to its proper order.

**Canaanite Myths** Baal appears in a set of Ugaritic myths called the Baal cycle. These stories describe Baal's rise to power and the challenges he faced from other deities and powerful forces. An underlying theme of the Baal cycle is the tension between the old god El and the young and

## The Invisible Queen

To the ancient Mesopotamians, light and darkness, life and death, were two halves of a whole. Inanna, the goddess of heaven, ruled the living world, and her sister Ereshkigal (pronounced ay-RESH-kee-gahl), or darkness, was queen of the dead. Neither sister could exist without the other; together they made existence complete. But while Inanna lived in the world that could be seen by humans, Ereshkigal was invisible. Mesopotamian artists never portrayed Ereshkigal directly, but they did create images of the monsters and demons that Ereshkigal sent to trouble the living.

vigorous Baal. Although El remained supreme, Baal became a king among the gods. He defeated Yam, also called **Leviathan** (pronounced luh-VYE-uh-thuhn), who represented the destructive force of nature and was associated with the sea or with **floods**. Baal also had to make peace with his sister Anat, a goddess of fertility, who conducted a bloody **sacrifice** of warriors. Finally, Baal and Anat went to the underworld to confront Mot, the god of death. El presided over the battle between Baal and Mot. Neither god won.

Other Ugaritic myths deal with legendary kings. Although these tales may have some basis in historical fact, the details are lost. One legend told the story of King Keret, who longed for a son. In a dream, El told Keret to take the princess of a neighboring kingdom as his wife. Promising to honor Anat and Ashera, the king did so, and his new wife bore seven sons and a daughter. However, Keret became ill and neglected the worship of the goddesses. Only a special ceremony to Baal could restore the king's health and the health of the kingdom. This myth illustrates the Semitic belief that the gods sent good or ill fortune to the people through the king.

**Jewish and Christian Myths** As Judaism developed over the centuries, new stories, sacred books, and commentary emerged to expand on the ancient texts. The term *midrash* refers to this large body of Jewish sacred literature, including a vast number of myths, legends, fables, and stories that date from the medieval era or earlier. These narratives are called the Haggadah (pronounced huh-GAH-duh), or "telling," and they are cherished as both instruction and entertainment.

Sometimes the Haggadah fills in the gaps that exist in older narratives. For example, Genesis contains an account of how Cain murdered Abel. The Haggadah adds the information that no one knew what to do with Abel's body, for his was the first death that humans had witnessed. Adam, the father of Cain and Abel, saw a raven dig a hole in the ground and bury a dead bird, and he decided to bury Abel in the same way.

Jewish tradition influenced Christianity, a monotheistic faith that began as an offshoot of Judaism. The two religions share many sacred stories and texts. The Tanach, especially the books of Genesis and Exodus, contains stories that are part of Christianity—God's creation of the earth, **Adam and Eve** in the Garden of **Eden**, Noah and the flood, and Moses and the Exodus. However, the New Testament of the Bible, which deals with the life and works of Jesus, is unique to Christianity.

**Islamic Myths** Like Christianity, Islam is a monotheistic Semitic faith that developed from Jewish traditions. Islam dates from 622 CE, when an Arab named Muhammad declared himself to be the prophet of God, or Allah (pronounced ah-LAH). Islamic tradition recognizes Abraham, Noah, Moses, and other ancient figures of Judaism as earlier prophets. Muslims, followers of Islam, also believe that Jesus was a prophet.

The word of Allah as made known to Muhammad is contained in the Islamic sacred text, the Qur'an or Koran. As time passed, Muslim scholars and teachers all over the Islamic world added more information about Muhammad and his followers, as well as interpretations of Islamic law and the sayings of the prophet. They incorporated elements of Semitic, Persian, and Greek mythology or stories about Muhammad, his family, and other key figures in Islamic history.

Although such storytelling was not officially part of Islam—and was sometimes vigorously discouraged by Islamic authorities—it appealed to many Muslims. As Islam spread to new areas, local traditions and legends became mingled with the basic Islamic beliefs. In Pakistan, for example, folk tales about girls dying of love came to be seen as symbols of souls longing to be united with Allah.

Many of the legends surrounding Muhammad credit him with miraculous events. Some tales say that Muhammad cast no shadow, or that when he was about to eat poisoned meat, the food itself warned him not to taste it. According to legend, the angel Gabriel guided Muhammad, who rode a winged horse called Buraq or Borak, on a mystical journey through heaven, where he met the other prophets.

Similarly, historical figures who founded mystical Islamic brotherhoods came to be associated with stories of miracles, such as riding on lions and curing the sick. In some cases, these legends have elements of traditional myths about pre-Islamic deities or **heroes**. Romantic tales about Alexander the Great may have colored some of the tales about Khir, an Islamic mythical figure and the patron of travelers, who is said to have been a companion of Moses.

## Key Themes and Symbols

Common themes of Semitic myths include creation, great floods, and heroes who overcome challenges. The body often appears as a symbol of the divine. In the ancient Babylonian myth of **Tiamat**, the goddess's body is used to create the heavens and the earth; in some Christian traditions, the body and blood of Jesus is symbolically consumed as a way to purify oneself. The flood that appears as a recurring theme in several cultures symbolizes a cleansing of humankind, or a purging of those unworthy in the eyes of the gods. Heroes in Semitic mythology are often celebrated for their ability to be like the gods or for their drive to become like the gods. Some themes, such as the death and rebirth of fertility deities, were rooted in the agricultural way of life of these Near Eastern peoples and represented the seasons of the year.

## Semitic Mythology in Art, Literature, and Everyday Life

Semitic mythology survives in modern times largely through its variations in modern Christian, Jewish, and Islamic beliefs. Tales like the Garden of Eden and Noah and the flood are familiar to people in many different cultures around the world. These tales have also been the inspiration for some of the greatest works of art ever created by artists such as Michelangelo, Hieronymus Bosch, and Albrecht Dürer.

Many specific characters from Semitic mythology are also still found in modern culture, though some came to be viewed differently over the centuries. Baal, now widely known as a demonic figure, appeared in the 1978 Robert R. McCammon horror novel of the same name. Marduk appeared as a character within another character's body in an episode of the animated television series *Sealab 2021* (2002). Perhaps the most enduring character is Gilgamesh, whose tale has been retold in many forms. Some notable versions of the tale include Robert Silverberg's

1984 novel *Gilgamesh the King*, the three-act opera *Gilgamesh* created by Rudolf Brucci in 1986, and *Never Grow Old: The Novel of Gilgamesh* (2007) by Brian Trent.

## Read, Write, Think, Discuss

Many of the tales from Semitic mythology have appeared in several different religious traditions, such as Christianity, Judaism, and Islam. However, followers of these religions are often quick to point out their differences; indeed, wars have been fought over the distinctions between these religions. Comparing the core myths of Christianity, Judaism, and Islam, do you think that there are more similarities or differences between these religions? Why do you think the differences are pointed out more frequently than the similarities?

SEE ALSO Devils and Demons; Floods; Persian Mythology; Satan

# Serpents and Snakes

## Theme Overview

Serpents and snakes play a role in many of the world's myths and legends. Sometimes these mythic beasts appear as ordinary snakes. At other times, they take on magical or monstrous forms. Serpents and snakes have long been associated with good as well as evil, representing both life and death, creation and destruction.

## Major Myths

Many mythical creatures, such as **dragons**, combine snake-like qualities with features of humans or animals. In **Greek mythology**, Echidna (pronounced i-KID-nuh) was a half-woman, half-serpent monster whose offspring included several dragons. Cecrops (pronounced SEE-krahps) had a man's head and chest on a snake's body and was a hero to the Athenians. In Toltec and **Aztec mythology**, **Quetzalcoatl** (pronounced keht-sahl-koh-AHT-l), the Feathered Serpent, held an important place. In medieval Europe, people told tales of the **basilisk** (pronounced BAS-

## Sea Serpents

Mysterious serpents occur not only in ancient myths but also in modern legends. For centuries, people have reported seeing huge snakes or snakelike monsters at sea or in lakes. Although many marine scientists admit that creatures yet unknown may inhabit the depths, no one has produced reliable evidence of an entirely new kind of sea serpent. Most likely the mysterious creatures seen swimming on the water's surface are masses of seaweed, floating logs, rows of porpoises leaping into the air, giant squid, or just common sharks or sea lions.

uh-lisk), a serpent with a dragon's body that could kill merely by looking at or breathing on its victims. Melusina (pronounced meh-loo-SEE-nuh), another figure in European folklore, was part woman, part fish and snake, and had to spend one day each week in water.

Myths that emphasized the frightening or evil aspects of serpents and snakes often portrayed them as the enemies of deities and humans. The Greek hero **Perseus** (pronounced PUR-see-uhs) rescued **Andromeda** (pronounced an-DROM-i-duh), who was chained to a rock, by slaying a sea monster that threatened to eat her. In **Norse mythology**, a monster called the Midgard serpent—also known as Jormungand (pronounced YAWR-moon-gahnd)—was wrapped around the earth, biting its tail. **Thor** battled the serpent, which lived in the sea, where its movements caused storms around the world. Another Norse monster, the Nidhogg (pronounced NEED-hawg), was an evil serpent coiled around one of the roots of **Yggdrasill** (pronounced IG-druh-sil), the World Tree. It was forever trying to destroy the tree by biting or squeezing it.

In the mythology of ancient Egypt, Apophis (pronounced uh-POH-fis) was a demon who appeared in the form of a serpent. Each night he attacked **Ra**, the **sun** god. But Mehen, another huge serpent, coiled himself around Ra's sun boat to protect the god from Apophis—a perfect illustration of how snakes can be symbols of both good and evil.

Mythological snakes that act as forces of good have various roles, such as creating the world, protecting it, or helping humans. Stories of the Fon people of West Africa tell of Da, a serpent whose thirty-five hundred coils support the cosmic ocean in which the earth floats. Another thirty-five hundred of its coils support the sky. Humans occasionally catch a glimpse of many-colored Da in a rainbow, or in light reflected on the surface of water.

The Aboriginal people of northern Australia tell how the Great Rainbow Snake Julunggul shaped the world. When human blood dropped into a waterhole, Julunggul grew angry. He sent a wave of water washing across the earth, and he swallowed people, plants, and animals. Julunggul reared up toward **heaven**, but an ant spirit bit him and made him vomit up what he had swallowed. This happened again and again until Julunggul departed from the earth, leaving people, plants, and animals in all parts of it.

According to a story of the Diegueño (pronounced dee-uh-GWAY-nyoh) Indians of California, humans obtained many of the secrets of civilization from a huge serpent named Umai-hulhlya-wit. This serpent lived in the ocean until people performed a ceremony and called him onto the land. They built an enclosure for him, but it was too small to hold him. After Umai-hulhlya-wit had squeezed as much of himself as possible into the enclosure, the people set him on **fire**. Soon the serpent's body exploded, showering the earth with the knowledge, secrets, songs, and other cultural treasures he had contained.

Hindu myths contain many tales of serpents. Kaliya (pronounced KAH-lee-yuh) was a five-headed serpent king who poisoned water and land until the god **Krishna** (pronounced KRISH-nuh) defeated him in battle. Kaliya then worshipped Krishna, who spared his life. Kadru was a snake goddess who bore one thousand children. Legend says that they still live today as snakes in human form. One of Kadru's children was the world snake Shesha that the gods used to turn a mountain and stir up the ocean, just as people churn milk into butter by using a rope coiled around a stick or paddle. As the gods churned the ocean with the snake, many precious things arose from it, including the moon, a magical tree, and the Amrita (pronounced uhm-REE-tuh), or water of life.

## Serpents and Snakes in Context

In religion, mythology, and literature, serpents and snakes often stand for fertility or a creative life force—partly because the creatures can be seen as symbols of the male sex organ. They have also been associated with water and earth because many kinds of snakes live in the water or in holes in the ground. The ancient Chinese connected serpents with life-giving rain. Traditional beliefs in Australia, India, North America, and

*The Hindu god Krishna defeated the five-headed serpent king Kaliya.* GIRAUDON/ ART RESOURCE, NY.

Africa have linked snakes with rainbows, which in turn are often related to rain and fertility.

As snakes grow, many of them shed their skin at various times, revealing a shiny new skin underneath. For this reason snakes have become symbols of rebirth, transformation, immortality (the ability to live forever), and healing. The ancient Greeks considered snakes sacred to Asclepius (pronounced uh-SKLEE-pee-uhs), the god of medicine. He carried a caduceus, a staff with one or two serpents wrapped around it, which has become the symbol of modern physicians.

For both the Greeks and the Egyptians, the snake represented eternity. Ouroboros (pronounced or-ROB-or-uhs), the Greek symbol of eternity, consisted of a snake curled into a circle or hoop, biting its own tail. The Ouroboros grew out of the belief that serpents eat themselves and are reborn from themselves in an endless cycle of destruction and creation.

Living on and in the ground, serpents came to be seen in some religions and mythologies as guardians of the **underworld**, or land of the dead. In this role they could represent hidden wisdom or sacred mysteries, but they also had other, more sinister meanings. The use of serpents as symbols of death, evil, or treachery may be related to the fact that some of them are poisonous and dangerous. **Satan** and other devils have frequently been portrayed as snakes, as in the biblical story of **Eden** where a sly serpent tempts Eve and Adam into disobeying God. Some Christian saints are said to have driven away snakes as a sign of miraculous powers given to them by God. According to legend, **St. Patrick** cleared Ireland of snakes.

The **Nagas** (pronounced NAH-gahz) of Hindu and Buddhist mythology show how serpents can symbolize both good and evil, hopes and fears. Although these snake gods could take any shape, including a fully human one, they often appeared as human heads on serpent bodies. The Nagas lived in underwater or underground kingdoms. They controlled rainfall and interacted with gods and humans in a variety of ways. Some were good, such as Mucalinda, the snake king who shielded Buddha from a storm. Others could be cruel and vengeful.

## Serpents and Snakes in Art, Literature, and Everyday Life

Even after many centuries, serpents and snakes have not lost their power to evoke a reaction in modern audiences. Though most depictions of snakes and serpents in modern art and literature do not qualify as mythical, there have been some notable examples of larger-than-life serpents, especially in films. The talking snake Kaa from Rudyard Kipling's *The Jungle Book* (1894), as well as the 1967 Disney animated

*Nagas were snake gods that could be both good and bad in Hindu and Buddhist mythology. This statue shows Buddha being protected by the Naga behind him.* ERICH LESSING/ ART RESOURCE, NY.

adaptation, has the ability to hypnotize his prey—though he is a helpful mentor to the main character in the book, and a villain in the film. The 1998 novel *Harry Potter and the Chamber of Secrets*, by J. K. Rowling, features an enormous basilisk, as does the 2002 film of the same name. The Harry Potter books also feature a giant snake named Nagini that is the close companion of the evil wizard Lord Voldemort. The 1997 horror film *Anaconda*, starring Jennifer Lopez and Jon Voight, also contains a mythically large and deadly snake as its main antagonist.

## Read, Write, Think, Discuss

Serpents and snakes in Western cultures have long been associated with evil. However, in some Asian cultures, serpents are accepted in a much more neutral or even positive light. Why do you think there is such a dramatic difference between how different cultures view snakes and serpents?

**SEE ALSO** Adam and Eve; Animals in Mythology; Basilisk; Dragons; Medusa; Nagas; Patrick, St.; Quetzalcoatl; Satan

# Set

**Nationality/Culture**
Egyptian

**Pronunciation**
SET

**Alternate Names**
Seth, Sutekh

**Appears In**
The Book of the Dead

**Lineage**
Son of Nut and Geb

## Character Overview

In **Egyptian mythology** Set (or Seth) was the evil brother of the god **Osiris** (pronounced oh-SYE-ris) and the goddesses **Isis** (pronounced EYE-sis) and Nephthys (pronounced NEF-this). The son of the earth god Geb and the sky goddess **Nut** (pronounced NOOT), Set tore himself from his mother's body before he was fully formed, and then used pieces of animals to complete his own body. Among the many animals associated with Set were the pig, donkey, scorpion, antelope, hippopotamus, and crocodile.

## Major Myths

Originally a sky and storm god, Set was highly regarded at first, and his cult—or organized body of worshippers—was one of the oldest in Egypt. Each day he rode across the sky in the **sun** ship of the great god **Ra** (pronounced RAH); each night as he traveled through the **underworld**, or land of the dead, he killed the mighty serpent Apophis (pronounced uh-POH-fis) to protect Ra. In time, however, Set became jealous of the other gods, and his treachery against them turned him into one of the chief forces of evil.

Above all, Set envied his brother Osiris, who ruled as king of Egypt while Set served only as lord of the desert. Determined to destroy his brother, Set arranged a great feast to which he invited Osiris and the other gods. He had carpenters construct a large and magnificently decorated box, which he placed at the entrance hall of his palace. When Osiris arrived, Set tricked him into getting inside the box. As soon as Osiris stepped into the box, Set ordered his servants to nail down the lid, seal it with molten lead, and throw it into the Nile River. Osiris drowned.

Their sister Isis, who was also Osiris's wife, searched for her husband and eventually found the box. She brought Osiris back to life long enough to conceive a son, **Horus** (pronounced HOHR-uhs). Set, however, found Osiris's body and cut it into pieces. Then he scattered the pieces throughout Egypt. Nephthys, Set's wife and sister, helped Isis locate the pieces and bring Osiris back to life. After that, Osiris went to rule the underworld as king of the dead.

Horus later fought Set to avenge his father's death. In a series of great battles, Horus defeated his evil uncle. Horus would have killed Set, but Isis took pity on Set and asked Horus to spare his life. Ancient Egyptians viewed the battle between Horus and Set as the ultimate struggle between good and evil.

As the cult of Osiris grew in Egypt, worship of Set declined. Eventually, Egyptian priests declared Set to be an enemy of the gods. His name and image were removed from many monuments, and he became associated with Apophis, the monstrous serpent that he had once defeated each night to protect Ra.

## Set in Context

The conflict between Set and Horus may reflect actual historical conflicts between the two regions of Egypt known as Upper Egypt and Lower Egypt. The Shabaka Stone, an artifact that contains a recording of an Egyptian document dating back to at least 2000 BCE, states that Geb solved the battle between Set and Horus by giving Horus the area of Lower Egypt to rule, and giving Set Upper Egypt to rule. This does mirror the historical division between the two halves of Egypt, and the subsequent takeover of Upper Egypt by Horus may reflect the eventual unification that brought together these two halves. The people of Upper and Lower Egypt often worshipped different gods, so real-life battles

*Egyptians carved this limestone stele in order to protect against the spells of the evil god Set.* ERICH LESSING/ART RESOURCE, NY.

for control of the region may explain the stories of two gods fighting for power.

## Key Themes and Symbols

The main themes of the myth of Set are envy and the lust for power. Set betrayed and killed his own brother because he was jealous of the region his brother controlled, and wished to take it as his own. Set then battled his nephew in an attempt to gain control of the lands. Earlier myths present Set as a dedicated protector of Ra, but these are not the most well-known or enduring tales associated with the god.

## Set in Art, Literature, and Everyday Life

In ancient Egyptian art, Set is often pictured with the head of an unidentified animal that resembles an anteater, or possibly a jackal—both animals that lived in the area. In modern times, Robert E. Howard introduced a god named Set in his *Conan the Barbarian* series of stories, but Howard's serpent god does not resemble the traditional Egyptian Set. The Marvel Comics series *Thor* also includes a character named Seth, based more closely on traditional Egyptian mythology.

## Read, Write, Think, Discuss

Set plans to murder his brother Osiris so that he can take over the kingdom of Egypt in addition to the desert he already controls. In this way, he resembles leaders such as Adolf Hitler and Alexander the Great, who conquered nearby lands in order to expand their own empires. Do you think conquering foreign lands and cultures to expand the size of an empire is by definition evil? Why or why not?

**SEE ALSO** Egyptian Mythology; Horus; Isis; Nut; Osiris; Ra; Serpents and Snakes

# Seth

*See* **Set.**

# Shamash

**Nationality/Culture**
Assyrian/Babylonian

**Pronunciation**
shah-MAHSH

**Alternate Names**
Utu, Babbar, Chemosh

**Appears In**
The *Epic of Gilgamesh*, *Great Hymn to Utu*,

**Lineage**
Son of the moon god Sin

## Character Overview

Shamash (also known as Utu in Sumerian) was the **sun** god in the Akkadian mythology of the ancient Near East. Associated with truth and justice, he was one of the most active gods in the pantheons (collection of recognized gods and goddesses) of ancient Sumer, Babylonia (bab-uh-LOH-nee-uh), and Assyria (uh-SEER-ee-uh). Shamash was responsible for maintaining the order of the universe; Hammurabi, the Babylonian king who oversaw the first written code of laws in recorded history, claimed that they were given to him by Shamash. Nothing could hide from his bright light, which banished darkness and revealed lies. In Babylon those who wished to know the future would call on Shamash, for it was said that his eye could see everything.

Shamash was considered the defender of the poor and the weak, and therefore the enemy of evil. Those who wished for defense against witchcraft would call on Shamash for help. Travellers prayed to him before setting out, as would armies, since Shamash himself travelled across the sky. In addition to these duties, Shamash also aided women in labor, freed captives, and healed the sick.

## Major Myths

Shamash was the son of the Akkadian moon god Sin (pronounced SEEN) and the brother of the goddess **Ishtar** (pronounced ISH-tahr). His wife Aya (meaning "youth") bore him four sons: Giru (fire), Kittum (truth), Mesharum (justice), and Nusku (light). As god of the sun, Shamash moved across the sky during the day; according to some legends, he also moved through the **underworld**, or land of the dead, during the night. In other stories, the god and his sons crossed the sky in a chariot by day and rested in a palace on a mountain at night. In the Babylonian heroic poem *Epic of Gilgamesh*, Shamash offered the hero help and advice in carrying out a dangerous quest for immortality, or the ability to live forever.

## Shamash in Context

The relation of Shamash to the other gods in the Assyrian/Babylonian pantheon reflects the type of society in which he was worshipped. For most societies based upon farming and agriculture, the sun is considered to be the most important element in nature, and is therefore worshipped as the main deity. The moon is often referred to as a child or sister of the sun god. In the case of the ancient Babylonians and Assyrians, however, the sun god is considered to be a child of the moon. This suggests that Shamash may have been worshipped prior to the widespread development of agriculture-based culture, at a time when the moon was seen by these ancient people as the ultimate supernatural figure.

## Key Themes and Symbols

To the ancient Babylonians and Assyrians, Shamash represented justice. Light was considered to be the force that revealed all by banishing

*Shamash was a Near Eastern sun god responsible for maintaining order in the universe. In this carving, he is shown dictating his laws to Hammurabi, the king of Babylon.* © LOUVRE, PARIS, FRANCE/ GIRAUDON/THE BRIDGEMAN ART LIBRARY.

shadows. The sun—the symbol of Shamash—was the revealer of secrets and bringer of truth. Shamash was also a symbol of protection from the darkness, which was thought to contain demons or evil spirits. Shamash is often shown as an old man with a long beard with sun rays rising from his shoulders, and his foot stepping on a mountain he has just cut with his saw-toothed knife. In ancient art, Shamash was usually shown as a disk or wheel, although sometimes he appeared as a king holding a staff of justice and a wheel of truth. A human-headed bull is sometimes with him, or he is attended by servants who open the gates of the dawn. His special symbol is the four-pointed star set in a disk with flames shooting out from between the star points. The winged disk was another of his symbols.

## Shamash in Art, Literature, and Everyday Life

Shamash enjoyed great popularity in the ancient cultures of the Near East, with temples erected to him in Babylon, Ur (pronounced OOR), and Nineveh (pronounced NIN-uh-vuh), among other places. Some scholars contend that the god was the source of the name given to the central stem of the Jewish menorah, a candle-holder that is a key symbol in Judaism.

## Read, Write, Think, Discuss

In ancient Babylonian culture, darkness was associated with evil and dangerous forces. The same still holds true today, even though much of our modern world is kept from darkness thanks to electricity. Why do you think the association of darkness with evil and danger has held true across so many cultures, and through so many centuries?

**SEE ALSO** Gilgamesh; Ishtar; Semitic Mythology; Sun

# Shiva

**Nationality/Culture**
Hindu

**Pronunciation**
SHEE-vuh

**Alternate Names**
None

**Appears In**
The Vedas

**Lineage**
None

## Character Overview

Shiva, the destroyer, is one of the three supreme gods in Hindu mythology. The other two are **Brahma** (pronounced BRAH-muh), the creator, and **Vishnu** (pronounced VISH-noo), the preserver. Shiva's destructive powers are terrifying, but they also have a positive side in that destruction usually leads to new forms of existence. In art, Shiva is often portrayed with four arms, five faces, and three eyes. A glance from the third eye in the center of his forehead has the power to destroy anything in creation, including humans and gods. In the Vedas, a collection of ancient sacred texts, Shiva is identified with the storm god Rudra (pronounced ROOD-ruh).

## Major Myths

According to one myth, Shiva first appeared when Brahma and Vishnu were arguing about which of them was more powerful. Their argument

*The Hindu god Shiva is often portrayed in art as dancing. This statue shows him dancing in a ring of fire, representing the cosmos, and squashing a dwarf, who represents ignorance.* THE ART ARCHIVE/ MUSÉE GUIMET PARIS/ GIANNI DAGLI ORTI/THE PICTURE DESK, INC.

was interrupted by the sudden appearance of a great blazing pillar whose roots and branches extended beyond view into the earth and sky. Brahma became a goose and flew up to find the top of the pillar, while Vishnu turned into a boar and dug into the earth to look for its roots. Unsuccessful in their search, the two gods returned and saw Shiva emerge from an opening in the pillar. Recognizing Shiva's great power, they accepted him as the third ruler of the universe.

Shiva is a complex god with many roles and powers. In the natural cycle of creation and destruction, Shiva represents destruction, out of which a new creation will be born. He has many postures, from the seated ascetic (one who lives a life of self-denial) to the dancing Shiva. As ascetic, Shiva sits in a meditative pose. He has matted hair, from which flow the sacred waters of the Ganges (pronounced GAN-jeez) River, and wears a garland of snakes around his neck, symbolizing his control over physical desires. Despite his destructiveness, Shiva can be helpful to humans and other gods. He acts as a divine judge who shows no mercy to the wicked. He gains spiritual strength from periods of meditation—deep thought—in the Himalayas (pronounced him-uh-LAY-uhz), a mountain range on India's northern border. When he dances, he represents truth, and by dancing he banishes ignorance and helps relieve the suffering of his followers. According to one myth, Shiva saved the gods and the world from destruction by swallowing the poison of Vasuki (pronounced VUH-soo-kee), a serpent the gods used to produce the water of life. Drinking the poison made Shiva's neck blue, and he is often shown that way in art.

One of Shiva's greatest services to the world was to tame the sacred Ganges River, which flows from the Himalayas. At one time, the Ganges passed only through the heavens, leaving the earth dry. After a wise man changed the course of the river, it became a raging torrent and threatened to flood the earth. Shiva stood beneath the river and let its waters wind through his hair to calm its flow.

In another story, the gods were threatened by demons and asked Shiva for help. He agreed—on the condition that the gods lend him some of their own strength. After defeating the demons, however, Shiva refused to return the borrowed strength. As a result, he became the most powerful being in the universe. Shiva also has many weapons that make him unbeatable, including a club with a skull on the end, a sword and spear made from thunderbolts, and a bow made from a rainbow.

## Shiva in Context

The many forms of Shiva reflect a combination of different religious traditions throughout India that span many centuries. Rudra, for instance, is a form that pre-dates Shiva and emphasizes the god's status as a bringer of storms. Two other forms of Shiva—as the Teacher and as the Lord of Dance—both originated in southern India and continue to

## Shiva's Consorts: Parvati, Durga, and Kali

Most Hindu gods have a female consort, or wife, who complements the powers of the male god. Shiva's consort is Parvati, a benign mother goddess. But Parvati has many other forms. As Durga, she is an armed warrior goddess who rides a lion and slays Mahisha, the Buffalo Demon. As Kali, the fierce dark goddess beloved in Bengal, she comes to Durga's aid and slays Raktabija, a demon who has the ability to reproduce himself each time a drop of his blood touches the ground.

According to myth, Durga battles Raktabija but cannot kill him because each time she wounds him, another demon appears where his blood touched the earth. In need of help, Durga calls on Kali, who destroys the demon by sucking the blood from his wounded body before it can touch the ground. Kali then begins her furious dance upon the corpses of the slain demons and accidentally steps on her own husband, Shiva, lying on the ground. She stops her dance of death only when she hears Shiva's screams, which calm her.

be popular there. Shiva in the form of a lingam—or phallus, symbolizing procreation—likely originated in northern India or Pakistan, which was once part of India.

## Key Themes and Symbols

As with many Hindu deities, Shiva's various forms and myths cover a wide range of themes that reflect his varied character. In many instances, Shiva is closely associated with destruction. This is illustrated by the devastating power of his third eye, his arsenal of weapons, and the necklace of skulls he is often shown to be wearing. His association with storms also reflects the theme of destruction. However, Shiva is also linked to the theme of change, which can be positive or negative. In particular, he is associated with teaching, especially the teaching of yoga and music.

## Shiva in Art, Literature, and Everyday Life

Shiva is portrayed in many forms throughout Hindu art. His most recognized form is as the Lord of Dance, which shows him poised in the middle of a dance of creation and destruction, surrounded by a circle of flames. Shiva is also often shown in meditation, a reflection of his status as the teacher of yoga and meditation. In this pose, he is shown with long matted hair wrapped in a swirl or bun, with a crescent moon on his head, holding a trident and a drum, and seated on a tiger skin. Like many other figures from mythology, Shiva has lent his name to an asteroid, and his name is also invoked in the Shiva Hypothesis, an attempt to explain the periodic mass extinctions that have been observed in the fossil record.

### Read, Write, Think, Discuss

*Shiva's Fire* (2000) by Suzanne Fisher Staples tells the tale of a girl named Parvati—the name of Shiva's wife according to myth—who discovers she has extraordinary abilities that seem to be accessed through dancing. Parvati travels from the poor, small village where she was born to attend dance school in the bustling city of Madras, beginning a journey of discovery, identity, and her connection to the Lord of Dance. Author Staples received a Newbery Honor for a previous book, *Shabanu: Daughter of the Wind* (1989).

**SEE ALSO** Brahma; Hinduism and Mythology; Vishnu

# Siberian Mythology

## Siberian Mythology in Context

Siberia is a vast region in northern Asia, stretching from the Ural Mountains in the west to the Pacific Ocean in the east. To the north lies the Arctic Ocean; to the south lie Mongolia, China, and Central Asia. European Russians have been settling in Siberia for several centuries, but the region's original inhabitants were hunting, fishing, and herding peoples whose cultures were related to those of other northern groups, such as the Inuit of North America. Siberian mythology and religion reflected a world in which humans depended on and respected animals, believing that the animals had spirits and could change form.

Traditionally, Siberians viewed the world as the middle realm in a series of three, five, or seven worlds that were stacked one on top of the other. As in many belief systems, the realms above belonged to good gods and spirits, those below to evil ones. A tree connected the worlds of

Siberian myths in the same way that the World Tree **Yggdrasill** (pronounced IG-druh-sil) linked realms in **Norse mythology**. The tree's roots and branches extended into all levels.

## Core Deities and Characters

The devil or chief evil spirit in Siberian mythology was named Erlik. He was sometimes said to have been a human who helped in the creation of the earth but then turned against Ulgan, the creator god. Erlik ruled the dead, and his evil spirits brought him the souls of sinners.

Shamans held a central role in Siberian religion and mythology. They were believed to travel between worlds by climbing the World Tree or by flying, and they communicated with the spirit world through ceremonies and trances. The healing magic of shamans involved finding or curing the lost or damaged souls of sick people.

Many Siberian myths deal with powerful shamans. The Buriat people of the Lake Baikal region told of Morgon-Kara, who could bring the dead back to life. This angered the lord of the dead, who complained to the high god of **heaven**. The high god tested the shaman by sealing a man's soul in a bottle. Riding his magic drum into the spirit universe, Morgon-Kara found the soul in the bottle. Turning himself into a wasp, he stung the high god's forehead. The startled god released the trapped soul, and the shaman carried it down to earth.

Animals appear in many myths, sometimes as the ancestors or mates of humans. The Yukaghir people, for example, told of an ancestral hero who was the offspring of a man who spent the winter in the cave of a female bear. The Evenk people had stories of mammoths, immense animals that roamed the land long ago. They explained how these creatures had shaped the earth by moving mud with their tusks, created rivers where they walked, and formed lakes where they lay.

## Major Myths

Siberian mythology, which includes the beliefs and myths of a number of different peoples, has many variations on the story of creation. In one, the gods Chagan-Shukuty and Otshirvani came down from heaven to find the world covered with water. Otshirvani sat on a frog or turtle while Chagan-Shukuty dove repeatedly to the bottom, bringing up a bit of mud each time. The gods piled the mud on the back of the animal, which eventually sank into the water, leaving only the earth on the

*Shamans are an important part of Siberian mythology, and were believed to be able to heal the sick by communicating with the spirit world. In this engraving, a Siberian shaman attempts to heal a sick person by banishing evil spirits.* 

surface. In other stories, Otshirvani took the form of a giant bird that fought a huge, evil serpent called Losy.

Siberian tradition includes myths about a great flood and a hero who saved his family. In one version, the creator god Ulgan told a man named Nama to build a boat. Into the boat Nama brought his wife, his three sons, some other people, and some animals. The boat saved them all from the flood, and they lived on the earth after it dried out. Years later

Nama was close to death. His wife told him that if he killed all the animals and people he had saved in his boat, he would become king of the dead in the **afterlife**. Nama's son argued that the killing would be a sin, so Nama killed his wife instead and took the virtuous son to heaven, where he became a constellation of stars.

Another Siberian myth tells of a hero who followed a golden bird up the World Tree. The bird changed into many shapes, finally becoming a woman, whom the hero wished to marry. First, however, he had to destroy an extra **sun** and moon that were making the world too hot and too cold. For help, the hero turned to a sea god, who boiled the hero in an iron kettle and then shaped the fragments into a new man of iron, armed with iron weapons. The hero used these to shoot the extra sun and moon.

## Key Themes and Symbols

The struggle between good and evil colors Siberian mythology. This is shown in the myth of creation involving Ulgan and Erlik. Ulgan symbolizes the most important positive aspects of Siberian life, including food, water and warmth. Erlik is a symbol of death and sickness, but also of overconfidence and lust for power.

The idea of rebirth is also found in the myths of the Siberian people. In the tale of the man who destroys the extra sun and moon, the destruction and remaking of the hero's body may symbolize the making of a shaman, during which the person is reborn with magical powers. This theme is also seen in the myth of Morgon-Kara, who could bring the dead back to life.

## Siberian Mythology in Art, Literature, and Everyday Life

Siberian mythology is largely unknown in other parts of the world, perhaps due to the remote nature of Siberian cultures and peoples. Even in Russia, knowledge of Siberian mythology is limited mostly to small cultural groups. Some anthropologists, such as Marya Antonina Czaplicka, have provided information to Westerners about the nature and details of Siberian myths, but even these accounts are scarcely known to most people in the modern world. There still remain isolated groups in Siberia that continue to practice traditional beliefs, and the advent of globalization has opened the door for a future sharing of these cultural riches.

## Read, Write, Think, Discuss

Siberia is often considered to be a harsh and difficult place to live, primarily due to its weather. What effect do you think weather and environment have on the myths and beliefs of a culture? For example, do you think a sun god would have the same importance for Siberians as he would for a culture from a tropical island? Why or why not?

**SEE ALSO** Creation Stories; Floods; Yggdrasill

# Siegfried

*See* **Sigurd.**

# Sigurd

**Nationality/Culture**
Norse

**Pronunciation**
SI-gurd

**Alternate Names**
Sivard, Siegfried (German)

**Appears In**
The *Volsunga Saga*, the *Nibelungenlied*

**Lineage**
Son of Sigmund and Hjordis

## Character Overview

In Norse myth and legend, the warrior Sigurd was a member of the royal family of Denmark and a descendant of the god **Odin** (pronounced OH-din). He was raised by a blacksmith named Regin (pronounced RAY-gin), who made him a special sword from pieces of a sword owned by Sigurd's father.

Sigurd used his sword to kill the dragon Fafnir (pronounced FAHV-nir) and so acquire its golden treasure. When Sigurd roasted and ate the beast's heart, he was able to understand the language of the birds around him. They warned him that Regin was going to betray him, so Sigurd beheaded the blacksmith. Sigurd took the treasure and put a ring on his finger. He was unaware that the ring bore a curse that brought misfortune to its wearer.

After slaying Fafnir, Sigurd came upon a castle where he awakened the warrior maiden **Brunhilde** (pronounced BROON-hilt), whom Odin had cast into a deep sleep. Sigurd gave his ring to Brunhilde and promised to return to marry her. But during his journey Sigurd was given a magic drink that made him forget Brunhilde, and he married the princess Gudrun (pronounced GOOD-roon) instead.

*Sigurd is a Norse warrior who acquired the ability to understand the language of birds after he roasted and ate a dragon's heart.* WERNER FORMAN/ART RESOURCE, NY.

Gudrun's brother Gunnar tried to win Brunhilde for himself, but Gunnar was unable to cross the wall of flames that surrounded Brunhilde's castle. Sigurd, having forgotten Brunhilde completely and wanting to help his brother-in-law, assumed Gunnar's shape and courted Brunhilde in his place. Believing that Sigurd had abandoned her, Brunhilde agreed to marry Gunnar, whom she did not love. When Brunhilde discovered that she had been tricked by Sigurd, she was both angry with Sigurd and heartbroken at the loss of his love. She had him slain and then killed herself.

## Sigurd in Context

Sigurd reflects the Norse idea of the ultimate human hero: strong, brave, clever, forthright, and willing to help others. Sigurd also reflects the human flaws that are seen in nearly all Norse characters, both god and human alike. He is susceptible to magic and deception, and falls victim to a curse about which he is not aware. This reflects Norse beliefs in fate and destiny: certain events are unavoidable no matter how hard one might struggle to prevent them.

## Key Themes and Symbols

The story of Sigurd largely deals with the themes of betrayal and vengeance. Sigurd is told that Regin, the man who raised him, is planning on betraying him for his treasure, so Sigurd cuts off Regin's head—itself an act of betrayal against the only father he has known. Later, Sigurd, under the power of a magical potion, betrays Brunhilde by marrying Gudrun, and deceives her when he pretends to be Gunnar. Brunhilde avenges this betrayal by killing Sigurd.

## Sigurd in Art, Literature, and Everyday Life

Aside from being the main tale of the *Volsunga Saga*, the story of Sigurd and Brunhilde is also told in slightly different form in the German epic poem ***Nibelungenlied***, where Sigurd is known by the German name Siegfried. This version of the story was central to Richard Wagner's series of operas known as *Der Ring des Nibelungen* (*The Ring of the Nibelung*), one opera of which is titled *Siegfried*. The *Volsunga Saga* was also used as the basis for the bleak and futuristic young adult novel *Bloodtide* (1999) by Melvin Burgess.

## Read, Write, Think, Discuss

In the myth of Sigurd, the hero's downfall occurs because of a cursed ring he obtains as part of a treasure when he kills Fafnir. In modern times, certain treasures are in a sense cursed because of their origins; so-called "blood diamonds," for example, are taken from war-torn areas and may be used to finance large-scale murder. As another example, many of the priceless valuables and heirlooms taken from Jewish families before they were imprisoned during World War II were kept by those who cooperated with the Nazis. Do you think items such as these carry with them a "curse"—even a symbolic one—for those that know their origins?

**SEE ALSO** Brunhilde; *Nibelungenlied, The*; Norse Mythology

# Sinbad

**Nationality/Culture**
Persian, Arabic

**Pronunciation**
SIN-bad

**Alternate Names**
Sindbad

**Appears In**
*One Thousand and One Nights*

**Lineage**
Son of a merchant

## Character Overview

Sinbad the Sailor appears in *One Thousand and One Nights*, a collection of Persian, Arab, and Indian tales written down between the 800s and the 1400s CE. A merchant from the city of Baghdad in the Near East, Sinbad made seven voyages to lands and islands around the Indian Ocean. He had great adventures, survived numerous dangers, and acquired many riches during his travels.

On Sinbad's first voyage, he and his crew visited an island that turned out to be a huge sleeping whale. When they lit a **fire**, the whale woke up and dived underwater. Sinbad was picked up by another ship and taken home. The second voyage took Sinbad to a desert island, where he discovered an enormous egg belonging to a giant bird called a roc. When the bird appeared, Sinbad grabbed its claw and was carried away to the Valley of Diamonds. Eventually rescued by merchants, he returned to Baghdad laden with the valuable jewels.

During Sinbad's third voyage, the hero was captured by dwarves and taken to the home of a one-eyed giant. The giant started eating members of his crew. Sinbad managed to escape but was lured to another island by a serpent that tried to swallow him. Once again, Sinbad got away and was rescued by a passing ship. Shipwrecked on his fourth voyage, Sinbad and his crew were taken prisoner by cannibals who planned to eat them. The hero escaped, arrived at a strange kingdom, and married the king's daughter. When she died, however, Sinbad was buried alive with her. He succeeded in getting away again.

On Sinbad's fifth voyage, his ship was destroyed by angry rocs, which dropped huge stones from the air. Washed ashore on an island, he met and killed the Old Man of the Sea. The sixth voyage saw Sinbad once again shipwrecked on an island. There he found precious stones

**World Travelers**

*Several world myths focus on the fantastic adventures of seafaring travelers.*

| Figure | Nationality | Myth Summary |
|---|---|---|
| Gilgamesh | Near Eastern | Gilgamesh undertakes dangerous quests. First, he and his friend Enkidu travel to the distant cedar forest to slay a demon. After Enkidu's death, he travels in search of Utnapishtim, who reportedly knows the secret of immortality. |
| Odysseus | Greek | Traveling home after many years served in the Trojan War, Odysseus hits many delays, including a nymph who falls in love with him and refuses to let him leave her island, a man-eating cyclops, and a powerful sorceress. |
| Sinbad | Persian and Arabian | Sinbad is a merchant from Baghdad who makes seven famous sea voyages and, after some ups and downs, ends his days fabulously wealthy. Like Odysseus, he faces a man-eating giant with one eye. |

ILLUSTRATION BY ANAXOS, INC./CENGAGE LEARNING, GALE.

and visited the city of Serendib, whose king sent him home with more wealth. Sinbad returned to Serendib on his final voyage. On the way home he was attacked by pirates, who sold him into slavery. While working as an elephant hunter for the merchant who bought him, Sinbad discovered an elephant burial ground and a huge store of ivory tusks. The merchant gave Sinbad his freedom and enough ivory to make him rich. His final adventure over, Sinbad returned home to Baghdad.

## Sinbad in Context

The cultures of the ancient Middle East placed great importance on the sea as a means of travel, exploration, and trade. While countries in the

Near East such as Turkey relied upon the Mediterranean Sea for trade, Persian and Arabian cultures viewed the Persian Gulf and Indian Ocean as a source of both adventure and riches. The tales of Sinbad emphasize this, as well as the egalitarian—or relatively classless and democratic—spirit of the culture. The tale of Sinbad opens with a poor soul bemoaning his impoverished existence; a wealthy man overhears this and tells the poor man how he came to be rich. The wealthy man also reveals that he was left with riches when his father died, but spent it all rashly and became poor—showing that shifts in social class can happen in both directions. The two men are both named Sinbad, and the message seems clear: for someone willing to work hard, a life on the sea can lead to adventure and riches. This is similar to later American myths of both the sea and the unexplored West, where hard-working individuals were encouraged to find their fortunes.

## Key Themes and Symbols

One of the main themes of the tales of Sinbad is the spirit of exploration and adventure. Even after Sinbad has made his first journey and earned great wealth, he is still drawn by a desire to see other lands and cultures. Although he faces great danger, he is always rewarded—perhaps by Allah (the Islamic name for God) himself—for his boldness and risk-taking. For Sinbad, as for many in the ancient Middle East, the sea represents the excitement of the unknown: both danger and opportunity, with the potential for both disaster and riches.

## Sinbad in Art, Literature, and Everyday Life

The tales of Sinbad were popularly known throughout the Middle East for centuries. They finally became popular in the English-speaking world through the 1885 translation of *One Thousand and One Nights* by Sir Richard Burton. Throughout Europe, the tales captured the imaginations of readers and artists alike. Russian composer Nikolai Rimsky-Korsakov wrote a symphonic suite in 1888 based on the tales from *One Thousand and One Nights*, largely focusing on the adventures of Sinbad.

Sinbad has been the subject of numerous television and film adaptations, most notably three popular movies featuring stop-motion special effects by Ray Harryhausen: *The 7th Voyage of Sinbad* (1958), *The Golden Voyage of Sinbad* (1974), and *Sinbad and the Eye of the Tiger* (1977). Sinbad's adventures were also featured in the animated

Dreamworks adaptation *Sinbad: Legend of the Seven Seas* (2003), which features Brad Pitt as the voice of the hero.

### Read, Write, Think, Discuss

In ancient cultures, the sea often symbolized adventure and the great unknown. In the modern world, where journeys across the ocean can take just a few hours and the Internet allows people of vastly different cultures to directly share information and experiences, the life of a sailor has lost much of its glamour. In your opinion, are there any modern occupations that offer the same level of adventure that sailors and explorers once enjoyed? If so, what are they and how are people in these occupations portrayed in mainstream culture? If not, how do you think this "loss of the unknown" has affected modern culture?

**SEE ALSO** Persian Mythology

# Sirens

**Nationality/Culture**
Greek

**Pronunciation**
SYE-rinz

**Alternate Names**
None

**Appears In**
Ovid's *Metamorphoses*, Homer's *Odyssey*

**Lineage**
Daughters of Achelous

### Character Overview

The Sirens were three female creatures from **Greek mythology** whose singing lured men to destruction. Descriptions of the Sirens vary from beautiful women to monsters with the bodies of birds and human heads.

The Sirens were the daughters of the river god Achelous (pronounced ay-kee-LOH-uhs). They lived on an island where they enchanted passing sailors with their songs. According to some sources, sailors died when their ships crashed on the rocks near the island. Others say that sailors stayed on the island and listened to the singing until they died.

Only on two occasions did the Sirens fail to enchant passing sailors. When **Jason** and the **Argonauts** (pronounced AHR-guh-nawts) were searching for the **Golden Fleece**, the musician **Orpheus** (pronounced OR-fee-uhs) sang so sweetly that none of the crew listened to the Sirens. In Homer's epic the ***Odyssey***, the hero **Odysseus** (pronounced oh-DIS-ee-uhs) made his men put wax in their ears so they could not hear the Sirens. Odysseus, wanting to hear the Sirens' song, had his crew tie him to the mast so he would not steer the ship toward the island. Some stories

## Endangered Mermaids

*Sirenia* is an order of plant-eating mammals that includes the manatee, found along warm coastlines of the eastern part of North and South America, and the dugong, found near Australia and New Guinea. Sailors sighting these creatures sometimes mistook them for mermaids, creatures with the torso and head of a woman and the tail of a fish. Sirens are sometimes pictured as mermaids.

Dugongs and manatees are considered endangered species. Manatees are slow-moving and curious, and so are at special risk of injury and death due to boat collisions. Dugongs were once found throughout the Indian and South Pacific oceans, but hunting and habitat loss have caused its numbers to diminish greatly.

say the Sirens were destined to live only as long as no sailor could resist their song; because Odysseus and his crew were able to sail safely past, the Sirens were transformed into rocks along the shore.

## Sirens in Context

The myth of the Sirens is a reflection of how important—and at the same time treacherous—travel by sea was to the ancient Greeks. They relied on the sea for both trade and exploration. The Sirens functioned as a warning to Greek sailors, reminding them to always be aware of nearby rocks that could potentially destroy their ships. The song of the Sirens might even be compared to the rhythmic pulse of the sea against the bow of a ship, which might lull a sailor to sleep and prevent him from properly avoiding obstacles such as rocks.

## Key Themes and Symbols

The Sirens represented both the allure and the danger of beauty. The danger arose from losing sense of one's duties or surroundings while being enchanted by the Sirens. In a more general sense, the Sirens symbolized the mysterious qualities of women to sailors, who were nearly always men living without female contact for days or weeks at a time. The bird-like features of the Sirens also associated them with the beautiful singing of songbirds, and enhanced their otherworldly nature.

## Sirens in Art, Literature, and Everyday Life

In ancient art, the Sirens were often depicted as having human heads and the bodies of birds, or as being human women with the legs of birds. Later depictions often downplay these bird-like features and instead depict the Sirens simply as beautiful young women, or even as **mermaids** who lure sailors to a watery grave. Many adaptations of the myths of Jason and Odysseus include depictions of the Sirens. One notable appearance of the Sirens is in the 2000 Coen brothers' film *O Brother, Where Art Thou?*, a retelling of the *Odyssey* set in the American South during the Great Depression.

The term "siren" lives on in modern times in two ways: first, it describes a loud, unavoidable warning signal, such as the ones used by police and other emergency vehicles; and second, it is used to describe a woman to whom men are inevitably drawn, even when it may lead to their downfall.

## Read, Write, Think, Discuss

*Secret of the Sirens* (2006) by Julia Golding is the first novel in the author's *Companions Quartet* series. The book focuses on Connie, an eleven-year-old girl sent to live with her aunt in a seaside British town.

**SEE ALSO** Argonauts; *Odyssey, The*; Orpheus

# Sisyphus

**Nationality/Culture**
Greek

**Pronunciation**
SIZ-ee-fuhs

**Alternate Names**
None

**Appears In**
Hyginus's *Fabulae*, Homer's *Odyssey*

**Lineage**
Son of King Aeolus and Enarete

## Character Overview

In **Greek mythology**, Sisyphus was famous for two things: his cleverness during life and the punishment he suffered after death. Although stories about Sisyphus differ somewhat in their details, he is usually referred to as the king of Corinth. He was one of the sons of King Aeolus (pronounced EE-uh-luhs) of Thessaly (pronounced THESS-uh-lee).

One story about Sisyphus involves Autolycus (pronounced aw-TOL-i-kuhs), a clever thief. Autolycus stole cattle by changing their color so they could not be identified. On one occasion, he happened to steal Sisyphus's cattle; Sisyphus outwitted him, however, by placing a mark on the cattle's hooves so he could follow the hoofprints to the stolen animals.

In another myth, Sisyphus saw the god **Zeus** (pronounced ZOOS) kidnap a river nymph, or female nature deity, and he promised to keep the hiding place secret. He betrayed Zeus, however, when he revealed the location to the nymph's father in exchange for a spring of pure water. Furious, Zeus sent Thanatos (pronounced THAN-uh-tohs), the god of death, to take Sisyphus to **Hades** (pronounced HAY-deez), the ruler of the land of the dead. About to be shackled, the clever Sisyphus managed to trick Thanatos into trying out the shackles first and trapped the god in his place. Because Thanatos was shackled and could not perform his duties, for several days no one on earth died.

**Ares** (pronounced AIR-eez), the god of war, went to free death and take Sisyphus to Tartarus (pronounced TAR-tur-uhs), a gloomy pit at the bottom of the **underworld**. Sisyphus called out to his wife not to offer the customary sacrifices usually made when someone dies, and she followed his orders. While in the underworld, he persuaded **Persephone** (pronounced per-SEF-uh-nee), the goddess of the underworld, to let him go back to earth long enough to arrange a proper funeral, since his wife was clearly not following tradition. After returning to Corinth, Sisyphus stayed there until his second, and final, death.

As punishment for tricking the gods, Sisyphus was placed on a hillside in the underworld with a heavy boulder above him. To escape being crushed, he had to push the boulder uphill. The gods told him that if he rolled the stone to the other side they would release him. Each time he reached the top, however, the boulder rolled back down to the bottom, forcing Sisyphus to start over.

## Sisyphus in Context

While the myth of Sisyphus might appear to be a reflection of ancient Greek values, particularly against those who are cunning or deceitful, this is not likely to be the case. There are many other examples of ancient Greek myths where cunning and cleverness is highly rewarded—particularly in the tales of **Odysseus** (pronounced oh-DIS-ee-uhs), a

*The gods condemned Sisyphus to push a boulder uphill, only to have the boulder roll back down the hill each time he got near the top. It was his punishment in the underworld for tricking the gods.* CAL. STATE CALIFORNIA HISTORY COLLECTION/GETTY IMAGES.

hero who is sometimes mentioned as the possible son of Sisyphus. Indeed, in the tales of Sisyphus, Autolycus—sometimes called the king of thieves—was impressed by the man's cleverness and the two became friends.

In fact, the reason for the harsh punishment of Sisyphus is established quite clearly: he betrayed a promise to Zeus, the king of the gods. Had it not been for that betrayal, Sisyphus would never have faced the wrath of the gods. In fact, the myth even suggests that the ancient

Greeks did not consider the gods all powerful, as the cleverness of Sisyphus nearly allows him to escape punishment altogether.

## Key Themes and Symbols

An important theme in the myth of Sisyphus is trickery. Throughout his tale, Sisyphus uses his cleverness to trick the gods and other characters. This is shown when he shackles Thanatos and when he convinces Persephone to let him go back to the world of the living. The gods also use trickery when they tell Sisyphus he can go free if he rolls the boulder over the top of the hill—an impossible task. To many, the labor of Sisyphus symbolizes futility, or the inability to ever achieve one's goals.

## Sisyphus in Art, Literature, and Everyday Life

Several examples of ancient pottery have been found that illustrate the myth of Sisyphus. For a myth that has survived with such popularity into modern times, however, there are relatively few examples of art featuring the clever character—a 1549 depiction by Titian being the most notable. The philosopher Albert Camus wrote an essay titled "The Myth of Sisyphus," in which the author compares the task of Sisyphus to the human struggle to find meaning in the world. Sisyphus has been featured in an animated commercial for the energy beverage Red Bull, and the myth has been referenced in songs by artists as varied as Pink Floyd and Marilyn Manson. In modern language, the phrase "labor of Sisyphus" refers to any hopeless task that must be repeated endlessly. The name Sisyphus has also been used to signify a type of dung beetle, known for rolling up large balls of dung not unlike the boulder in the myth.

## Read, Write, Think, Discuss

A "Sisyphean task" is a job that seemingly never ends because the work needed to complete a given goal must often be repeated many times. Sisyphus is punished with such a task. Can you think of any jobs in modern society that might be considered "Sisyphean"? Why do you think people take on such jobs? Should they be pitied? Or should they be considered heroic for their persistence?

**SEE ALSO** Greek Mythology; Hades

# Sphinx

**Nationality/Culture**
Greek and Egyptian

**Pronunciation**
SFEENKS

**Alternate Names**
Phix

**Appears In**
Hesiod's *Theogony*, Seneca's *Oedipus*

**Lineage**
Offspring of Typhon and Echidna

## Character Overview

The Sphinx was a legendary winged monster of **Greek mythology** that had the body of a lion and the head of a woman. Her siblings were **Cerberus** (pronounced SUR-ber-uhs), Hydra (pronounced HYE-druh), and the Nemean (pronounced ni-MEE-uhn) Lion. The Sphinx lived on a rock outside the city of Thebes (pronounced THEEBZ), where she terrified the local people. Some sources say **Hera** (pronounced HAIR-uh), the wife of **Zeus** (pronounced ZOOS), sent the Sphinx to punish the king of Thebes for carrying off one of the children of Zeus. Others claim that the god **Apollo** (pronounced uh-POL-oh) sent the monster because the Thebans failed to honor him properly.

The Sphinx posed a riddle to any passerby: "I have four legs in the morning, two legs at noon, and three legs in the evening, but I am weakest when I have the most legs. What am I?" No one was able to solve the riddle, and the Sphinx killed and devoured anyone who failed to answer correctly. Finally, the Greek hero **Oedipus** (pronounced ED-uh-puhs) provided the correct answer: "A human being crawls on all fours as a baby, on two legs as an adult, and with a crutch as a third leg when he grows old." Upon hearing Oedipus's answer, the Sphinx killed herself.

## The Sphinx in Context

Egyptian sculpture also included a type of figure called a sphinx, which had a lion's body and the head of the pharaoh, or ruler of Egypt, or sometimes an animal representing one of the Egyptian gods. Many of these included the likenesses of male figures, but some—just like some pharaohs—were female. Egyptian sphinxes, which guarded temples and monuments, were unrelated to the Greek Sphinx, though it is possible—likely, even—that ancient Egyptian art inspired the Greek legends. The Egyptian sculptures existed nearly two thousand years before the rise of ancient Greek culture, and were located just across the Mediterranean Sea from Greece. With many ships crossing the Mediterranean as part of established trade routes, it would make sense that these figures were known to early Greeks, and their foreign location may have inspired the

*The sphinx was a winged monster in Greek mythology. It is best known for its role in the tragic tale of Oedipus, in which it asked a riddle of anyone attempting to enter the city of Thebes; failure to answer the riddle correctly resulted in the sphinx devouring that person. Oedipus, however, correctly answered the riddle, and the phoenix killed itself.* THE BRIDGEMAN ART LIBRARY.

tale of an exotic or fantastic creature previously unknown to Greeks. In fact, the name "sphinx" is actually a Greek term, used for both the mythological character and the Egyptian sculptures because there is no indication that the Egyptians gave their figures any sort of name.

## Key Themes and Symbols

One of the main themes of the tale of the Sphinx is the victory of shrewdness over violence. The Sphinx destroys all those who cannot solve her clever riddle; when Oedipus figures out the solution, she kills herself. Oedipus does not have to resort to violence to defeat her. Another theme is the vengeance of the gods, since the Sphinx is sent to terrorize Thebes at the request of one of the gods.

### The Sphinx in Art, Literature, and Everyday Life

The tale of Oedipus and the riddle of the Sphinx remains one of the best-known tales from Greek mythology. Many painters have created their own depictions of the Sphinx, including Ingres and Gustave Moreau. The figure became very popular in European decoration during the sixteenth century, rendered with the realistic face and chest of a beautiful young woman and usually referred to as a "French sphinx." In modern times, the best-known Sphinx is undoubtedly the Great Sphinx of Giza found in Egypt, which has been featured in many films; however, this monument is not directly connected to the character found in Greek myth.

### Read, Write, Think, Discuss

The Sphinx challenges travelers with a riddle. See if you can come up with a riddle to challenge your friends. Use the riddle of the Sphinx as a model: think of a thing, and describe it in a way that would require creative thinking. Make sure your clues make sense, but do not reveal the answer too easily. Example: "I tumble over a cliff, but even when I hit the bottom, I never stop falling. What am I?" Answer: a waterfall!

**SEE ALSO** Oedipus

# Spider Woman

**Nationality/Culture**
Navajo/Hopi

**Pronunciation**
SPY-dur woo-muhn

**Alternate Names**
Spider Grandmother

**Appears In**
Navajo and Hopi oral creation myths

**Lineage**
None

### Character Overview

Spider Woman appears in the mythology of several American Indian tribes, including the Navajo, Keresan, and Hopi. In most cases, she is associated with the emergence of life on earth. She helps humans by teaching them survival skills. Spider Woman also teaches the Navajos the art of weaving. Before weavers sit down at the loom, they often rub their hands in spiderwebs to absorb the wisdom and skill of Spider Woman.

In the Navajo creation story, Spider Woman (called Na'ashjéiiasdzáá by the Navajo) helps the warrior **twins**, Monster Slayer and Child of Water, find their father, the Sun. The Keresan say that Spider Woman gave the **corn** goddess Iyatiku a basket of seeds to plant.

According to the Hopi, at the beginning of time Spider Woman controlled the **underworld**, the home of the gods, while the **sun** god Tawa ruled the sky. Using only their thoughts, they created the earth between the two other worlds. Spider Woman molded animals from clay, but they remained lifeless. So she and Tawa spread a soft white blanket over them, said some magic words, and the creatures began to move. Spider Woman then molded people from clay. To bring them to life, she clutched them to her breast, and together with Tawa, sang a song that made them into living beings. She divided the animals and people into the groups that inhabit the earth today. She also gave men and women specific roles: women were to watch over the home, and men were to pray and make offerings to the gods.

Another Hopi myth states that Tawa created insect-like beings and placed them in the First World. Dissatisfied with these creatures, Tawa sent Spider Woman to lead them, first to the Second World and then to the Third World, where they turned into people. Spider Woman taught the people how to plant, weave, and make pottery. A hummingbird gave them **fire** to help them warm themselves and cook their food. However, when sorcerers brought evil to the Third World, Spider Woman told the people to leave for the Fourth World. They planted trees to climb up to the Fourth World, but none grew tall enough. Finally, Spider Woman told them to sing to a bamboo plant or reed so that it would grow very tall. She led the people up the hollow tube of the bamboo stalk to the Fourth World, the one in which the Hopi currently live.

## Spider Woman in Context

Spider Woman may be related to a Mexican deity known as the Great Goddess of Teotihuacán (pronounced TAY-aw-tee-wah-KAHN). She is known mainly from ancient murals, where she is shown surrounded by or covered in spiders and spiderwebs. Many scholars speculate that this goddess is associated with vegetation, like Spider Woman, and with the underworld—much like Spider Woman led the first people through the successive layers of the underworld to reach the surface. Both goddesses reflect the importance of agriculture in these early cultures, where hunting and gathering alone could not support larger communities.

## Key Themes and Symbols

Spider Woman represented wisdom and education. She provided the first people with the skills they needed to survive, such as planting crops and weaving. The spider so closely associated with the goddess is a symbol of the ability to weave and to create something from one's own body, just as a spider makes silk.

## Spider Woman in Art, Literature, and Everyday Life

Spider Woman is an important part of American Indian mythologies throughout the Southwest, but is not well known outside of these cultures. Playwright Murray Mednick wrote a series of one-act plays called *The Coyote Cycles* (1993) that featured Spider Grandmother as a main character. It is worth noting that the term "Spider Woman" has been used by many other characters—ranging from the villain of a 1940s Sherlock Holmes film to a series of Marvel Comics superheroines—that have no connection to the Spider Woman of American Indian myth.

## Read, Write, Think, Discuss

Using your library, the Internet, or other available resources, research Spider Rock in the Canyon de Chelly National Monument. How is this formation related to Spider Woman? What does Spider Rock reveal about the significance of Spider Woman to the Navajo people?

**SEE ALSO** Animals in Mythology; Changing Woman; Corn; Creation Stories; Native American Mythology

# Styx

*See* **Underworld.**

# Sun

## Theme Overview

The largest object in the sky, the sun is the source of light, heat, and life. It can also be a symbol of destructive power. Since earliest times, people in all parts of the world have observed the position of the sun and its rising and setting throughout the year. Many cultures have created solar calendars to use for planting crops and timing religious festivals. They have also given the sun a major place in their mythologies, often as a deity, or god.

## Major Myths

Some solar myths explain the sun's daily movement across the sky from east to west and its disappearance at night. Such stories often take the form of a journey, with the sun deity traveling across the heavens in a chariot or boat. Helios (pronounced HEE-lee-ohs), a Greek solar deity later identified with **Apollo**, was a charioteer who drove his fiery vehicle through **heaven** by day. At night he floated back across the ocean in a golden bowl, only to mount his chariot again the next morning. The Navajo people of the American Southwest portray their sun god as a worker named Jóhonaa'éí, or sun bearer. Every day Jóhonaa'éí laboriously hauls the sun across the sky on his back. At night, he hangs the sun from a peg in the wall and rests.

The Egyptian sun god **Ra** made a similar circuit. Each day he traveled across the sky in his sun boat, and at night he passed through the **underworld**, or land of the dead, greeting the dead and facing many dangers. Ra's daily cycle was more than a journey, though—it was a daily rebirth. Dawn saw the newborn sun god rise in the sky. During the morning he was a child, at noon he was mature, and by sunset he was an old man ready for death. Each sunrise was a celebration of the god's return, a victory of life over the forces of death and darkness.

In some solar myths the sun is paired with the moon. The two may be husband and wife, brother and sister, or two brothers. In the mythology of many Native Americans, the sun god and moon god are sister and brother who also become forbidden lovers. The moon god's face is smeared with ash from the sun's fires, which accounts for the dark

## Too Many Suns

If one sun is good, are ten suns ten times better? Not according to the Chinese myth of Yi and the ten suns. Yi, a famous soldier, was an archer of great skill. At that time, ten suns lived in the Fu Sang tree beyond the eastern edge of the world. Normally the suns took turns lighting the earth, one sun at a time. The suns grew rebellious, and one day all ten of them rose into the sky at the same time. The extra light and heat pleased the people below—until their crops shriveled and their rivers began to dry up. The Lord of Heaven sent Yi, the divine archer, to handle the problem. Yi shot nine of the suns out of the sky.

patches on the moon's surface. In some accounts, the moon flees in shame when he learns that his lover is also his sister. This is why the moon leaves the sky when the sun comes near.

Many cultures have myths of monsters or evil spirits that steal or devour the sun, or stories of the sun falling from the heavens or withdrawing its light for a time. Some of these myths may explain eclipses, times when the earth's shadow temporarily blots out the sun or moon. A solar eclipse creates a period of eerie near-darkness in the middle of the day—an event that would surely cry out for a reassuring explanation. A well-known myth about the Japanese sun goddess **Amaterasu** (pronounced ah-mah-te-RAH-soo), tells how she became so angry with her brother, who was misbehaving, that she retreated into a cave. The goddess's withdrawal deprived the world of light and warmth. Finally, the other gods tricked her into emerging.

According to a traditional myth from the Hindu Kush mountains of Afghanistan, the giant Espereg-era once stole the sun and the moon. The hero god Mandi disguised himself as a child and tricked the giant's mother into adopting him. After a time with the **giants**, Mandi rescued the sun and moon and rode off with them on a magical horse. The supreme god then hurled them into the sky to shine on the world.

## The Sun in Context

The mythologies of many cultures have included a sun deity, usually a god but occasionally a goddess. Some myths reflect the sun's vital role in

*Throughout history, many different cultures had solar deities and myths about the sun. This head of the Mayan sun god was excavated in Chiapas, Mexico.* WERNER FORMAN/ ART RESOURCE, NY.

supporting life: solar deities are often creators who bring people into existence. Native Americans from the Pacific Coast, for example, tell how the sun god Kodoyanpe and the trickster Coyote together created the world and set about making people to live in it.

Solar deities have also been associated with fertility of people and the earth. The Hittites of ancient Turkey worshiped Arinna, an important goddess of both the sun and fertility. In traditional myths from Uganda in Central Africa, the creator god Ruhanga, the sun god Kazooba, and the giver of life Rugaba are all the same deity.

In some mythologies, sun gods have healing powers. **Shamash** (pronounced shah-MAHSH), the solar god of the Babylonian people of the ancient Near East, was known as "the sun with healing in his wings." Ancient Celtic peoples had Belenus (pronounced BEHL-eh-nuhs), the god of sunlight: besides driving away the predawn mists and fogs each day, Belenus could melt away disease from the sick. When the Romans conquered the Celts, they identified Belenus with their own sun god, Apollo (pronounced uh-POL-oh), who was also a god of healing.

As the most important and splendid deities of their pantheons, some solar deities have been associated with earthly rulers, the most powerful people in society. The Incas of Peru in South America regarded the sun god Inti (pronounced IN-tee), their chief deity, as the ancestor of the Inca royal family. According to Japanese tradition, the country's imperial family is descended from Amaterasu, the sun goddess.

## The Sun in Art, Literature, and Everyday Life

The sun is perhaps the most universally depicted object in all of mythological art. It appears in ancient Egyptian and Persian art as well as in some of the first examples of Nordic art. Some of the most enduring depictions of the sun in mythological art include the ancient Egyptian god Ra, usually pictured with the head of a falcon crowned with a sun disk; the Greek gods Helios and Apollo, often shown pulling the sun through the sky with a chariot; and the Japanese goddess Amaterasu, shown exiting the cave where she hides to bring sunlight back into the world. In modern times, the image of the sun is still used in advertising and art to symbolize life, purity, health, and happiness.

## Read, Write, Think, Discuss

Sun deities are often thought of as male figures. However, many sun deities in cultures around the world are female, such as Amaterasu. Using your library, the Internet, or other available resources, research various cultures with either male or female sun deities. Why do you think some cultures view the sun as a male figure, while others view it as a female figure? What do you think this might indicate about those cultures?

**SEE ALSO** Amaterasu; Apollo; Aten; Lug; Ra; Shamash

# Sundiata

*See* **Sunjata.**

# Sunjata

**Nationality/Culture**
African

**Pronunciation**
soon-JAH-tuh

**Alternate Names**
Sundiata

**Appears In**
The Epic of Sunjata

**Lineage**
Son of the king of Manding

## Character Overview

Sunjata is the hero of an African epic popular among the people of Mali in the Sahel region of West Africa. He may be based on a king named Sundiata or Sundjata, who founded the kingdom of Mali around 1240 CE. His story is filled with supernatural elements, from the hero's mysterious birth to his extraordinary strength.

The epic of Sunjata begins with the hero's childhood. The son of the king of Manding, Sunjata was born under unusual circumstances. His mother was pregnant with him for eight years when a magical spirit called a jinni (or genie) told Sunjata's father that the boy would someday become a great king.

As a child, Sunjata performed many amazing deeds and earned the name Mari Djata (the Lion of Manding) because he could transform himself into a lion. Sunjata's father grew afraid of him and used his power to paralyze the boy. But after seven years the king recognized Sunjata's wisdom and restored his son to health. Sunjata's miraculous deeds continued. He taught wild animals to gather firewood and helped a group of witches bring back to life a boy they had killed.

Sunjata lived in the countryside, killing eight hundred elephants and eight thousand lions. However, on the death of his father, he returned to Manding and won a competition against one of his brothers to become king. The young ruler's first task was to kill a terrible beast—a witch in the shape of an animal—that had been terrorizing the people. The old

*The African hero Sunjata may have been based on a king named Sundiata who founded the kingdom of Mali around 1240 CE. The town of Kirina, shown here, was one of three towns that formed the foundation for the empire.* WERNER FORMAN/ART RESOURCE, NY.

witch was so impressed by Sunjata's kindness and wisdom that she told him how to kill her. He did so and became a hero. Later, Sunjata went to war against a wicked king who claimed his throne. After defeating this demon king with the help of his sister, Sunjata went on to conquer an extensive area that became the empire of Mali. According to legend, Sunjata ruled with fairness and in peace.

## Sunjata in Context

It is generally acknowledged that Sunjata was a historical figure who lived around the thirteenth century CE. Sumanguru, the evil king in the legend, is believed to be responsible for killing several of Sunjata's siblings in an attempt to protect his kingdom from the royal Keita family, which had rightful claim. Sunjata was exiled at a young age, but gained support from surrounding leaders who all wished to see Sumanguru dethroned. Sunjata eventually led an army against Sumanguru at the Battle of Kirina in 1235 and defeated him. Sunjata spent the next several years reclaiming his kingdom and creating a capital at the important trade center of Niani. As the most important figure in the creation of the Mali Empire, it is not surprising that the people of Mali would expand upon these facts to create an enduring legend about Sunjata.

## Key Themes and Symbols

One central theme in the myth of Sunjata is the idea of the rightful heir to the throne. Sunjata and his siblings, as members of the royal Keita family, were by tradition the rightful inheritors of the kingdom. Although Sunjata was exiled, he eventually claimed his rightful place by defeating Sumanguru. Sunjata himself was able to transform into a lion, which has long been considered a symbol of fierceness, nobility, and leadership.

## Sunjata in Art, Literature, and Everyday Life

The Epic of Sunjata is an important part of West African culture and is still performed by griots, traveling artists who function as musicians, singers, poets, and historians. Many of the most popular musical artists in Mali are griots who have adapted traditional songs and tales into modern compositions. The internationally known singer-songwriter Salif Keita, though not a griot, is acknowledged to be a descendant of Sunjata. The legend of Sunjata, who has historically been referred to as "the lion king of Mali," may have also loosely inspired the 1994 Disney animated film *The Lion King*.

## Read, Write, Think, Discuss

*Sundiata: A Legend of Africa* (2003) by Will Eisner is a retelling of the Sunjata myth in comic book form. The book includes a brief historical introduction to its subject. Eisner is best known as the creator of the influential comic series *The Spirit* (begun in 1940) and the graphic novel *A Contract with God, and Other Tenement Stories* (1978).

**SEE ALSO** African Mythology; Heroes; Witches and Wizards

# Surya

**Nationality/Culture**
Hindu

**Pronunciation**
SOOR-yuh

**Alternate Names**
Vivasvat, Mitra, Savita, Ravi

**Appears In**
The *Ramayana*, the *Mahabharata*

**Lineage**
Son of Kasyapa

## Character Overview

In Hindu mythology, Surya is recognized as the god of the **sun**. He rides across the sky each day in a chariot pulled by seven horses, and is worshipped as the most visible of all the gods, seen by followers every single day. He is the son of Kasyapa (pronounced kahsh-YUH-puh), and is sometimes said to be in the form of one of the three principal deities: **Brahma** (pronounced BRAH-muh), **Vishnu** (pronounced VISH-noo), or **Shiva** (pronounced SHEE-vuh).

## Major Myths

Some Hindus believe that Surya takes the form of the three gods of the Trimurti (pronounced tri-MOOR-tee), the main gods of the Hindu pantheon, as it travels across the sky. In the morning, the sun is Brahma, the creator god. As it reaches the height of its power, it is Vishnu, the preserver. As it descends and ultimately leaves the world in darkness, it is Shiva, the destroyer.

Surya's most notable appearances in myth are found in the ***Mahabharata*** and the ***Ramayana***, two important Hindu epics. In the *Mahabharata*, Surya is accidentally summoned by princess Kunti (pronounced KOON-tee), who is given the ability to call upon any god and have a child with him. Not believing the power is real, she calls Surya and he appears. He insists on fulfilling his duty, and Kunti immediately gives birth to a son. Ashamed and scared, she abandons the baby in a basket and floats it down the river. The boy grows up to become Karna, one of the central figures in the *Mahabharata*, where he battles the hero Arjuna (pronounced AHR-juh-nuh) at Kurukshetra (pronounced khuh-rook-SHAY-truh). In the *Ramayana*, Surya is the father of the monkey king Sugriva (pronounced soo-GREE-vuh), who pledges his armies to help Rama after Rama assists him in reclaiming his throne.

## Surya in Context

A symbol commonly associated with Surya, and found frequently in ancient Hindu texts, is the bent-cross design called the swastika. The symbol was originally meant as a sign of good luck or well-being. From India, the symbol spread across Asia and even into Europe, all the while retaining its meaning as a symbol of good fortune (though it was not usually seen as a symbol of the sun, as in Hinduism). Pilots frequently wore the symbol as a good luck charm, or had it painted somewhere on their plane in hopes of safe passage. In the 1920s, however, the Nazi Party of Germany appropriated the symbol as their own in an effort to draw a connection between Germans and the ancient Aryan peoples of India and Iran, who they believed were the most superior race of all humankind. Although in India the symbol is still used in Hindu and other religious decorations, in the West it is now largely associated with the hatred and genocide brought about by the Nazis before and during World War II.

## Key Themes and Symbols

As the embodiment of not one but all three of the gods of the Trimurti, Surya symbolizes the entire cycle of the universe, from creation to preservation to destruction, in a single day. Surya himself is represented by the sun. The seven horses of Surya's chariot are meant to represent the seven *chakras* (pronounced CHUK-ruhz), or centers of spiritual energy within the body.

## Surya in Art, Literature, and Everyday Life

Surya is often depicted as a golden figure riding through the sky in a chariot pulled by seven horses. He is sometimes shown holding lotus flowers, and is usually depicted with four arms. Many temples have been built throughout India in honor of Surya, including a well-known temple built in the thirteenth century CE in the town of Konark; the entire structure was designed to resemble the sun god's chariot. In yoga, Surya Namaskara, which means "salute to the sun," is the name given to a popular sequence of yoga positions usually performed at sunrise.

## Read, Write, Think, Discuss

The swastika was a well-regarded religious symbol for centuries before the Nazis adopted it for their own purposes. For this reason, while some people might be offended by the appearance of a swastika in Hindu religious art, others might see it as an expression of traditional ways and beliefs. Do you think the government should have the right to restrict the display of certain symbols if they are viewed negatively by most citizens? Why or why not? What if the symbol were a Confederate flag—flown by the South during the American Civil War—instead of a swastika?

**SEE ALSO** *Mahabharata, The*; *Ramayana, The*; Shiva; Vishnu

# T

## Tammuz

*See* **Ishtar.**

## Tellus

*See* **Gaia.**

## Tezcatlipoca

### Character Overview

Tezcatlipoca was one of the most important gods of the Aztecs of central Mexico. His name, meaning Lord of the Smoking Mirror, refers to the mirrors made of obsidian, a shiny black stone that Aztec priests used in divination, or attempts to predict the future. Tezcatlipoca played many contradictory roles in **Aztec mythology**. Like other Aztec deities, he could be both helpful and destructive. As a god of the **sun**, he ripened the crops but could also send a burning drought that killed the plants. The protector of helpless people, such as orphans and slaves, he was also associated with royalty, and he gloried in war and human **sacrifice**. Another of Tezcatlipoca's roles was to punish sinners and cheats, even though he himself was often portrayed as untrustworthy.

**Nationality/Culture**
Aztec

**Pronunciation**
tehs-cah-tlee-POH-cah

**Alternate Names**
Titlacauan

**Appears In**
Aztec creation myths

**Lineage**
None

Although associated with the sun, Tezcatlipoca was even more strongly linked with night and its dark mysteries, including dreams, sorcery, witches, and demons. Legend said that he roamed the earth each night in the form of a skeleton whose ribs opened like doors. If a person met Tezcatlipoca and was bold enough to reach through those doors and seize his heart, the god would promise riches and power in order to be released. He would not keep his promises, though.

## Major Myths

As a trickster god, Tezcatlipoca delighted in overturning the order of things, causing conflict and confusion. Sometimes these disruptions could also be a source of creative energy and positive change. Tezcatlipoca's ultimate trick was one he played on his fellow god **Quetzalcoatl** (pronounced keht-sahl-koh-AHT-l). After introducing Quetzalcoatl to drunkenness and other vices, he used his mirror to show Quetzalcoatl how weak and degraded he had become. Quetzalcoatl fled the world in shame, leaving it to Tezcatlipoca. He did, however, promise to return at the end of a fifty-two-year cycle.

Indeed, the battles between Quetzalcoatl and Tezcatlipoca led to the creation and destruction of the five different worlds in Aztec mythology. In the first world, Tezcatlipoca created himself as the sun, but Quetzalcoatl defeated him, so he then transformed into a jaguar. Tezcatlipoca led other jaguars in the destruction of all people, which ended the world of the first sun. After that, Quetzalcoatl became the second sun, and ruled his people until Tezcatlipoca turned them all into monkeys for not respecting the gods. This fight between the two gods continued until the establishment of the world of the fifth sun, which is what exists today.

## Tezcatlipoca in Context

Tezcatlipoca reflects the Aztec belief that change—especially change through conflict or disorder—is an essential part of life. Tezcatlipoca is an instrument of change throughout Aztec creation mythology, and while these changes are sometimes positive and sometimes negative, they ultimately reflect the progression of people to their current civilized state. Tezcatlipoca changes all the people into monkeys when they become complacent; this again reflects the importance, in the eyes of the Aztecs, of a human culture that always changes and progresses.

*This mask of the Aztec god Tezcatlipoca is made from a human skull decorated with turquoise and lignite.* ERICH LESSING/ART RESOURCE, NY.

## Key Themes and Symbols

Like many **tricksters**, Tezcatlipoca was a symbol of disorder and mischief. He often tried to interfere with the actions of the other gods, such as when he shamed Quetzalcoatl. One of the main themes running throughout the Aztec creation myths is the conflict between Tezcatlipoca and Quetzalcoatl, and how this leads to the creation of each of the different worlds.

## Tezcatlipoca in Art, Literature, and Everyday Life

Tezcatlipoca was often depicted with yellow and black stripes across his face, and with his right foot replaced by a snake or an obsidian mirror. Sometimes Tezcatlipoca was depicted in the form of a jaguar, a reference to the myth of the world of the first sun. In modern times, Tezcatlipoca has appeared in the 2001 science fiction novel *Smoking Mirror Blues* by Ernest Hogan. The book tells the story of how a version of the god, created by computer programmers, becomes conscious and takes over the body of a human.

## Read, Write, Think, Discuss

Using your library, the Internet, or other available resources, research the use of obsidian by Aztec and other early Central American tribes. Where did they get it? What was it used for? Why do you think it played a part in Aztec mythology?

**SEE ALSO** Aztec Mythology; Quetzalcoatl

# Theseus

**Nationality/Culture**
Greek

**Pronunciation**
THEE-see-uhs

**Alternate Names**
None

**Appears In**
Plutarch's *Life of Theseus*, Hyginus's *Fabulae*

**Lineage**
Son of King Aegeus and Aethra

## Character Overview

Theseus, a hero of **Greek mythology**, is best known for slaying a monster called the **Minotaur** (pronounced MIN-uh-tawr). His life and adventures illustrate many themes of Greek myths, including the idea that even the mightiest hero cannot escape tragedy if that is his fate.

**Mysterious Origins** Like many other **heroes** of myth and legend, Theseus was born and raised in unusual and dramatic circumstances. His mother was Aethra (pronounced EE-thruh), daughter of King Pittheus (pronounced PIT-thee-uhs) of Troezen (pronounced TREE-zen). Although some accounts name **Poseidon** (pronounced poh-SYE-dun) as his father, most say that Theseus was the son of King Aegeus (pronounced EE-joos) of Athens, who had stopped at Troezen after consulting the oracle at **Delphi** (pronounced DEL-fye).

The oracle had warned Aegeus not to get drunk or father a child on his way home to Athens, or one day he would die of sorrow. However, at Troezen, Aegeus ignored the warnings and became Aethra's lover. Before leaving for Athens, he placed his sandals and sword under a boulder and told Aethra that if she bore a son who could lift the boulder, that son would inherit the throne of Athens.

Their son Theseus grew into a strong young man, and one day he easily lifted the boulder and retrieved the sandals and the sword. He then set off for Athens to claim his heritage. On the way, he faced a series of challenges: three vicious and murderous outlaws; a monstrous pig that was destroying the countryside; a king who challenged travelers to fatal wrestling matches; and an innkeeper named Procrustes (pronounced proh-KRUS-teez) who tortured people by either stretching them or chopping off their limbs to make them fit his beds. Theseus overcame these dangerous opponents and killed them by the same methods they had used against their victims.

**Meeting the Minotaur** Upon arriving in Athens, Theseus found King Aegeus married to an enchantress named **Medea** (pronounced me-DEE-uh). Medea tried to poison Theseus, but when Aegeus saw the young man's sword and sandals, he realized that Theseus was his son and saved him from the poison. Medea fled, and Theseus became heir to the Athenian throne. He continued his heroic feats, defeating a plot against his father and destroying a savage wild bull.

Athens labored under a terrible curse. Earlier, Aegeus had sent another warrior, the son of King Minos (pronounced MYE-nuhs) of Crete, against the bull. The prince had died, and in revenge King Minos called down a plague on the Athenians. Only by sending seven young men and seven young women to Crete every year could they obtain relief. In Crete the youths were sacrificed to the Minotaur, a monstrous man-bull that lived below Minos's castle in a maze called the Labyrinth (pronounced LAB-uh-rinth).

Determined to end this grim practice, Theseus volunteered to be one of the victims. When the Athenians reached Crete, Minos's daughter **Ariadne** (pronounced ar-ee-AD-nee) fell in love with Theseus. Before Theseus entered the Labyrinth, Ariadne gave him a ball of yarn and told him to unwind it on his way in so that he could find his way out again. Deep in the maze Theseus met the Minotaur and killed it with a blow from his fist. He and the other Athenians then set sail for Athens, taking Ariadne with them. Along the way, they stopped at the island of Naxos (pronounced NAK-suhs), where Theseus abandoned Ariadne.

Theseus had promised his father that if he returned safely to Athens he would raise a white sail on his homecoming ship. He forgot to do so, however, and left the black sail hoisted. When Aegeus saw the black-sailed vessel approaching, he killed himself in grief, thus fulfilling the prophecy he had heard at Delphi.

**Later Adventures** On his father's death, Theseus became king of the city-state of Athens, where he won honor and was credited with enlarging the kingdom. His name sometimes appears in myths about heroic deeds, such as a battle against the **centaurs** (half-man, half-horse creatures), or the quest of **Jason** and the **Argonauts** (pronounced AHR-guh-nawts) for the **Golden Fleece**. Theseus also went to war against the female warriors known as **Amazons** (pronounced AM-uh-zonz), and he captured and married one of them—either Hippolyta (pronounced hye-POL-i-tuh), the Amazon queen, or her sister Antiope (pronounced an-TEE-oh-pee). This wife bore him a son, Hippolytus (pronounced hye-POL-i-tuhs).

After his Amazon wife died, Theseus eventually married Phaedra (pronounced FEE-druh), said to be a sister of Ariadne. Phaedra fell passionately in love with her stepson, Hippolytus, who rejected her love. The scorned Phaedra hanged herself, leaving a letter in which she accused Hippolytus of raping her. Furious, Theseus asked the god Poseidon to destroy Hippolytus, and the god fulfilled the king's wish. Later, Theseus learned the truth and knew that he had wrongly caused the death of his only son.

Theseus's final adventures were less than glorious. Seeking another wife, he kidnapped a daughter of **Zeus** (pronounced ZOOS), the king of the gods. He also became involved in a plot to carry off **Persephone** (pronounced per-SEF-uh-nee), queen of the **underworld**. These events brought trouble upon Athens, and the people drove Theseus away. Now a lonely old man, Theseus took refuge on the island of Skyros (pronounced SKY-rohs), but the local king, regarding Theseus as a possible rival, pushed the hero off a cliff to his death.

## Theseus in Context

The myth of Theseus and the Labyrinth may reflect ancient relationships between the Minoan civilization and the ancient Greeks. Minoan civilization was established on the island of Crete long before mainland Greek culture rose to prominence, with the Minoans lasting until about the fifteenth century BCE. It is quite possible that, in the final days of Minoan prominence, rulers on Crete clashed with Greek forces in an attempt to maintain control of their empire. Ultimately, the ancient Greeks flourished and assumed control of Crete. This history mirrors the myth, with King Minos threatening to attack Athens after his son is killed, and provides an explanation for the tension between the two cultures.

## Key Themes and Symbols

One of the themes found in the myth of Theseus is the idea that one cannot escape destiny—the path of one's life as determined by the gods. This was true for Theseus's father, who ignored warnings not to father a

*Theseus, a hero of Greek mythology, is best known for slaying a half-man, half-bull monster called the Minotaur.* HULTON ARCHIVE/STRINGER/GETTY IMAGES.

child. Ultimately, this led to his death by sorrow when he thought his son had been killed. Another interesting theme in the myths of Theseus is the appearance of false messages. When Theseus returned from Crete, he forgot to change the color of the sails on his boat, which caused his father to think he was dead. Later, his wife Phaedra left a letter that falsely accused Hippolytus of raping her, which led Theseus to ask the gods to kill his son.

The myths of Theseus also focus on the theme of ill-fated love. Although Ariadne fell in love with Theseus and helped him escape the Labyrinth, he abandoned her on Naxos as soon as he was able. Later, he fell in love with an Amazon, but she died. He then married Phaedra, who, instead of loving Theseus, loved his son. Theseus then tried to kidnap another wife, a plan that failed and brought him disgrace.

### Theseus in Art, Literature, and Everyday Life

The myth of Theseus and the Minotaur is one of the best-known tales of Greek mythology. Perhaps because of this, the character of Theseus has made several appearances in other works unrelated to the myth. These include a tale from Geoffrey Chaucer's *Canterbury Tales*, and William Shakespeare's plays *A Midsummer Night's Dream* and *The Two Noble Kinsmen*. Modern retellings of the myth include "The House of Asterion" (1949) by Argentinian fantasist Jorge Luis Borges, and two novels from Mary Renault, *The King Must Die* (1958) and *The Bull from the Sea* (1962), each of which covers different periods of the life of Theseus.

### Read, Write, Think, Discuss

*Lost in the Labyrinth* (2002) by Patrice Kindl offers a unique retelling of the myth of Theseus, Ariadne, and the Minotaur. The story is told from the point of view of Ariadne's younger sister, Xenodice. In this version of the tale, the Minotaur is mostly gentle but misunderstood, while Ariadne and Theseus may be less heroic than they appear—and it is up to Xenodice to straighten things out.

**SEE ALSO** Amazons; Argonauts; Ariadne; Delphi; Greek Mythology; Heroes; Medea

# Thor

**Nationality/Culture**
Norse/German

**Pronunciation**
THOR

**Alternate Names**
Donner (German)

**Appears In**
The Eddas, Germanic myths

**Lineage**
Son of Odin and Jord

### Character Overview

Thor was the god of thunder and of the sky in Norse and early Germanic mythology. Though **Odin** (pronounced OH-din) held a higher rank,

Thor seems to have been the best loved and most worshipped of the Norse deities (gods). He belonged to the common people, while Odin appealed to the educated and noble classes. A protector of farmers, Thor was associated with weather and crops. Although he could be fearsome, many myths portray him in a comic and affectionate way.

Thor appears throughout **Norse mythology** as a huge, strongly built, red-bearded fellow with a huge appetite. Some myths say that Thor was the son of Odin and Jord (pronounced YORD), the earth goddess. His wife was the beautiful goddess Sif, who seldom appears in myths and remains a somewhat mysterious figure.

Generally good-natured, Thor had a hot temper and his anger was dreadful to behold. He was a fierce enemy of the frost **giants**, the foes of the Norse gods. When people heard thunder and saw lightning in the sky, they knew that Thor was fighting these evil giants.

The thunder god's chief weapon was his mighty hammer Mjolnir (pronounced MYAWL-nir), or Crusher, which the dwarves had forged for him. When he threw Mjolnir, it returned magically to his hand like a boomerang. Among Mjolnir's other powers was the gift of restoring life to the dead. The connection of Thor's hammer with life and fertility gave rise to the old Norse customs of placing a hammer in a bride's lap at her wedding and of raising it over a newborn child.

Thor's treasures included a magical belt that doubled his strength whenever he wore it. He also had a pair of goats, Tanngniost and Tanngrisni, that pulled his chariot across the sky. Whenever he was overcome with hunger, Thor would devour his goats, only to return them to life with Mjolnir.

## Major Myths

According to one well-known myth about Thor, Thrym, king of the giants, came into possession of Mjolnir and declared that he would give it back to Thor only if the beautiful goddess **Freyja** (pronounced FRAY-uh) agreed to marry him. She angrily refused, and the trickster god **Loki** (pronounced LOH-kee) came up with a clever plan to recover Mjolnir. Using women's clothing and a bridal veil to disguise Thor as Freyja, Loki escorted "Freyja" to Jotunheim (pronounced YAW-toon-heym), the home of the giants. Thrym greeted his bride, though he was surprised at her appetite at the wedding feast. "Freyja" consumed an entire ox, three barrels of wine, and much more. Loki explained that she had been unable to eat for a week because of her excitement at marrying Thrym. The giant accepted this explanation, and the wedding proceeded. When the time came for a hammer to be placed in the bride's lap according to custom, Thor grabbed Mjolnir and threw off his disguise. Then he used the hammer to smash the giants and their hall.

During another visit to Jotunheim, Thor and Loki met Skrymir (pronounced SKREE-mir), an especially large giant. He was so big that when they wandered into one of his gloves, they thought they were in a mansion and slept in one of the fingers. In the morning they found Skrymir sleeping, and Thor tried to crush the giant's head with Mjolnir. Skrymir simply brushed away the blow as though it were no more than a falling leaf.

The gods traveled on to Utgard (pronounced OOT-gard), a city of giants, where the giants challenged Thor to drain their drinking cup and lift their cat from the floor. He could not do either—the cup was connected to the sea, and the cat was really Jormungand (pronounced YAWR-moon-gahnd), the serpent that encircles the world. Although Thor failed the tests, he came close to draining the ocean and removing the world serpent.

Several early Norse sources recount the myth of Thor's encounter with the giant Hymir. Thor disguised himself as a young man and went fishing with Hymir, first killing the giant's largest ox to use for bait. Thor then rowed their boat far out of sight of land and cast his hook. Something bit at the ox, and Thor drew up his line to discover that he had hooked Jormungand, the giant serpent. Placing his feet on the ocean floor, Thor pulled and pulled on the line, while the serpent spit out poison. Just as Thor was about to strike Jormungand with his hammer, Hymir cut the line and the serpent sank back down to the depths. Many myths say, however, that Thor and Jormungand remained bitter enemies, fated to fight again on the day called **Ragnarok** (pronounced RAHG-nuh-rok), the end of the world, when they will kill one another.

## Thor in Context

For the Germanic and Norse people, Thor represented much more than just the god of thunder. In the final years of Germanic dominance, Thor became a symbol of pre-Christian beliefs, embraced by many who held onto their traditional roots and condemned by those attempting to expand Christianity throughout northern Europe. A tree known as

*Thor holding his hammer and riding his chariot pulled by two goats, Tanngniost and Tanngrisni.* © CHARLES WALKER/TOPFOTO/THE IMAGE WORKS.

Thor's Oak was considered sacred by the Germanic tribe called the Chatti.

When a Christian missionary—later known by the name St. Boniface—arrived in the area in an attempt to convert the locals, he noted the importance of the tree in their beliefs. He had the tree cut down to prove the superiority of Christianity; when Thor did not strike the missionary dead with lightning for this act, many of the Chatti agreed to convert to Christianity. Afterward, Christian missionaries often singled out Thor as an example of a false god who had to be renounced in order to prove one's faith in God. Legends and beliefs about Thor continued, however, as part of a German folk tradition that could not be erased by the spread of Christianity.

## Key Themes and Symbols

To the Norse and Germanic people, Thor represented the devastating power of storms. The pounding of his hammer symbolized the crackle of thunder; storms were thought to represent Thor's battles against the giants. One of the main themes in the tales of Thor is the ongoing battle between the giants and the Norse gods. Most of his tales center on exacting revenge against the giants, or battling with them in a prelude to the final war against the giants at Ragnarok.

## Thor in Art, Literature, and Everyday Life

In Norse art, Thor is depicted as having red hair and a red beard, holding his trusted hammer Mjolnir and often being pulled in his chariot by his trusted goats. In modern times, Thor is perhaps the best-known god in Norse mythology. This is primarily due to the popularity of the Marvel Comics superhero Thor, based on the mythical god. Thor has appeared in this form in countless comic books and in several animated television series and video games. Thor also appears under his German name, Donner, as a character in Richard Wagner's series of operas known as *Der Ring des Nibelungen* (*The Ring of the Nibelung*).

## Read, Write, Think, Discuss

Though most of Scandinavia was converted to Christianity by about the twelfth century, the Sami people of northern regions of Finland, Norway, and Russia remained particularly devoted to Thor until they were forcibly converted in the seventeenth and eighteenth centuries. Today, the Sami maintain a distinctive culture in which many ancient cultural influences are detectable. Using your library and the Internet, find out more about Sami culture. Write a paper summarizing your findings.

**SEE ALSO** Loki; Norse Mythology; Odin

# Thoth

**Nationality/Culture**
Egyptian

**Pronunciation**
TOHT

**Alternate Names**
Djehuty, Sheps, Asten

**Appears In**
Egyptian *Book of the Dead*

**Lineage**
Son of Ra

## Character Overview

Thoth was the Egyptian god of wisdom and knowledge. Honored as the inventor of writing and the founder of branches of learning, such as art, astronomy, medicine, law, and magic, he was the god associated with scribes, the official writers who documented ancient Egyptian culture and beliefs. Ancient Egyptians associated Thoth with the moon and identified him as the son of **Ra**, the supreme **sun** god. According to legend, Thoth possessed books of wisdom that contained secret information about nature and magic. Although the books were hidden, certain scribes had access to them.

## Major Myths

Thoth played a key role in the Egyptian story of the **afterlife**. Known to be fair and impartial, Thoth judged the souls of the dead by weighing their hearts against a feather that represented truth. After recording the results, he told **Osiris** (pronounced oh-SYE-ris), ruler of the **underworld** or land of the dead, whether the individual had led a just life.

Thoth also played an important role in the creation of the Egyptian pantheon, or collection of recognized gods. According to myth, the goddess **Nut**—who had married her twin brother Geb against the wishes of Ra—was not allowed to have children during any month of the year, which originally consisted of only 360 days. Thoth felt sorry for Nut and gambled with the moon in an effort to win a portion of its light. Thoth won and turned that light into five additional days for each year. During those five days, Nut gave birth to her five children: Osiris, **Isis** (pronounced EYE-sis), **Set** (pronounced SET), Nephthys (pronounced NEF-this), and **Horus** (pronounced HOHR-uhs).

## Thoth in Context

The nature of the god Thoth reflects the importance of the moon and calendars in ancient Egypt. Thoth was originally seen as a moon god, with the curve of the beak on his ibis head even resembling a crescent moon. As the observation of the moon became a crucial part of determining the passage of months and seasons—the basis for early

*The Egyptian god Thoth writing on a tablet. Thoth is credited with the invention of writing.* © CHARLES WALKER/ TOPFOTO/THE IMAGE WORKS.

Egyptian calendars—Thoth came to be seen as the god of wisdom and knowledge. The Egyptians used these calendars to determine when to plant and harvest crops, and were one the first societies to establish a month and year cycle similar to what is still used today. The first month of the Egyptian year was even named after their god of the moon and wisdom, Thoth.

## Key Themes and Symbols

Thoth represented wisdom to the ancient Egyptians. He was also known as the "tongue of Ra," the tongue symbolizing his eloquence of speech as the speaker for the supreme god. He was seen as a force of levelheadedness and compromise among the gods, as shown in his acquisition of five extra days in each year for Nut.

## Thoth in Art, Literature, and Everyday Life

In works of art, Thoth appears as either a human with the head of an ibis—a bird with a long, curved bill—or a baboon that supports the moon on its head. In modern times, Thoth was popularized by occult author Aleister Crowley in *The Book of Thoth*, which outlined the proper use of a deck of Tarot cards he created known as the Thoth Tarot. The Thoth Tarot has gone on to become one of the most popular decks of Tarot cards ever created.

## Read, Write, Think, Discuss

Calendars played a crucial role in ancient societies. Nearly all important tasks, including religious rituals and agricultural tasks, relied upon knowledge of dates and seasons. Using your library, the Internet, or other available resources, research the ancient Egyptian calendar. How does it differ from the calendar we use today? Does it have any advantages over our modern calendar? Does it have any disadvantages? Does the Egyptian calendar reflect ancient Egyptian beliefs? If so, how?

**SEE ALSO** Afterlife; Egyptian Mythology; Osiris; Ra; Underworld

# Thunderbird

**Nationality/Culture**
American Indian

**Pronunciation**
THUHN-der-burd

**Alternate Names**
Animikii (Ojibwa), Jojo (Kwakiutl)

**Appears In**
Various American Indian oral mythologies

**Lineage**
Varies

## Character Overview

An important figure in American Indian mythology, the Thunderbird represents the natural forces of thunder, lightning, and storms. It is also believed to protect humans by fighting evil spirits. Many different cultural groups have their own stories about the bird, and some cultures even refer to groups or races of such birds.

## Major Myths

The Thunderbird is thought by some to be one of the main gods of the sky. It creates thunder by flapping its wings and causes lightning by opening and closing its beak and eyes. Usually described as a huge bird, the Thunderbird is large enough to carry off a whale to eat and to split open trees to find insects for food.

The Algonquian people consider Thunderbirds to be ancestors of the human race, involved with the creation of the universe. According to a Shawnee tale, Thunderbirds appear as boys and can speak backwards. Other cultures believe in four Thunderbirds that guard a nest holding an egg, which hatches all other birds of their type.

A Lakota Sioux (pronounced SOO) myth says that the great Thunderbird was the grandson of the sky spirit that created the world and put people on it. But the water spirit Unktehi (pronounced UN-teh-hee) thought the people were lice, and she and her followers tried to drown them. The people retreated to the highest hill they could find and prayed for help. The Thunderbird came to fight Unktehi and sent lightning crashing to earth. The ground split open, and Unktehi and her followers drained into the cracks. As a result, humankind was saved.

## The Thunderbird in Context

Though no evidence exists of gigantic birds that existed during the time of humans, the American Indian myth of the Thunderbird may have some basis in scientific fact. According to legend, the birds are the bringers of storms, which means they would appear in front of approaching storm clouds. Storm clouds generally form at the boundary between air masses of different pressures; this collision of air masses can also result in a strong updraft, or a wind that flows upward. Zoologists are already familiar with large birds that use updrafts as a way to fly without wasting energy; it is possible that the "thunderbirds" of American Indian legend were based on sightings of large birds, such as eagles or condors, that utilized the updrafts created at storm fronts in order to glide with little effort. To some, it might appear that such birds were leading the storm across the sky.

*A Haida thunderbird sculpture.* © PRIVATE COLLECTION/ PETER NEWARK WESTERN AMERICANA/THE BRIDGEMAN ART LIBRARY.

## Key Themes and Symbols

The Thunderbird is an embodiment of the thunderstorm: its wings are associated with thunder and wind, and its eyes are linked to lightning. Although the Thunderbird is associated with fierce power, in many myths it also represents a protective or helpful force for humankind. The Thunderbird was viewed as a provider, since rain was necessary for the growth of crops and for the grasses that fed the buffalo.

## The Thunderbird in Art, Literature, and Everyday Life

The Thunderbird is found in many American Indian cultures. It is often seen on the totem poles of the Kwakiutl (pronounced kwah-kee-OOT-l) of the Pacific Northwest and in the art of the Navajo and Sioux. In modern times, the mythical creature is believed by some to be a real animal that has so far escaped human study, similar to Bigfoot. The legendary bird also loosely inspired a Marvel Comics superhero of the same name, an Apache with superhuman strength and speed whose costume was decorated with an image of the Thunderbird. Many commercial products have borrowed the name of Thunderbird, including a brand of bass guitar, an inexpensive wine, and a line of Ford automobiles, among many others.

## Read, Write, Think, Discuss

Many products and services in modern times take their names from mythical figures. The Ford Thunderbird is one example, and the Venus women's razor is another. See if you can think of another example that has not already been mentioned. Why do you think so many products are named after characters from mythology? Do you think this reveals anything about the place of mythology in modern society?

**SEE ALSO** Native American Mythology

# Tiamat

**Nationality/Culture**
Babylonian

**Pronunciation**
TYAH-maht

**Alternate Names**
Thalatte (Greek)

**Appears In**
The *Enuma Elish*

**Lineage**
None

## Character Overview

Tiamat was an ancient goddess of salt waters and chaos, or disorder. She is mentioned in the Babylonian (pronounced bab-uh-LOH-nee-uhn) creation story called the ***Enuma Elish***, found inscribed on clay tablets dating back to around 1100 BCE. She is the mother of the gods, and her body was used to make the world.

## Major Myths

At the beginning of the universe, Tiamat and Apsu (pronounced AHP-soo), the spirit of fresh waters, gave birth to all the gods. She also gave birth to all manner of beasts, such as serpents and scorpion-people. Tiamat's son Ea (pronounced AY-uh, also known as Enki) soon challenged and

### Divine Creation

A theme repeated throughout world mythologies is the creation of heaven and earth through the sacrifice of a deity or primal being. Marduk split Tiamat in half and shaped heaven and earth from her ribs. Her tears became the source of the two major rivers in Mesopotamia, the Tigris and the Euphrates. In Indian mythology, Purusha, the original being, is sacrificed by the gods and from his body are created the sky, moon, earth, sun, and the four castes of Indian society. These creation stories indicate that people have always sought a divine origin for their existence.

killed Apsu, but he could not defeat Tiamat. Ea then enlisted the help of his son **Marduk**, who destroyed the legions of monsters Tiamat created as her army. Then he rode out in a chariot to do battle with Tiamat in the form of a dragon. As Marduk approached, Tiamat opened her mouth to swallow him, but Marduk threw a storm into Tiamat's mouth and prevented her from closing it. Then he killed her by shooting an arrow into her belly. After cutting Tiamat's body into pieces, Marduk used them to create the heavens and the earth.

## Tiamat in Context

In the myth of Tiamat and Marduk, it is important to understand that Marduk was the patron, or protector god, of Babylon. When Babylon rose to prominence in the ancient world, stories that glorified their chosen god were favored. Earlier versions of the myth developed before the rise of Babylonian civilization may have differed in details related to Marduk. Some scholars have suggested that the killing of Tiamat by Marduk reflects a Babylonian victory over an earlier, matriarchal society where women hold the ruling power. However, this theory is not widely accepted.

## Key Themes and Symbols

The myth of Tiamat emphasizes the connection between the world and the gods, and also highlights the split nature of the universe. The world and the heavens are created from the dead body of the goddess; similarly, the blood of her ally Kingu (pronounced KIN-goo) is used to make humankind. This reflects the presence of the divine in all parts of the world. The split nature of the universe is shown in the presence of two ancient forces—one a creation of salt water and one of fresh water. This is also shown in Tiamat's defeat, when Marduk slices her in two to create the heavens from one half and the earth from the other half.

## Tiamat in Art, Literature, and Everyday Life

Tiamat is mostly known from the *Enuma Elish*, which was rediscovered by modern scholars in the nineteenth century. In mainstream culture, Tiamat is a well-known deity in the *Dungeons & Dragons* role-playing game universe, though she is depicted as a multi-headed dragon and is only marginally connected with the original Babylonian goddess. Tiamat also appeared in the animated television series *Dungeons & Dragons* (1983), and in several video games, including *Golden Sun* for Nintendo's Game Boy Advance and the *Final Fantasy* series.

## Read, Write, Think, Discuss

The creation myth of the Babylonians is based on the deities of the waters. Using your library, the Internet, or other available resources, locate Babylon on a map of the ancient world. What sources of fresh water are located near it? What sources of salt water can be found nearby? Why do you think the goddess of salt water is depicted as more powerful and chaotic than the god of fresh water?

**SEE ALSO** Creation Stories; *Enuma Elish*; Marduk; Semitic Mythology

# Titans

**Nationality/Culture**
Greek

**Pronunciation**
TYE-tuhnz

**Alternate Names**
None

**Appears In**
Hesiod's *Theogony*

**Lineage**
The children of Uranus and Gaia

## Character Overview

The Titans were gigantic, powerful, ancient beings that loomed in the background of many Greek myths and tales. Children of **Uranus** (pronounced YOOR-uh-nuhs) and **Gaia** (pronounced GAY-uh), the

Titans ruled the world before they were overthrown by the god **Zeus** (pronounced ZOOS) and his brothers and sisters. Originally there were twelve Titans. The Greek writer Hesiod listed six male Titans—Oceanus (pronounced oh-SEE-uh-nuhs), Coeus (pronounced SEE-uhs), **Cronus** (pronounced KROH-nuhs), Crius (pronounced KRYE-uhs), Hyperion (pronounced hy-PEER-ee-on), and Iapetus (pronounced eye-AP-uh-tus)—and six female Titanesses—Tethys (pronounced TEE-this), Themis (pronounced THEEM-is), Phoebe (pronounced FEE-bee), Mnemosyne (pronounced nee-MOSS-uh-nee), Theia (pronounced THEE-uh), and Rhea (pronounced REE-uh). Some accounts add the brothers **Prometheus** (pronounced pruh-MEE-thee-uhs), Epimetheus (pronounced ep-uh-MEE-thee-uhs), **Atlas** (pronounced AT-luhs), and the moon goddess Selene (pronounced suh-LEE-nee) to this group of Titans. These four gods and a few others are more often described as children of the original twelve Titans.

## Major Myths

The most important tales of the Titans involve the overthrow of their father Uranus and their own battle against the Olympian gods. Uranus hated the children born from his wife Gaia, so he forced her to keep the Titans in Tartarus (pronounced TAR-tur-uhs), a dismal pit deep within Gaia's bowels. This caused Gaia much pain, and she asked her sons to help her defeat Uranus by cutting off his genitals with a sickle. Only her youngest son, the Titan Cronus, was willing to do it. After he was successful, the Titans were freed from Tartarus and ruled the heavens. Cronus, with his sister Rhea at his side, was their leader.

However, Cronus was told that when he had children, one of his sons would overthrow him—just as he had done to his own father. To avoid this fate, Cronus swallowed each of his children as soon as they were born. Rhea managed to save only one child, Zeus, by hiding him and feeding Cronus a stone in the baby's place. When Zeus grew older, he gave his father a potion that made him vomit out his other siblings. These children, known as the Olympians, then waged an eleven-year war against the Titans. The Olympians eventually won and cast many of the Titans back into Tartarus, where Uranus had imprisoned them long before. However, several of the Titans—including Oceanus and all the female Titans—did not participate in the war against the Olympians, and therefore were able to remain free.

*Oceanus was one of six male Titans—giant, powerful, and primeval beings that were overthrown by the Greek gods.* VANNI/ART RESOURCE, NY.

## Titans in Context

Some scholars suggest that the reign—and ultimate defeat—of the Titans in **Greek mythology** reflects the conquest of an earlier culture by the one we now associate with the ancient Greeks. This earlier culture is believed to have been matriarchal, meaning women held the primary positions of power within the society. This is suggested by the Titans' close association with their mother, Gaia, and poor relationship with their father Uranus. The ancient Greeks, being a patriarchal society (where men held the most power), were similar to the Olympian gods who take control of the heavens. The regions of the world were divided among the three sons—Zeus, **Poseidon** (pronounced poh-SYE-dun), and **Hades** (pronounced HAY-deez)—while the daughters were not given direct rule over anything. If this idea is correct, the myths of the ancient Greeks would be a direct reflection of ancient cultural clashes in the region.

## Key Themes and Symbols

The Titans represent huge, primitive, hard-to-control forces; indeed, many of the Titans are embodiments of the forces of nature and are born from Mother Earth (Gaia). They also symbolize a spirit of rebellion against the authority of the gods, as in the story of the Titan Prometheus, who helped human beings against Zeus's will. The myth of the Titans and their downfall includes a theme common throughout Greek mythology: the fate of a god or person cannot be avoided, no matter how hard one might try to change it.

## Titans in Art, Literature, and Everyday Life

The Titans are featured in ancient art primarily in depictions of the war between them and the Olympian gods. Although some Titans, such as Prometheus, appear in other myths, they were not generally considered important subjects for literature or art. Instead, throughout the centuries, the Olympian gods dominated art influenced by Greek mythology. The most notable exception is Cronus, also referred to by his Roman name, Saturn. One of the most famous images of Saturn is Francisco Goya's grisly painting *Saturn Devouring One of His Children* (1823), which depicts the myth of the Titan leader consuming one of his children in order to keep from being overthrown. Another famous image of Cronus/Saturn eating one of his children was created by Peter Paul Rubens in 1636. More recently, the 1997 Disney animated film *Hercules* included a plot by Hades to release the Titans from their imprisonment and take control of Greece and Olympus. In modern usage, the immense size of the Titans has led to the word "titanic," meaning extremely large.

## Read, Write, Think, Discuss

The myths of the early Greek gods include two examples of sons overthrowing their fathers for control of the heavens—first Cronus defeating Uranus, and then Zeus defeating Cronus. In both cases, the sons are raised by mother figures and have very little or no contact with their fathers. What do you think this theme of conflict between fathers and sons reflects about ancient Greek family life?

**SEE ALSO** Atlas; Cronus; Gaia; Greek Mythology; Prometheus; Uranus; Zeus

**Rama Fighting the Demon Ravana**

Rama, sitting on the shoulders of Hanuman, fought the demon king Ravana in the Hindu epic the *Ramayana*.
*See Ramayana, The.*

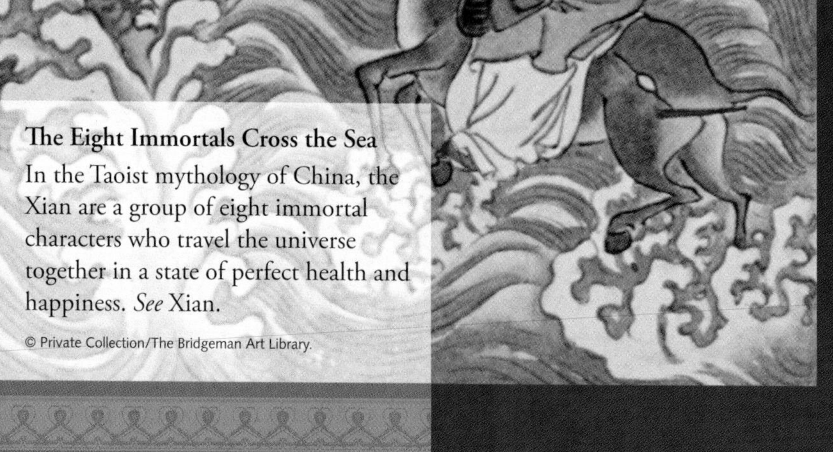

**The Eight Immortals Cross the Sea**
In the Taoist mythology of China, the Xian are a group of eight immortal characters who travel the universe together in a state of perfect health and happiness. *See* Xian.

**The Hindu God Surya Riding His Chariot**

*See* Surya.

Jalaram Temple, Bilimora, Gujarat, India/ Dinodia/The Bridgeman Art Library.

**The Samsara Being Turned by Yama**

According to Buddhist belief, Yama, the Lord of Death, spins the wheel that causes people to continue the cycle of reincarnation until they achieve the highest level of spiritual development. *See* Reincarnation.

**Abraham's Sacrifice of Isaac**

Abraham's near-sacrifice of his son Isaac on orders from God illustrated his faith and obedience in the Bible. *See* Sacrifice.

Scala/Art Resource, NY.

**Zeus Throws Lightning from a Cloud**

One of the primary weapons of the Greek god Zeus was the thunderbolt. *See* Zeus.

Erich Lessing/Art Resource, NY.

**The Sirens Call to Odysseus**

Most sailors who heard the sirens' song met an unfortunate end; the Greek hero Odysseus avoided this fate by instructing his crew to tie him to the mast of the boat to prevent him from jumping into the ocean when he heard the sirens. The crew were safe because they stopped up their ears so they could not hear. *See* Sirens.

Herbert James Draper/The Bridgeman Art Library/Getty Images.

**A Unicorn with a Maiden**

The unicorn was a mythological creature that served as a symbol of purity. According to tradition, one way to capture a unicorn was to send a young virgin into the forest, and the unicorn would be drawn out of hiding by her purity. *See* Unicorns.

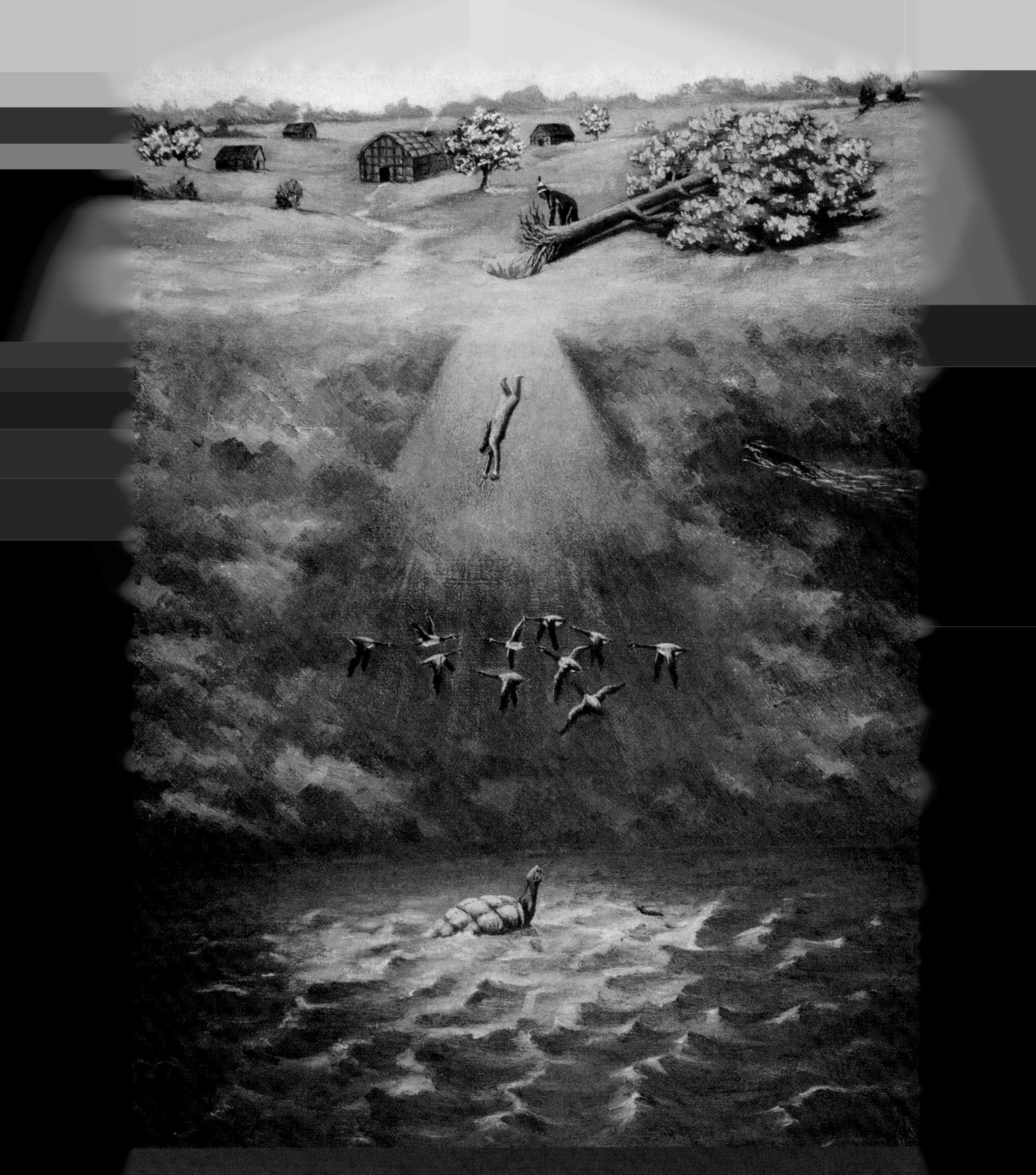

**Sky Woman Falls from Heaven**

According to an Iroquois creation myth, the earth came to be after Sky Woman fell from heaven through a hole left by the uprooted Tree of Life. Flying ducks slowed her descent, and a large turtle kept her afloat in the primal waters until she gave birth. Her children created the features of the earth and sky. *See* Woman Who Fell from the Sky.

**The Sun God Ra in His Solar Barque with Apophis Below**

This detail from an Egyptian coffin shows the sun god Ra in his solar barque. Below him is the serpent Apophis, which Ra battles every evening. Egyptians believed that the victory of Ra over Apophis showed the victory of the sun over darkness. *See* Ra.

# Tlaloc

**Nationality/Culture**
Aztec

**Pronunciation**
TLAH-lok

**Alternate Names**
Tohil, Chac (Mayan)

**Appears In**
Aztec oral myths and codices

**Lineage**
Unknown

## Character Overview

To the Aztecs of central Mexico, Tlaloc was a god of rain and fertility. Associated with lightning, thunder, and vegetation, he appeared as a man with circles around his eyes and fangs like the teeth of a jaguar. Tlaloc shared the main temple in the Aztec capital of Tenochtitlán (pronounced teh-nowch-TEE-tlan) with the gods **Quetzalcoatl** (pronounced keht-sahl-koh-AHT-l) and **Huitzilopochtli** (pronounced wee-tsee-loh-POCH-tlee). The Maya called him Chac, and the Quiché of Guatemala knew him as Tohil.

Tlaloc had both helpful and harmful aspects. He carried four water jugs: one gave rain, but the others poured disease, frost, and drought onto the world. He and his wife, Chalchiuhtlicue (pronounced chahl-kwee-TLEE-kway), supervised the Tlaloque, spirits in charge of weather and mountains. The Tlaloque delivered rain to the earth and produced thunder by clashing their water jugs together.

One level of the Aztec heavens was named Tlalocan after the god. It was a place of abundant vegetation and everlasting spring. The souls of the dead who were sacred to Tlaloc—victims of drowning, lightning, and certain diseases, such as leprosy—went to this lush garden paradise.

## Major Myths

In the myths of the Aztec, there are five different worlds that have come to pass. Each world was destroyed and replaced by the next. The first world was presided over by **Tezcatlipoca**, and was known as the World of the Jaguar Sun. The second world, ruled by Quetzalcoatl, was the World of the Wind Sun. The third world was ruled by Tlaloc, and was known as the World of the Rain Sun. In Tlaloc's world, all people lived on water lilies and were changed into animals, such as dogs and butterflies. Tlaloc's reign ended when Quetzalcoatl destroyed everything in a rain of **fire**. The current age is the fifth world, the World of the Earthquake Sun—which, according to Aztec myth, will end in a series of devastating earthquakes.

*The symbol of Tlaloc.* WERNER FORMAN/ART RESOURCE, NY.

## Tlaloc in Context

Tlaloc reflected the Aztec belief that human **sacrifice** was an important part of pleasing the gods and maintaining order in the natural world. For Tlaloc, the Aztecs believed that the sacrifice of children—usually viewed as the most perfect or purest members of the society—was required. Priests sacrificed children to Tlaloc during five of the eighteen months that made up the Aztec year. According to tradition, if the victims cried during the proceedings, their tears were a sign of plentiful rain to come. The Aztecs believed that if they failed to sacrifice children, Tlaloc would withhold rain, killing their crops.

## Key Themes and Symbols

Tlaloc, as a god of rain, represented growth and life to the Aztec people. This is shown in the Aztec vision of Tlalocan, which is thought to be always lush and green. The Aztecs also drew a direct connection between human tears and rain, just as they equated blood with the life-giving energy of the **sun**.

## Tlaloc in Art, Literature, and Everyday Life

Tlaloc appears in many Aztec codices—written documents of Aztec beliefs, calendars, and other cultural information created shortly after Spanish explorers conquered their society. Sculptures of Tlaloc have also been found at various Aztec sites. He is generally depicted as a blue being surrounded by clouds and holding rattles that are used to create thunder.

## Read, Write, Think, Discuss

Human sacrifice may be difficult for people in modern societies to accept or understand, but it was practiced in many areas of the world, and is even mentioned in the Bible when God tells Abraham to sacrifice his son Isaac. Using your library, the Internet, or other available resources, research human sacrifice in several different societies. What were some of the underlying cultural beliefs or philosophies about human sacrifice in those societies? How has the practice of sacrifice to the gods developed throughout history? What does sacrifice mean in contemporary Western societies?

**SEE ALSO** Aztec Mythology; Huitzilopochtli; Mayan Mythology; Quetzalcoatl

# Tricksters

## Theme Overview

Tricksters are among the most entertaining characters in world mythology. Usually male, they delight in breaking rules, boasting, and playing tricks on both humans and gods. Most tricksters are shape-changers who can take any form, though they often appear as animals. Tricksters play a prominent role in African and Native American mythologies. They can also be found in the myths of Europeans, Asians, Pacific Islanders, and the Aborigines of Australia. Many gods, demigods, and **heroes** from around the world are described as having trickster qualities.

## Major Myths

**African Tricksters** Eshu, a West African trickster also known as Legba, is associated with travel, commerce, and communication—or miscommunication. He often creates quarrels among people or between people and gods. In one myth, he caused conflict between a man and his two wives. Disguised as a merchant, Eshu sold one of the wives a fine hat, which pleased the husband but made the other wife jealous. Eshu then sold a more splendid hat to the second wife. The competition continued, making the husband and both wives miserable. According to another myth, the High God became so disgusted with Eshu's trickery that he left the world, ordering Eshu to remain as his link with it.

Eshu is just one of the many tricksters in **African mythology**. A trickster hare appears in some myths, and tales about a trickster spider called **Anansi** are widespread in West Africa. Anansi is a cunning fellow who acts as God's assistant, although some stories reveal him trying to trick God.

Occasionally the trickster himself falls victim to a trick. One myth about Anansi tells how he cheated the chameleon out of his field. For revenge, Chameleon created a fine cloak of vines decorated with buzzing flies. Everyone wanted the cloak, but Chameleon would sell it only to the spider. The price, he told Anansi, was merely a little food, just enough to fill the tiny hole that was his storehouse. The spider agreed and sent two of his children with grain. However, Chameleon had secretly dug the deepest hole that anyone had ever seen. Anansi's children poured grain into the hole for weeks, and still it was not full. Chameleon ended up with most of the spider's wealth. Anansi received only a few withered vines for his part of the bargain and fled from the mocking laughter of the people. According to the myth, this explains why spiders hide in the corners of houses.

**Native American Tricksters** Tricksters figure prominently in the mythologies of Native Americans. They usually take the form of animals, although they also have some human qualities and may appear human if it suits their purposes. The most common trickster figure is Coyote, but Raven, Crow, Bluejay, Rabbit, Spider, Raccoon, Bear, and others appear in the trickster myths of different Native American groups.

A myth of the Coeur d'Alene people illustrates the sly and bumbling side of Coyote. The first people selected Coyote as their moon. But when they learned that he spied on them from the sky and told their secrets, they replaced him with a chieftain who turned the tables by keeping watch on Coyote. Then, because the **sun** had killed some of Coyote's children, the trickster cut out the sun's heart, plunging the world into darkness. Coyote wanted to take the heart home with him, but he kept stumbling in the dark. In the end he had to return the heart to the sun, which restored light to the world.

Myths of the Algonquian-speaking people tell of a trickster named **Gluskap**. Gluskap lived in the cold north, but during a journey to the warm south, he tricked Summer, a beautiful female chieftain, into returning north with him. After she melted the cold of Winter, Gluskap let her return to her home.

*This statue of of the West African trickster Eshu was made by the Yoruba people of Nigeria.* © ROYAL ALBERT MEMORIAL MUSEUM, EXETER, DEVON, UK/THE BRIDGEMAN ART LIBRARY.

**Other Tricksters Maui**, the trickster hero of the Polynesian Islands in the Pacific Ocean, created the world while he was fishing. He let out a long fishing line and reeled in island after island from the bottom of the ocean. Later, Maui stole **fire** from the **underworld** and gave it to humans.

**Greek mythology** also includes a trickster associated with the gift of fire. The god **Prometheus** tricked **Zeus** and the other gods into granting humans the best part of an animal killed for a **sacrifice**. Angry at having been tricked, Zeus refused to let humans have fire, but Prometheus stole a burning ember from the gods for people to use.

Myths from the Micronesian islands of the western Pacific tell of Olifat, son of a human woman and a sky god, who used cleverness, trickery, and magic to obtain the food, drink, and women he wanted. The trickster's greed turned to jealousy and spite when he discovered that he had a brother who had been raised in secret. Olifat caught the brother and cut off his head, offering it to his father in place of the fish that was expected. The sky god restored Olifat's brother to life and turned in anger to Olifat. The trickster slyly pleaded innocence, arguing that since his father had told him he had no brother, he could not have killed a brother who did not exist.

A trickster may be a go-between or messenger between the human and divine worlds. **Hermes** (pronounced HUR-meez), the messenger of the gods in Greek mythology, was the god of travelers and trade but also of thieves and deceit. As a child, Hermes demonstrated his cleverness by stealing cattle from **Apollo**. He hid their tracks by tying tree bark to their hooves.

The Norse trickster **Loki** was originally a friend of the gods, but eventually they became tired of his tricks and grew to dislike him. In one tale, Loki stole the hair of **Thor**'s wife, Sif. In order to appease Thor, Loki convinced two dwarf craftsmen to each create three magnificent gifts that he could present to Thor. Loki turned himself into a stinging fly in an attempt to distract the second craftsman, Sindri, and his brother Brock, since Loki had wagered his head that the second dwarf could not possibly create gifts more magnificent than the first. When Thor received the gifts, he chose Sindri's gifts as the better of the two. When Brock tried to claim Loki's head, Thor cautioned that he cannot touch Loki's neck, since it was not mentioned in the wager. Brock satisfied himself with sewing Loki's mouth shut.

## Tricksters in Context

Some scholars have suggested that the trickster is one of the oldest figures in mythology. A chaotic and disorderly character, he acts out many human urges and desires that people living in communities learn to control to maintain social order. Trickster myths, especially those in which the trickster's deeds backfire against him in some way, may have developed to teach a moral lesson about the penalties of misbehavior.

Tales in which the trickster is a small but clever animal that emerges victorious teach a different lesson. They show how a seemingly powerless creature can triumph over a mighty one.

While not typically considered purely good or evil, tricksters operate outside the rules of society. Often childish, greedy, lustful, and even nasty, tricksters can also be friendly, helpful, clever, and wise. Sometimes they appear to be clownish, clumsy, or foolish, although they usually possess amazing powers of survival. A trickster may come to a sorry end in one story but then, after being miraculously brought back to life, reappear in other tales. Sometimes a trickster is a creator or culture hero whose activities explain how some aspect of the world came into being. While tricksters are often shown to be selfish, silly, or wrongheaded, they also help people identify with the situations and lessons contained in these myths. In addition, tricksters provide entertaining moments that remind readers and listeners that myths are meant to be enjoyed and shared from generation to generation.

## Tricksters in Art, Literature, and Everyday Life

Over the years, because of the entertaining appeal of this type of character, many trickster characters have been borrowed from their native mythology and incorporated into newer works. Loki, for example, appears in Marvel comics as a villain who fights against superheroes, including Thor. **Brer Rabbit**, a popular African American trickster derived from other West African tricksters such as Anansi, became the focus of the *Uncle Remus* books by Southern journalist Joel Chandler Harris in the late 1800s. In William Shakespeare's *A Midsummer Night's Dream*, the character of Puck incorrectly distributes a love potion among several couples, creating chaos and compounding the romantic problems of all the main characters.

The trickster character also appears in many popular films. One recent example is Captain Jack Sparrow from Disney's *Pirates of the Caribbean* films. Jack shows the classic trickster traits of greed, self-importance, and foolishness, but at the same time he uses his cleverness as a way out of the predicaments he creates for himself.

## Read, Write, Think, Discuss

*Trickster Tales From Around The World* (2001) by Ila Lane Gross offers a diverse selection of trickster tales from countries such as China, Saudi

Arabia, South Africa, and Brazil. Virginia Hamilton and Barry Moser's *A Ring of Tricksters: Animal Tales from America, the West Indies, and Africa* (1997) is an illustrated book aimed at younger readers, but provides excellent versions of several popular trickster myths, as well as useful information about the cultures in which the various myths evolved.

**SEE ALSO** African Mythology; Anansi; Animals in Mythology; Brer Rabbit; Hermes; Krishna; Loki; Maui; Native American Mythology

# Tristan and Isolde

**Nationality/Culture**
French/British

**Pronunciation**
TRIS-tuhn and i-SOHL-duh

**Alternate Names**
Tristram and Iseult

**Appears In**
Sir Thomas Malory's *Le Morte d'Arthur*, the *Prose Tristan*

**Lineage**
Son of Blancheflor (Tristan) and daughter of Queen Isolde of Ireland (Isolde)

## Character Overview

The legend of Tristan and Isolde is the tragic tale of two lovers fated to share a forbidden but undying love. Scholars of mythology believe that the legend originated in Brittany, in western France. In time it was associated with the **Arthurian legends** and became part of the mythology of medieval Europe, told and retold in various versions and many languages.

Tristan (also called Tristram), the nephew of King Mark of Cornwall, was a brave and honorable young man. Some accounts also claim that he was a brilliant harp player. According to the most detailed versions of this legend, the king of Ireland sent a champion named Morholt to demand tribute, or payment, from Cornwall, and Tristan fought Morholt in single combat. Tristan killed Morholt, leaving a broken piece of his sword in the fatal wound. The piece remained in Morholt's body when it was carried back to Ireland. Morholt had wounded Tristan as well, and when the wound did not heal, the young knight went to Ireland, in disguise, to seek help from an Irish princess named Isolde (or Iseult) who was skilled in healing.

After Isolde healed Tristan, he lingered at the Irish court for a while. On his return to Cornwall he praised Isolde so highly that King Mark resolved to marry her. Loyal and obedient to his uncle and king, Tristan agreed to return to Ireland and seek Isolde's hand for Mark.

Back in Ireland, Tristan found that the country was being terrorized by a fearsome dragon. Tristan succeeded in killing the beast. While Isolde was nursing him back to health after the fight, she discovered his broken sword and realized that he was the warrior who had killed Morholt, her uncle. At first she wanted to avenge her uncle's death. However, Tristan had endeared himself to the Irish people by killing the dragon, so Isolde forgave him and agreed to marry King Mark. She set off with Tristan for Cornwall.

Many versions of the legend say that Tristan and Isolde had already begun to care for one another. Their sense of honor might have prevented them from letting their feelings show, but fate now took a hand. Isolde's mother had prepared a magical drink for Isolde to share with Mark—a potion that would make them love each other forever. During the voyage to Cornwall, Isolde and Tristan drank the potion, not knowing what it was, and fell deeply in love.

Although Isolde went through with the marriage to Mark, she could not stop loving Tristan, who was fated to love her in return. They tried to keep their passion a secret, but eventually it became known. Some accounts of the story contain episodes of intrigue and suspense in which King Mark or various knights try to trap the lovers and obtain proof of their guilt. In the end, Tristan fled from Cornwall in despair.

By the 1200s, the legend of Tristan had been interwoven with the Arthurian legends. Tristan had become a noble knight and appeared in some of the stories about Arthur, **Lancelot**, and the Knights of the Round Table. By this time, storytellers had also begun to portray King Mark as cruel or cowardly, perhaps to create a stronger contrast between Mark and Tristan, though in earlier versions of the legend Mark was an honorable man.

Tristan finally settled in Brittany, where he married another Isolde, known as Isolde of the White Hands. His love for Isolde of Cornwall had never died, though. In time Tristan was wounded in battle, and his wife could not cure him. He sent for Isolde of Cornwall, hoping that she could once again heal him. He requested that the ship coming back from Cornwall should have white sails if it carried Isolde and black ones if it did not.

Tristan lay on his sickbed and waited. Finally the ship appeared on the horizon, bearing white sails. Too sick to sit up, Tristan asked about the color of the sails. Jealous of his passion for the first Isolde, his wife lied and said that they were black. Tristan fell into despair, believing that

*Tristan and Isolde accidentally drank a love potion intended for Isolde and the man she was supposed to marry. They fell hopelessly in love with each other, with tragic consequences.* © PRIVATE COLLECTION/ ARCHIVES CHARMET/THE BRIDGEMAN ART LIBRARY.

Isolde had refused to help him, and died. When Isolde arrived and learned of his death, she too died of grief. The two were buried in Cornwall. From Isolde's grave a rose tree grew, and from Tristan's came a vine that wrapped itself around the tree. Every time the vine was cut, it grew again—a sign that the two lovers could not be parted, even in death.

## Tristan and Isolde in Context

The myth of Tristan and Isolde reflects a fundamental fascination with the idea of doomed love throughout European culture. The first versions of the tale appear to have originated in northern France, but it quickly traveled across the region, with new additions and variations to the same core story. Versions of the tale—usually featuring character names similar to the original tale, but adjusted for local languages—have appeared in Britain, Scandinavia, Italy, Spain, Germany, and even as far east as Poland and Croatia. The tale became commonly known among even the peasant classes, and is remarkable for its similarity across the various cultures of Europe.

## Key Themes and Symbols

The central theme in the story of Tristan and Isolde is forbidden but irresistible love. The two characters are drawn together just as strongly as they are forced apart. Just as Isolde begins caring for Tristan, she discovers he is the killer of her uncle. Though Tristan begins to fall in love with Isolde, he knows she is promised to Mark. The love potion binds them together even as outside forces attempt to separate them.

## Tristan and Isolde in Art, Literature, and Everyday Life

The legend of Tristan and Isolde, with its emphasis on a love that cannot be denied even when it leads to tragedy, has continued to appeal to artists since medieval times. It inspired three English poems of the 1800s: Matthew Arnold's *Tristram and Iseult*, Algernon Swinburne's *Tristram of Lyonesse*, and Alfred, Lord Tennyson's "The Last Tournament," one of the Idylls in the Arthurian poem *Idylls of the King*. American poet E. A. Robinson based his *Tristram* on the legend. One of the most influential works to draw on the story was the opera *Tristan und Isolde*, by German composer Richard Wagner. The story has also appeared in many film adaptations, with filmmakers such as Jean Cocteau and Francois Truffaut working on different versions over the years. The most recent was the 2006 film *Tristan & Isolde*, starring James Franco and Sophia Myles as the doomed lovers.

## Read, Write, Think, Discuss

The tale of Tristan and Isolde is one of the best-known examples of the theme of doomed love. The story of Romeo and Juliet, popularized by William Shakespeare, is another. Can you think of a modern tale that centers on this same theme? It can be in a book, a film, or a television show. How does your modern example differ from the myth of Tristan and Isolde? Do these differences reflect cultural differences between modern audiences and medieval European audiences? How? What parts of the tale remain timeless?

**SEE ALSO** Arthurian Legends; Celtic Mythology

# Trojan War

*See* ***Iliad, The.***

# Trolls

**Nationality/Culture**
Norse/Scandinavian

**Pronunciation**
TROHLZ

**Alternate Names**
Huldrefolk, Vitterfolk

**Appears In**
Norse and Scandinavian folk tales

**Lineage**
Varies

## Character Overview

Trolls were creatures in Norse myth and legend who became part of the folklore of Scandinavia and northern Europe. Generally trolls were thought to be evil and dangerous, although sometimes they interacted peacefully with people. They were clever at building and making things of stone and metal, and often lived in caves or among rocks.

Early stories described trolls as **giants** who lived in castles and roamed during the night. When exposed to sunlight, trolls turned to stone. The stone crags of a place called Trold-Tindterne (Troll Peaks) in central Norway are said to be two armies of trolls that once fought a great battle until sunrise caught them and turned them to stone. Over time, trolls came to be portrayed as being about the size of humans or, in some cases, as small as dwarves.

In one popular myth, a man named Esbern loved a girl whose father would not let her marry until Esbern built a fine church. A troll agreed to build the church for Esbern on the condition that if Esbern could not

*A troll carved from wood in Grodas, Norway. Trolls are prominent figures in Scandinavian folklore.* © E & E IMAGE LIBRARY/HIP/THE IMAGE WORKS.

discover the troll's name by the time the job was done, the troll would have Esbern's eyes and his soul. Try as he might, Esbern could not learn the troll's name. He was in despair until the girl he loved prayed for him. At that moment Esbern heard the troll's wife singing to her baby, and her song contained the name of her husband.

## Trolls in Context

The treatment of trolls in northern European folklore over the centuries can be viewed as a reflection of that region's relationship with Christianity. Early tales of trolls describe them as mystical nature beings or distant relatives of the gods. After the people of northern Europe converted to Christianity, many of their stories featured prayer as a weapon against trolls, who were portrayed as wicked. One folk tale even describes trolls as the unclean siblings of humans who were hidden from God out of shame.

## Key Themes and Symbols

A common theme in stories of trolls is a bargain between a troll and a human, in which the human must outwit the troll or suffer a sad fate. This is shown in the tale of Esbern, where the man must discover the troll's name or he will die. This also illustrates the theme of trolls as clever or crafty **tricksters**, occasionally helping humans but often causing problems.

## Trolls in Art, Literature, and Everyday Life

Trolls are one of the few mythical creations associated specifically with northern Europe, and they appear frequently in Scandinavian art. Many Scandinavian depictions of trolls resemble squat, stone-like figures with long, flowing hair—similar to the stones seen beneath waterfalls throughout the region, believed by some to be trolls who had been turned to stone by the **sun**. Folk tales of trolls are common in literature, and some early twentieth century illustrators such as Jon Bauer helped to define and popularize the modern image of a troll. Modern fantasy writers beginning with J. R. R. Tolkien have made trolls a standard creature in their fantasy worlds. Although trolls are mostly limited to children's tales in Scandinavia, many people still hold superstitious beliefs about the creatures and will avoid disturbing areas thought to be inhabited by the creatures.

## Read, Write, Think, Discuss

*Troll Fell* (2004) by Katherine Langrish tells the story of Peer, a Scandinavian boy who is forced to live with his evil uncles after his father dies. Even worse, his uncles live in a forest surrounded by mischievous trolls and they plan to offer Peer as a gift to the creatures. The novel is the first in Langrish's *Troll Trilogy*, which also includes *Troll Mill* (2005) and *Troll Blood* (2007).

SEE ALSO Dwarfs and Elves; Norse Mythology

T

# Twins

## Theme Overview

As two children born on the same day to the same mother, twins have a unique sense of identity. They have more in common with one another than any two ordinary people, especially if they are identical twins. Yet twins are also separate beings who may be very different in character. Myths about twins—as partners, rivals, opposites, or halves of a whole—are rooted in this basic mystery of sameness and difference. Twins appear in the myths and legends of many cultures, but they are especially important in African and **Native American mythology**. In some traditions, two children may be considered twins if they are born to two sisters at the same time.

## Major Myths

The mythology of ancient Egypt includes examples of twinship operating in different ways. According to one version of the Egyptian creation myth, the earth god Geb and the sky goddess **Nut** (pronounced NOOT) were twins and also lovers, locked together in a tight embrace. The great god **Ra** separated them with air, leaving Nut arched across the heavens above Geb. Nut and Geb are complementary symbols, meaning that the two complete each other, forming a whole.

Similar myths from around the world associate twins with complementary features of the natural world, such as male and female, day and night, and **sun** and moon. The Xingu (pronounced shing-GOO) people of Brazil, for example, have stories about the twin brothers Kuat and Iae who forced the vulture king Urubutsin to give light to the dark world. Kuat occupied the sun, and Iae the moon. Their wakefulness keeps light in the world, except for a brief time each month when they both sleep and the world experiences nights without a visible moon (also known as a "new moon").

Twins can also be rivals. **Egyptian mythology** explores this aspect of twin relationship in the stories about the gods **Osiris** (pronounced oh-SYE-ris) and **Set**, twin sons of Nut and Geb. Set was so determined to be born first that he tore his way out of his mother's womb before he was fully formed. He hated his brother Osiris and eventually killed him. In the mythology of ancient Persia, some accounts of **Ahriman** (pronounced AH-ri-muhn), the spirit of evil, say that he too was a twin who forced his way out of the womb so that he could be born first. Ahriman and his twin and enemy **Ahura Mazda** (pronounced ah-HOO-ruh MAHZ-duh), the spirit of good, are symbols of opposing moral forces that struggle for control of the universe.

Many myths of the Melanesian islands in the southwest Pacific Ocean tell of twin brothers who are rivals or enemies. Often, one twin is wise and the other foolish, as in the case of To Kabinana and To Karvuvu. The stupidity of To Karvuvu led to unpleasant or dangerous things. For example, he created the shark, thinking it would help him catch more fish. Instead, the shark ate the fish—and people. When To Karvuvu's mother shed her old, wrinkled skin and became young, he wept because he could not recognize her. To calm him she put on her old skin again. Ever since that time, people have had to grow old and die.

Twins often appear as partners or companions who share a bond deeper than ordinary friendship or even brotherly affection. This is illustrated in the myth of **Castor and Pollux** (pronounced PAHL-uhks). Some versions of their story say that although they were born to the same mother, they had different fathers. Pollux, son of the god **Zeus** (pronounced ZOOS), was able to live forever; Castor, son of a human, was not. When his beloved brother was killed, Pollux gave up half of his immortality to restore Castor to life. As a result, each twin could live forever, but they had to divide their time between Mount Olympus (pronounced oh-LIM-puhs) and the **underworld**, or land of the dead. The Greeks identified Castor and Pollux with a constellation, or star group, known as Gemini, the Twins.

Aborigines of Australia also associated this constellation with twins. According to a myth told in central Australia, twin lizards created trees, plants, and animals to fill the land. Their most heroic deed was to save a group of women from a moon spirit who wanted to mate with them. The women went into the sky as the cluster of stars widely known as the Pleiades (pronounced PLEE-uh-deez) while the lizard twins became Gemini.

Because the birth of twins is a rare occurrence, some cultures believed that certain gods and **heroes** were twins. In **Greek mythology**, notable sets of twins included the deities **Apollo** (pronounced uh-POL-oh) and **Artemis** (pronounced AHR-tuh-miss), and two remarkable sisters, **Helen** and Clytemnestra (pronounced klye-tem-NES-truh), who were also the sisters of Castor and Pollux. Some myths of community origins featured royal twins, or those born to gods. The Greeks said that Amphion (pronounced AM-fee-uhn) and Zethus (pronounced ZEE-thuhs), twin sons of Zeus, had founded the city of Thebes (pronounced THEEBZ), while the Romans claimed that the founders of their city were the twin brothers **Romulus and Remus**, sons of Mars.

**Twins in African Mythology** The theme of twins is common to the creation myths of some West African peoples. To the Dogon of Mali, twins represent completeness and perfection. The symbol of this wholeness is the deity Nummo, who is really a set of twins, male and female. The act of creating the other gods and the world required the **sacrifice** of one part of Nummo. From that time on, all beings were either male or female, lacking Nummo's divine completeness.

The supreme creator deity of the Fon people of Benin is Mawu-Lisa, a being both male and female who is sometimes described as a pair of twins. Mawu is the moon and the female element of the deity, while Lisa is the sun and the male part. They gave birth to all of the other gods, who also were born as pairs of twins.

Among the Yoruba people of Nigeria, twins are called *ibejis* after Ibeji, the protector deity of twins. People believe that, depending on how they are treated, twins can bring either fortune or misfortune to their families and communities. For this reason, twins receive special attention. One myth links the origin of twins with monkeys. According to this story, monkeys destroyed a farmer's crops, so he began killing all the monkeys he could find. When the farmer's wife became pregnant, the monkeys sent two spirits into her womb. They were born as the first human twins. To keep these children from dying, the farmer had to stop killing monkeys.

**Twins in American Indian Mythology** The role of twins in American Indian mythology is complex. Some pairs of twins combine heroism with the mischievous behavior of **tricksters**. Occasionally, twins represent opposing forces of good and evil. The Huron people of northeastern North America tell of Ioskeha and Tawiskara, twins who fought to decide who would rule the world. The evil Tawiskara, who fought his way out of the womb, used a twig as his weapon against his brother, while Ioskeha used the horn of a stag. Ioskeha, a positive creative force, won the conflict. In the same way, **Gluskap** (pronounced GLOOS-kahb), the creator god and hero of many northeastern myths, had to defeat Malsum, his evil twin who was the source of all harmful things and the ruler of demons. In Iroquois mythology, Good Mind helps his grandmother, the Woman Who Fell from the Sky, place useful and beautiful items on the earth. His twin, Warty One, creates unpleasant things, such as mosquitoes and thorny bushes.

Rather than enemies, twins in Native American mythology are often partners in a task or a quest. In myths from the Pacific Northwest, the twins Enumclaw (pronounced EE-nuhm-klaw) and Kapoonis sought to

*Twins that appear in the myths and legends of Africa can bring fortune or misfortune to families and communities. These figures from Yoruba,* **ibejis**, *are named after the deity of twins, Ibeji.* PRIVATE COLLECTION/ PHOTO © HEINI SCHNEEBELI/ THE BRIDGEMAN ART LIBRARY.

obtain power over **fire** and rock from the spirits. Their activities became so threatening that the sky god made them into spirits themselves. Enumclaw ruled lightning and Kapoonis controlled thunder.

Hunahpú (pronounced WAH-nuh-pwuh) and Xbalanqúe (pronounced shi-BAY-lan-kay), hero twins of **Mayan mythology**, descended into the underworld to restore their father to life. They then escaped from the lords of the underworld by outwitting them. Masewi (pronounced mah-SEH-wee) and Oyoyewi (pronounced oh-yo-YEH-wee), culture heroes in the myths of the Acoma Indians of the American

Southwest, made a journey to their father, the sun. The theme of twins in search of their father also appears in the myth of Ariconte and Tamendonare of the Tupinamba people of Brazil. Setting out on a quest to learn their father's identity, these twin sons faced many dangerous trials. Each twin died once, only to be brought back to life by his brother. In the end, they learned that they had different fathers, one immortal and one mortal. Because the twins did not know which of them had the immortal father, they protected one another forever.

Navajo myths tell of Monster Slayer (Naayéé'neizghání) and his twin brother, Child of Water (Tó bájísh chíní). Their father carried the sun across the sky and was too busy to pay attention to his sons. One day the twins went in search of him. After enduring a series of ordeals, they at last found their father, and he equipped them to roam the world fighting monsters.

## Twins in Context

It is easy to see why twins would be considered special in many cultures. Currently, about one in every fifty people around the world is a twin; only one in every five hundred people is an identical twin. For some cultures, the occurrence of twins is rare enough to be thought of as possibly supernatural in origin. At the same time, twins appear frequently enough for most people to be familiar with the notion, which makes twin births ideal for indicating the special qualities of characters in myths and legends. In the United States, the rate of twin births in the twenty-first century has been on the rise, with about one in every seventeen children being born a twin in 2001—most likely due to the use of fertility drugs, which can cause multiple eggs to be available for fertilization at the same time. Studies have also shown that diet may also affect the rate of twin births in a society, with mothers who consume more meat producing twins more often than those who do not eat meat. This—along with the risks associated with bringing two infants to term instead of one—may mean that twins were even more rare in ancient times, and therefore more special.

## Twins in Art, Literature, and Everyday Life

As indicated in the previous myths, twins were common fixtures in the stories of cultures around the world. The twins most often found in ancient art are those from the Greek and Roman cultures, such as Castor and Pollux or Apollo and Artemis. In modern times, twins have also appeared in supernatural or mythical roles: one well-known example is Luke Skywalker and Princess Leia Organa from the *Star Wars* series of films by George Lucas.

## Read, Write, Think, Discuss

In modern times, as in many myths, twins are often depicted as having opposite natures or personalities. However, stories of many real-life twins indicate that they share remarkable similarities in thought and behavior, and even consider themselves to have a supernatural bond with each other. Why do you think twins in myth are so often portrayed as opposites?

**SEE ALSO** Ahriman; Ahura Mazda; Castor and Pollux; Helen of Troy; Hunahpú and Xbalanqúe; Masewi and Oyoyewi; Osiris; Romulus and Remus; Set

# Tyr

**Nationality/Culture**
Norse

**Pronunciation**
TEER

**Alternate Names**
Tiw (Old English), Tiwaz (proto-Germanic)

**Appears In**
The Eddas

**Lineage**
Son of Odin

## Character Overview

In **Norse mythology**, Tyr was worshipped as a god of war, justice, and order. One of his roles was to guarantee that contracts and oaths were not broken. Although he appears to have been worshipped earlier than many other Norse gods, he is generally considered to be the son of **Odin** (pronounced OH-din), the leader of the gods.

## Major Myths

Although Tyr appears in very few legends, the best-known story about him involves the fierce wolf **Fenrir** (pronounced FEN-reer) that no chain could hold. The wolf was so frightening that only Tyr was brave enough to feed him. As Fenrir continued to grow, the gods knew he would have to be restrained somehow. The supreme god Odin ordered the dwarves to make a magical ribbon so strong that Fenrir could not break it. Fenrir was suspicious when the gods wanted to tie the ribbon around him. But he allowed himself to be bound after brave Tyr put his hand in the wolf's

*The most famous myth regarding the Norse god Tyr is the story of how he had his hand bit off by the monstrous wolf Fenrir after the gods tried to bind Fenrir.* WERNER FORMAN/ART RESOURCE, NY.

mouth, swearing an oath to free him if he could not free himself. However, when Fenrir realized that he could not escape, the gods refused to set him free and he realized he had been tricked. The wolf bit off Tyr's hand in anger, but the brave god did not even cry out in pain.

## Tyr in Context

The story of Tyr and Fenrir reflects the value and importance of stoicism in Norse culture. Stoicism is the tendency to not display emotions openly to others; feelings of joy, pain, sadness, or anger would not appear obvious in the expression or behavior of a stoic person. This quality was seen as a positive thing to the Norse, because it reflected bravery and total self-control. The Norse characteristic of "fearlessness in the face of death" may also reflect their belief that a brave death would be rewarded by entrance to **Valhalla** (pronounced val-HAL-uh), the heavenly hall of Odin.

## Key Themes and Symbols

One of the central themes in the myth of Tyr is **sacrifice**. Tyr was the only god willing to place his hand in Fenrir's mouth so the wolf could be tied up. He sacrificed his hand in order to protect the rest of the world from Fenrir's ferocity. Tyr was also associated with victory, and warriors engraved a symbol associated with Tyr known as a *t-rune* on their weapons to ensure victory in battle.

## Tyr in Art, Literature, and Everyday Life

Early Germanic peoples associated Tyr with Mars, the Roman god of war. The third day of the week, known as *dies Martis* (Mars's Day) in Latin, became known as *Tyrsdagr* to the Norse and entered English as Tuesday. In modern times, Tyr has not enjoyed the same level of popularity as other Norse gods like Odin or **Thor**. However, both DC Comics and Marvel Comics have featured characters based on Tyr—the former was a villain, while the latter more closely resembled the Tyr of Norse myth.

## Read, Write, Think, Discuss

When Tyr sacrifices his hand in order for the gods to secure Fenrir, he does not cry out in pain. For the Norse, such stoicism was considered to be a sign of strength and bravery. Do you think stoicism is still considered a value in contemporary societies? Give examples to support your opinion.

**SEE ALSO** Fenrir; Norse Mythology

# U

## Ulysses

*See* **Odysseus.**

## Underworld

### Theme Overview

From all parts of the world come myths and legends about the underworld, a mysterious and shadowy place beyond ordinary human experience. The underworld is the realm of the dead, the destination of human souls in the **afterlife**. In some traditions, it is also the home of nonhuman, supernatural, or otherworldly beings, such as fairies, demons, **giants**, and monsters. Although usually portrayed as a terrifying, dangerous, or unpredictable place, the underworld appears as a source of growth, life, and rebirth in some myths. Many descriptions of the underworld include elements of earthly life, such as powerful rulers and palaces.

The most common idea of the underworld is that it lies beneath the everyday world. The passage from this world to the other may begin by descending into a cave, well, or pit. However, the distance between the two worlds is more than physical, and the spiritual journey involved often includes great peril. The souls of the dead are the principal travelers, but sometimes living **heroes**, mystics, and religious leaders also make the journey.

## Major Myths

Some of the earliest descriptions of the underworld occur in myths from ancient Mesopotamia (pronounced mess-uh-puh-TAY-mee-uh). One tells how the fertility goddess **Ishtar** (pronounced ISH-tahr) descends into the kingdom of the dead, ruled by her sister Ereshkigal (pronounced ay-RESH-kee-gahl). Ishtar is killed trying to overthrow Ereshkigal. The other gods convince Ereshkigal to release Ishtar, but Ishtar cannot leave the underworld without finding someone to take her place. She determines that her husband, Tammuz (pronounced TAH-mooz), should be her substitute. Some scholars believe that this myth is related to the annual death and rebirth of vegetation.

The underworld Ishtar visits is the same as that described in the Mesopotamian *Epic of Gilgamesh*, in which the character Enkidu (pronounced EN-kee-doo) has a vision of himself among the dead. The underworld described is a dim, dry, dreary place called the House of Darkness, a house that none who enter leave. The dead dwell in darkness, eating dust and clay. Although recognizable as individuals, they are pale and powerless shadows of their former selves.

This image of the underworld also appears in early Jewish mythology. The Jewish underworld was Sheol (pronounced SHEE-ohl), which means "pit." It held all the dead who had ever lived. Over time, as the idea of judgment in the afterlife took root in Jewish and then Christian belief, the early, neutral concept of the underworld changed. Sheol became a place of punishment and torment for the souls of sinners.

The ancient Greek vision of the underworld was, at first, much like that of the early Semitic cultures. All the dead went to the same place—a vague, shadowy underworld populated by the ghosts, or shades, of the dead. This realm is sometimes called **Hades** (pronounced HAY-deez), after the god who ruled it. Gradually the underworld of Greek and then **Roman mythology** became more elaborate. The kingdom of Hades was said to lie either beyond the ocean or deep within the earth, separated from the world of the living by five rivers: Acheron (pronounced AK-uh-ron, meaning "woe"), Styx (prounounced STIKS, meaning "hate"), **Lethe** (pronounced LEE-thee, meaning "forgetfulness"), Cocytus (pronounced koh-SEE-tuhs, meaning "wailing"), and Phlegethon (pronounced FLEG-uh-thon, meaning "**fire**"). **Cerberus** (pronounced SUR-ber-uhs), a fierce, three-headed, dog-like monster, guarded the entrance to the underworld, which consisted of various regions. The souls of the good dwelled in the Elysian (pronounced eh-LEE-zee-uhn) Fields or Islands of the Blessed, while those who deserved punishment went to a deep pit called Tartarus (pronounced TAR-tur-uhs).

To the Maya of Mesoamerica—a region that encompassed a large area of what is now Central America—the underworld was a dreadful place, but not one limited to sinners. Only people who died a violent death went to a **heaven** in the afterlife. Everyone else entered Xibalba (pronounced shi-BAHL-buh), the underworld, whose name meant "place of fright." Any cave or body of still water was an entrance to Xibalba. The dead were not confined to the underworld forever. In the Mayan sacred book, ***Popol Vuh***, the Hero Twins Hunahpú (pronounced WAH-nuh-pwuh) and Xbalanqúe (pronounced shi-BAY-lan-kay) outwitted the lords of Xibalba and left the land of death. The souls of kings and nobles could also escape from Xibalba if they were summoned by living relatives during the Serpent Vision ceremony. The Aztecs of central Mexico believed that the underworld consisted of eight layers, each with its own dangers, such as drowning or sharp blades. Souls descended through the layers until they reached Mictlan (pronounced MEEKT-lahn), the bottommost part of the underworld.

The underworld of **Japanese mythology** was Yomi (pronounced YOH-mee), land of night or gloom. It was empty until the creator goddess Izanami (pronounced ee-zuh-NAH-mee) died after giving birth to the god of fire. The maggots that appeared in her dead body grew into a host of demons who populated Yomi and tormented the souls of the wicked. Although Yomi was said to be a dark region of barren plains and lonely tunnels, artists often portrayed it as an underground palace crowded with the dead and demons. Also there was Emma-Ô (the Japanese version of Yama, the Buddhist god of death), who judged the souls as they arrived in Yomi.

**Journeys to the Underworld** Many myths tell of heroes who entered the underworld while still alive. Those who survived the ordeals of the journey often returned to the living world transformed by the experience, perhaps bearing special wisdom or treasure. Some heroes wished to rescue or reclaim a loved one who had died. In **Greek mythology**,

**Demeter** (pronounced di-MEE-ter) went down to the underworld to try to bring back her daughter, **Persephone** (pronounced per-SEF-uh-nee), whom Hades (pronounced HAY-deez) had carried off. The Greek hero **Orpheus** (pronounced OR-fee-uhs) traveled to the underworld in search of his wife **Eurydice** (pronounced yoo-RID-uh-see).

Chinese Buddhist mythology tells of a hero named Radish, a follower of Buddha (pronounced BOO-duh). Before leaving on a journey, Radish gave his mother, Lady Leek Stem, money for begging monks. The mother failed to give the money to the monks, but she lied to her son and said that she had done so. When Lady Leek Stem died, she went to **hell**. Radish became so holy that he was made a saint named Mulian. With Mulian's enlightenment, or elevation of spirit, came the knowledge of his mother's torment. He went to hell to save her, although Yama, the king of hell, warned him that no one had the power to change a sinner's punishment. On his way Mulian had to travel past fifty demons, each with the head of an animal and swords for teeth. By waving a wand that Buddha had given him, he was able to make them disappear. Finally Mulian found his mother nailed to a bed, but he could not release her; only Buddha could change a sinner's fate. Mulian asked Buddha for mercy for his mother, and after the proper prayers, Buddha released Lady Leek Stem from hell.

The Ashanti people of Africa have a myth about Kwasi Benefo, who made a journey to the underworld. Kwasi Benefo married four women in turn, and each one died. Miserable and alone, he decided to go to Asamando, the land of the dead, to seek his lost loves. He went to the place of burial and then beyond it, passing through a dark, silent, trackless forest. He came to a river. On the far side sat Amokye, the old woman who greets dead women's souls. She felt sorry for Kwasi Benefo and allowed him to cross the river, though normally the living are forbidden to enter Asamando. Soon Kwasi Benefo found the invisible spirits of his wives. They told him to marry again, promising that his fifth wife would live and that they would be waiting for him in the underworld when his time came to die. Kwasi Benefo fell asleep and awoke in the forest. He brought from the underworld the precious gift of peace of mind, which allowed him to marry and live a normal life for the rest of his days.

**The Other World** In some myths the underworld is a kind of alternative reality, a land not merely of the human dead but of different beings who live according to different rules. **Celtic mythology** contains many accounts of an otherworldly realm. Its location was said to be far away on remote islands or lying beneath the sea or the ground. Certain caves or hills were believed to be entrances to this other world.

In Wales the other world was called Annwn (pronounced AHN-oon), which means "not-world." It had a number of different sides. Primarily, the other world was the kingdom of the dead, and its grim ruler was known as Arawn (pronounced AHR-oun) to the Welsh and Donn to the Irish. The other world, however, could also be a joyous and peaceful place or a source of wisdom, magic, and enchantment. The fairies, demons, spirits, and other supernatural beings who lived there were neither purely good nor purely evil. Depending on the circumstances, they could bring humans either harm or good fortune.

Celtic folklore is filled with legends of living people who entered the other world. Some went voluntarily, like King **Arthur** of Britain, who led an army into Annwn to capture a magical cauldron (kettle). Others were lured into the other world by fairies, sometimes in human or animal form. The theme of a human straying into the other world appears in many European fairy tales that draw on the old notion of the underworld as a supernatural realm. In such stories, a human who ate or drank while in the other world could never leave. Those who resisted food and managed to leave found that time had different meanings in the two worlds. After spending a single night in the other world, a person might return to the world above to find that years had passed.

The underworld is sometimes a mirror image of the world above. According to some African myths, the underworld is just like the ordinary world except that it is upside down: its people sleep during the day and are active during the night. In the Congo, tradition says that the world of the living is a mountain and the underworld of the dead is another mountain pointing downward. Chinese myths tell of "China plowed under," an underworld inside the earth that mirrors every province and town in the world above.

**The Underworld as a Source of Life** The underworld does not always represent the kingdom of the gloomy dead or the home of dangerous beings. In some myths it serves as the point of contact between the surface world of the living and the earth's powerful creative forces. Among the Ibo people of Western Africa, Ala, the goddess of the underworld, is also the earth goddess who protects the harvest, which emerges from the ground. Ala receives the dead; burial is thought to be placing the dead in her pocket or womb. However, Ala also ensures life by making people and animals fertile.

The creation myths of many American Indian cultures say that people and animals emerged from an underworld or series of underworlds. In these stories the underworld is a womb in which life is nurtured, or prepared, until the time is right for it to enter the world. One of many such myths is told by the Zuni, who say that the Ahayuuta **twins** were sent deep into the earth by their father the **sun** god to guide unformed creatures up to the daylight. Once above the ground, the creatures changed into human beings.

According to the Jicarilla (pronounced hee-kuh-REE-uh) Apache of New Mexico, in the beginning all people, animals, and plants lived in the dark underworld. Those who wanted light played a game with those who liked darkness. The light-lovers won, and the sun and stars appeared. Then the sun, looking through a hole in the roof of the underworld, saw the surface of the earth, which was covered with water. Eager to reach this hole in the underworld, the people built four great hills that grew upward. But after girls picked the flowers from the hills, the hills stopped rising. Then the people climbed to the roof on ladders made of buffalo horns. They sent the moon and sun through the hole to light the world and dispatched the winds to blow away the water. Next they sent out animals. Last of all, the people climbed up into the new world. Once they reached the surface, they spread out in four directions. Only the Jicarilla stayed in the original homeland near the hole that led up from the underworld.

## The Underworld in Context

Many cultures believe that after death the soul travels to the underworld. In some traditions, the passage to or through the underworld is part of a process that involves judgment of the individual's deeds when alive, and perhaps punishment for evil deeds. In others, the underworld is simply the destination of all the dead, good and bad alike. The different variations of the underworld myth reflect the values of the cultures in which they arose. For cultures that are built on the belief in a mythic struggle between good and evil, the underworld usually represents a place of torment for those not worthy of heaven. For cultures that emphasize the importance of the land as a provider, the underworld might be a source of life instead of just a repository for the dead. For cultures in which the soul is believed to last forever, the underworld can be a temporary station between lives.

## The Underworld in Art, Literature, and Everyday Life

Various versions of the underworld appear throughout art and literature. The most common depictions are of the Christian hell, with notable examples being Dante's *The Divine Comedy*, an epic poem that provides detailed descriptions of each level of hell, and the Hieronymus Bosch painting *Garden of Earthly Delights*, created in the early sixteenth century. The Mayan underworld of Xibalba was featured as a central element in the 2006 Darren Aronofsky film, *The Fountain*, which tells three stories about death and the quest for eternal love.

## Read, Write, Think, Discuss

Using your library, the Internet, or other available resources, find another example of a mythical underworld that has not already been mentioned. What culture does it come from? What kind of underworld is it? How do you think this underworld reflects the beliefs of the culture that created it?

**SEE ALSO** Afterlife; Hades; Hell; Ishtar; Izanagi and Izanami; Orpheus; Persephone

# Unicorns

**Nationality/Culture**
Various

**Pronunciation**
YOO-nuh-kornz

**Alternate Names**
Qilin (Chinese), Kirin (Japanese)

**Appears In**
Aelian's *On Animals*, the Bible

**Lineage**
Varies

## Character Overview

The word *unicorn* comes from the Latin for "one-horned" and refers to an imaginary beast that appears in the legends of China, Japan, India, Mesopotamia, and Europe. Since medieval times the unicorn has often been portrayed as a horse with a single horn growing from its forehead. Descriptions of the animal in various sources differ somewhat, but they all agree on the horn. According to ancient Greek sources, the unicorn has the tail of a lion and split hooves like a boar. Some images of unicorns were probably based on real animals, such as the one-horned rhinoceros or the narwhal—a small whale with a single long tooth or tusk that resembles a spiral ivory horn.

In Chinese tradition, the unicorn was one of four magical or spiritual creatures—along with the **phoenix**, tortoise, and dragon—that were regarded as signs of good fortune. The appearance of a unicorn signaled the birth or death of a great person; one was said to have appeared when Confucius (pronounced kuhn-FYOO-shuhs), a famous wise man, was born.

Although unicorns were thought to be fierce fighters, they were also symbols of purity. Perhaps this was because the ancient Greeks and Romans had associated them with virgin goddesses, such as **Artemis**, whose chariot was said to be drawn by eight unicorns. According to tradition, one way to capture a unicorn was to send a very young virgin into the forest. The unicorn would be attracted to her and would rest its head in her lap, at which point a hunter could catch the animal.

## Unicorns in Context

The Western image of the unicorn comes in part from the Hebrew Bible. During its translation into Greek, a Hebrew word for "wild ox" was changed to a Greek word that people interpreted as a reference to either a unicorn or a rhinoceros. Around 400 BCE, the Greek historian Ctesias (pronounced TEE-shee-uhs) wrote of a wild beast in India that had a single horn and fought elephants. It was probably the rhinoceros, though later writers developed an image that much more closely resembled a horned horse.

By the Middle Ages, Europeans had come to believe that these horse-like unicorns really existed in remote parts of the world. Among the legends linked to them was the belief that water touched by a unicorn's horn became safe for animals and people to drink. From this tradition developed the idea that powdered unicorn horn offered protection against poison and possibly cured disease as well. Rich and important people treasured horns and powders said to have come from unicorns. Some kings, fearing that rivals might try to poison them, drank from vessels that they believed to be unicorn horns.

## Key Themes and Symbols

The unicorn is most commonly associated with purity. This is shown in the idea that a unicorn's horn could purify a poisoned drink, and in the legend that one could catch a unicorn only by its attraction to a pure young woman. The unicorn's white color also represents purity.

## Unicorns in Art, Literature, and Everyday Life

The unicorn has endured through the centuries as one of the most popular mythical creatures ever conceived. Throughout medieval Europe, the unicorn appeared as a symbol of heraldry on the coats of arms of cities and many noble families. In modern times, the unicorn remains a popular decorative image on posters and other items. Unicorns have appeared in books, such as the Peter Beagle novel *The Last Unicorn* (1968) and the *Chronicles of Narnia* series by C. S. Lewis. The Chinese *qilin* is very popular in Asian animated series and video games, and the Japanese *kirin* is used as the logo for a popular beer of the same name.

## Read, Write, Think, Discuss

*The Last Unicorn* (1968) by Peter S. Beagle tells the story of a unicorn who may be the last surviving member of her species in a mythical land. She embarks on a journey to discover the truth about the fate of the other unicorns, and to try and find others like her that are still alive. Along the way, she joins with various other misfits and outcasts who assist her with her quest.

**SEE ALSO** Animals in Mythology

# Uranus

**Nationality/Culture**
Greek

**Pronunciation**
YOOR-uh-nuhs

**Alternate Names**
Caelus (Roman), Aeon (Roman)

**Appears In**
Hesiod's *Theogony*

**Lineage**
Son of Gaia

## Character Overview

Uranus, who represented the sky, was one of the original deities (gods and goddesses) of **Greek mythology**. He was the son of **Gaia** (pronounced GAY-uh), the earth, who also became his wife. Together they had many children, including the **Titans** and the **Cyclopes** (pronounced sigh-KLOH-peez). He was eventually overthrown by his son **Cronus** (pronounced KROH-nuhs).

## Major Myths

Uranus detested the children he had with Gaia. As soon as they were born, he forced them into Tartarus (pronounced TAR-tur-uhs), a dark place deep beneath the surface of the earth. This caused Gaia great pain. She asked her children to stop Uranus, but only her son Cronus came to her aid. Cronus cut off his father's sex organs with a flint-bladed sickle and threw them into the sea. According to myth, **Aphrodite** (pronounced af-ro-DYE-tee) was born from the foam where they landed. Uranus became the sky that surrounds the earth, and Cronus replaced his father as king of the universe. But Cronus was later defeated by his son **Zeus** (pronounced ZOOS) who, together with **Hera** (pronounced HAIR-uh) and other Olympian gods, overthrew the Titans and took their place ruling the universe.

## Uranus in Context

To the ancient Greeks, the mention of the sickle having a flint blade was significant, and puts the era of the old gods into a proper context. Flint, an easily splintered stone, was used in the creation of tools and weapons long before humans had mastered the art of metalworking. Ancient cultures throughout Greece and the surrounding regions were effectively creating bronze tools and weapons at least two thousand years before the writings of mythographers like Hesiod, and in fact were mastering the creation of iron and steel products by that time. For the myth of Uranus to specifically mention a flint blade, then, reflects either the original age of the myth or an attempt to illustrate that the tales of the old gods took place in the very distant past of the ancient Greeks.

## Key Themes and Symbols

One of the central themes in the myth of Uranus is the overthrow of the heavenly hierarchy. This is shown in Cronus's rebellion against Uranus, as well as by the prediction that Cronus will suffer the same fate as his father. For the ancient Greeks, Uranus represented the most ancient of beliefs and traditions, two generations removed from their own beliefs in the Olympian gods.

## Uranus in Art, Literature, and Everyday Life

Though he lies at the heart of an ancient Greek creation myth, Uranus was seldom worshipped and only occasionally depicted in art. Roman artists sometimes showed a slightly different version of Uranus, known as Aeon and considered to be the god of time, standing over Gaia and holding the wheel of the zodiac (another representation of time). In 1781, when the sixth planet of our solar system was discovered by William Herschel, it was named Uranus in honor of the oldest god.

## Read, Write, Think, Discuss

Most of the planets in our solar system are named after gods and goddesses from Greek and **Roman mythology**. For several, their names were determined based on similarities to their mythical counterparts. Based on what you know about classical mythology, can you figure out why the planets Mercury, Jupiter, Saturn, and Uranus were named the way they were? You may have to do some research about the planets in order to find the answers.

SEE ALSO Cronus; Titans

# V

Character

Deity

Myth

Theme

Culture

## Valentine, St.

**Nationality/Culture**
Christian

**Pronunciation**
saynt VAL-uhn-tye-n

**Alternate Names**
Valentinus

**Appears In**
Voragine's *The Golden Legend*, Chaucer's *Parliament of Fowls*

**Lineage**
Unknown

### Character Overview

According to tradition, St. Valentine is the saint associated with courtship, travelers, and young people. Early celebrations in honor of St. Valentine took place in the middle of February, around the time of an ancient Roman festival known as the Lupercalia (pronounced loo-pur-KAY-lee-uh). It was customary for men to draw the name of a young girl from a box and celebrate the festival with her. The Christian church substituted names of saints for the women, and individuals who picked them were supposed to draw inspiration from the lives of the saints. During the Middle Ages, St. Valentine's feast day on February 14 became known as a day for lovers. Though a popular theory for many years, modern scholars have discounted the idea that St. Valentine's Day served as a replacement for the Roman Lupercalia.

One story says that Valentine was a Roman priest who became a martyr—a person punished or killed due to his or her beliefs—because he helped persecuted Christians around 270 CE. Sent to prison, he restored the sight of a blind girl, who fell in love with him. According to another tale, Valentine was a young man awaiting execution. He loved the jailer's daughter and signed a farewell message to her: "From your Valentine."

## St. Valentine in Context

The oldest sources of the legend of St. Valentine contain no reference to love or lovers. In fact, the first connection between St. Valentine and romance was offered by English author Geoffrey Chaucer, whose poem *Parliament of Fowls* (1382) suggested that St. Valentine's Day was the occasion on which birds chose their mates. At the time, there were several days dedicated to different saints named Valentine; one of these days was May 2. Chaucer's poem was actually written to honor King Richard II of England, who had gotten engaged on May 2 of the previous year, and this is the date the author refers to as St. Valentine's Day.

## Key Themes and Symbols

The central theme in the myth of St. Valentine is doomed romantic love. St. Valentine fell in love just before he was scheduled to die and could do nothing about it except write a message expressing his love. The myth also symbolizes the importance of religious conviction above all else—including romance.

## St. Valentine in Art, Literature, and Everyday Life

St. Valentine has one of the most recognized saintly names in modern times, yet he is known mostly for the romantic holiday he indirectly inspired. The messages of love that pass between two people on that special day are commonly known as valentines, and the term "valentine" is sometimes used to refer to any message of love sent to another person on any day. Unfortunately for St. Valentine, the mythical figure most closely associated with the holiday that bears his name is not Valentine, but the Greek god of love **Eros**—also known by his Roman name, Cupid.

## Read, Write, Think, Discuss

The modern holiday known as Valentine's Day is an example of how beliefs from different cultures can combine to create something new that still retains elements from radically different belief systems. Can you think of any other examples of a holiday that combines beliefs or characters from two or more cultural traditions? Be specific about which elements come from which culture; you may need to do some research about the holiday to find these answers.

# Valhalla

**Nationality/Culture**
Norse

**Pronunciation**
val-HAL-uh

**Alternate Names**
None

**Appears In**
The Eddas

## Myth Overview

In **Norse mythology**, Valhalla was the great hall of **Odin** (pronounced OH-din), the chief of the gods. It was located in Asgard (pronounced AHS-gahrd), the home of the gods of war and the sky. According to legend, the heroic warriors slain in battle gathered in Valhalla. There they enjoyed a glorious **afterlife** and awaited **Ragnarok** (pronounced RAHG-nuh-rok), a time of great destruction when they would join the gods to wage a final battle against the forces of evil. Valhalla had more than 640 doors, each wide enough to allow hundreds of warriors to leave at the first sign of threat. Filled with shields and armor, the enormous hall was also the haunt of wolves, ravens, a boar that could be eaten and brought back to life, and a goat that provided an unlimited supply of an alcoholic drink called mead.

The **Valkyries** (pronounced val-KEER-eez), the battle maidens of Odin, selected the warriors worthy enough to live in Valhalla. These warriors entered the palace when they died, and their wounds were healed miraculously. They spent their days feasting and improving their battle skills in preparation for Ragnarok. Those warriors who were killed during practice each day were brought back to life and healed each evening.

## Valhalla in Context

The people of the Norse culture valued bravery in warfare as one of their most important cultural traits. This is reflected in the different versions of the **underworld** that the Norse believed in. Valhalla was the most heavenly, with constant feasting and merriment; it was reserved for those who died bravely in battle in foreign lands, fighting for the advancement of the Norse culture. Those who died fighting to preserve their own lands were next, taken in by the goddess **Freyja** (pronounced FRAY-uh).

*A Valkyrie welcomes dead soldiers to Valhalla, the resting place for those who died on the battlefield.* SNARK/ART RESOURCE, NY.

Those who died in other ways were considered to be without glory, and went to the relatively dismal underworld watched over by **Hel**.

## Key Themes and Symbols

For the Norse people, Valhalla represented the rewards of bravery. Valhalla also represented the ideal life to a Norseman: all the food, drink, and song one could ever hope for, with beautiful maidens as servants and plenty of opportunities to engage in battle. Valhalla also stood as a symbol of preparedness, since it served as a temporary home for soldiers who would ultimately be called upon to fight at Ragnarok, and was designed to allow them to be ready to fight at a moment's notice.

## Valhalla in Art, Literature, and Everyday Life

Valhalla is the most well-known realm of the dead in Norse mythology, probably because it is also the most heavenly. The grand-scale descriptions of the hall found in the Eddas—the most significant literary source of Norse myths—are not often depicted by artists, perhaps because the immense dimensions would be difficult to capture. The name Valhalla has been used as the title of a long-running Danish comic series begun in 1978; the comic is an adaptation of many of the stories found in the Eddas, and is scheduled to conclude with the events leading to Ragnarok. DC Comics has also borrowed the name for its Valhalla Cemetery, a fictional resting place for superheroes who have died while performing their duties—much like the Norse warriors in the Valhalla of myth.

## Read, Write, Think, Discuss

In Norse mythology, dying bravely in battle was the only way to gain entrance to Valhalla. In the history of religion, there are many examples of religious groups who believe that a special paradise is reserved in the afterlife for martyrs, or those who die for their beliefs. Using your library, the Internet, or other available resources, research the idea of martyrdom in one of the major world religions. Are there important differences between the Norse cultural ideal and religious beliefs about martyrdom? If so, what are they?

**SEE ALSO** Heroes; Norse Mythology; Odin; Ragnarok; Valkyries

# Valkyries

**Nationality/Culture**
Norse

**Pronunciation**
val-KEER-eez

**Alternate Names**
None

**Appears In**
The Eddas

**Lineage**
Varies

## Character Overview

Female spirits in **Norse mythology**, the Valkyries were servants of the god **Odin** (pronounced OH-din). Originally, the Valkyries were fierce creatures who took part in battles and devoured bodies of the dead on battlefields. They later emerged as beautiful female warriors—clad in armor on horseback—who rode over battlefields selecting the bravest slain warriors to enter **Valhalla**, Odin's great hall in Asgard (pronounced AHS-gahrd). During battles the Valkyries carried out Odin's commands, bringing either victory or defeat according to his wishes. After leading slain warriors to Valhalla, the Valkyries waited on them, serving them food and drink, while they awaited their time to do battle once again at **Ragnarok** (pronounced RAHG-nuh-rok), the final battle between the gods and their enemies.

In several myths, the Valkyries appeared as giant beings with supernatural powers who could cause a rain of blood to fall upon the land, or who rowed ships across the sky on rivers of blood. Some Valkyries caused warriors to die, while others served as protectors, guarding the lives of those most dear to them. Valkyries were often shown as wives of **heroes**. **Brunhilde** (pronounced BROON-hilt), one of the most famous Valkyries in mythology, disobeyed Odin and was placed in an enchanted sleep within a wall of **fire** as punishment.

## Valkyries in Context

Although the origin of the myth of the Valkyries is not known, some historians believe that they may reflect religious rituals among the early Norse people. The worship of Odin was sometimes carried out through human sacrifices, with the most likely victims being fallen enemy warriors. Some believe that these sacrifices may have been performed by female priests; in later centuries, stories of these women could have evolved into the legend of the Valkyries. This would explain the main function of the Valkyries: leading fallen warriors from the battlefield to the **afterlife**.

## Key Themes and Symbols

One of the central themes in the legend of the Valkyries is the rewarding of bravery on the battlefield. This is ultimately the main purpose of the Valkyries, as they choose the best warriors to reside in Valhalla until the coming of Ragnarok. In addition, Valkyries may have represented the typical Norseman's view of the ideal woman: brave and independent, yet also beautiful and willing to be a servant to men.

*Valkyries were beautiful female warriors and servants of the Norse god Odin. They influenced human battles and served the slain in Valhalla, the resting place for the bravest warriors.* THE ART ARCHIVE/RICHARD WAGNER/ MUSEUM BAYREUTH/GIANNI DAGLI ORTI.

## Valkyries in Art, Literature, and Everyday Life

While Valkyries do not appear frequently in older Norse art, the image of the warrior maiden captured the imagination of nineteenth-century painters such as Peter Nicolai Arbo and Edward Robert Hughes. The German composer Richard Wagner based part of his opera cycle *The Ring of the Nibelung* on the legend of Brunhilde. One of the most famous pieces of music from the entire opera cycle—and indeed, one of the most readily recognized pieces of all classical music—is popularly known as "The Ride of the Valkyries." Valkyrie was also the name of a superheroine in the Marvel Comics Universe, and Valkyries—or similar warrior maidens who make use of the name—have appeared in numerous video games, such as *The Legend of Valkyrie* and *Valkyrie Profile*.

## Read, Write, Think, Discuss

Valkyries are often described as "warrior maidens." In **Greek mythology**, the **Amazons** were also warrior maidens. Using your library, the Internet, or other available resources, research both Valkyries and Amazons. How are they similar or different? What do you think these myths suggest about the role of women in Norse and Greek societies?

SEE ALSO Brunhilde; Norse Mythology; Odin; Valhalla

# Venus

*See* **Aphrodite.**

# Viracocha

**Nationality/Culture**
Incan

**Pronunciation**
vee-ruh-KOH-chuh

**Alternate Names**
Con Tiqui Viracocha, Huiracocha

**Appears In**
Inca creation mythology

**Lineage**
None

## Character Overview

Viracocha was the god who created the world and human civilization in **Inca mythology**. His name means "sea foam," and one legend states that he rose from Lake Titicaca and transformed the universe from a place of empty darkness. He is a god of both the **sun** and storms, and is said to have destroyed the world once with a great flood. He was also referred to as Old Man of the Sky and Lord Instructor of the World.

## Major Myths

After rising from the lake and bringing light into the darkness, Viracocha created a world with people made from stone. He was unhappy with the

*The Incan god Viracocha.* THE ART ARCHIVE/MUSEO PEDRO DE OSMA LIMA/MIREILLE VAUTIER/THE PICTURE DESK, INC.

result, since the people were disrespectful and ill-suited to becoming civilized. He destroyed the creatures with a great flood, and tried again by fashioning new people out of clay. These were much better at learning civilized ways, and Viracocha's son Inti (pronounced IN-tee) sent his own son and daughter to teach the people how to live and show them the land upon which they should found their society. (In some versions, Viracocha himself wandered the land in disguise, teaching humans the finer points of civilized life.) The location they chose for their society was named Cuzco (pronounced KOOZ-koh), the center of the Inca empire. One of the greatest leaders of the Incas, Pachacuti, was said to be connected to Viracocha. He ordered the creation of a temple and a golden statue of Viracocha at Cuzco.

## Viracocha in Context

According to Inca tradition, one day Viracocha walked off across the sea and vanished. One day, he would return to the Inca people when he was needed. Viracocha had a bearded face and pale skin, similar to the Spanish soldiers who encountered the Inca people during their conquest of the New World. This may have allowed the Spanish to subdue the Incas easily, since the explorers were viewed as gods by the Inca people.

## Key Themes and Symbols

One of the central themes in the myth of Viracocha is the quest for human advancement. Viracocha destroys his first attempt at people because they are unwilling to better themselves. He then sends his son to ensure that the new people are taught civilized ways and do not fall back into beastly habits. The fact that Viracocha is considered both a sun god and a storm god suggests his complete power over the sky and weather.

## Viracocha in Art, Literature, and Everyday Life

Viracocha was commonly depicted as a golden figure with a head that resembled the sun with rays of light extending outward from it, and holding staves in his hands. One well-known representation of Viracocha can be found on the Sun Gate, a stone monument at Tiahuanaco in Bolivia. Explorer and author Thor Heyerdahl borrowed one of Viracocha's names, Kon-Tiki, as the name of a raft he built for a trip across the Pacific Ocean in 1947. Heyerdahl also used it as the name of a subsequent book he wrote about the experience, as well as a 1951 documentary film on the subject, which won an Academy Award.

## Read, Write, Think, Discuss

The Inca people believed that Viracocha walked off across the ocean and would return someday when his people once again needed him. Compare this to the myth of King **Arthur** and his final journey to Avalon. Do you think King Arthur and Viracocha both qualify as hero figures for their cultures? Why or why not? What is the significance of two vastly different cultures—Romano-British and Inca—both having such similar legends?

**SEE ALSO** Creation Stories; Inca Mythology

# Vishnu

**Nationality/Culture**
Hindu

**Pronunciation**
VISH-noo

**Alternate Names**
Narayana, Rama, Krishna

**Appears In**
The Vedas, the *Mahabharata*, the *Ramayana*

**Lineage**
None

## Character Overview

Known as the preserver, Vishnu is one of three supreme Hindu deities, along with **Brahma** (pronounced BRAH-muh) and **Shiva** (pronounced SHEE-vuh). Vishnu's role is to protect humans and to restore order to the world. His presence is found in every object and force in creation, and some Hindus recognize him as the divine being from which all things come. Vishnu appears in a number of Hindu texts, including the Vedas, the ***Mahabharata*** (pronounced muh-hah-BAHR-ruh-tuh), and the ***Ramayana*** (pronounced rah-MAY-yah-nuh).

## Major Myths

Associated with the power of light, Vishnu floated on the surface of the ancient ocean on top of a thousand-headed snake called Shesha. Vishnu's most famous feat in the Vedas was to take the three steps that measured the extent of the world, an act that was part of creation. Some stories credit Vishnu with a major role in creation; others say he assisted the god **Indra** (pronounced IN-druh).

According to Hindu mythology, Vishnu comes to earth in a variety of animal and human forms called avatars. These avatars are embodiments of the god that contain part of his divine spirit and power. Hindus believe that an avatar of Vishnu appears whenever the world or humans are in danger, and in this way, the god helps to overcome evil, bring justice, and restore order.

Vishnu had ten principal avatars. The first, Matsya (pronounced MAHT-see-yah), was a fish that saved the first human, **Manu** (pronounced MAN-oo), from a great flood by leading his ship to safety. Kurma (pronounced KOOR-muh), the second avatar, was the tortoise that recovered some precious objects that the gods had lost during

*The Hindu god Vishnu had ten different forms.* HIP/ART RESOURCE, NY.

another great flood. Also saved from the flood was Lakshmi (pronounced LAHK-shmee), a goddess of fortune and beauty who became Vishnu's wife. Vishnu appeared on earth a third time as Varaha (pronounced VAH-rah-hah), the boar. Varaha rid the world of a demon giant named Hiranyaksha (pronounced HAHR-nah-kahsh), who had dragged the earth to the bottom of the ocean and threatened to keep it there. After a thousand-year struggle, Varaha killed the demon.

Vishnu's fourth avatar, the man-lion Narasimha (pronounced nah-rah-SIM-hah), freed the world from another demon, Hiranyakashipu, who had forbidden worship of the gods. When the evil King Vali (pronounced VAH-lee) gained control of the world, Vishnu appeared on earth a fifth time as Vamana (pronounced vuh-MAH-nah), the dwarf. Vamana persuaded Vali to give him whatever land he could cover in three steps. The dwarf then changed into a giant, and his steps extended over both **heaven** and earth. Vishnu's sixth avatar was Parasurama

### Lakshmi, Wife of Vishnu

Vishnu's consort, or wife, is Lakshmi, the goddess of wealth, love, and beauty. One of her symbols is the lotus blossom, which in Hinduism is associated with creation, purity, and spiritual power. Lakshmi is called the "daughter of the sea" because in Indian mythology she arose from the ocean, like the Greek goddess Aphrodite. Lakshmi has other incarnations: she is Sita, the wife of Rama (an avatar of Vishnu) in the Hindu epic the *Ramayana*, and she is Rukmini, the wife of Krishna, another avatar of Vishnu. Hindus believe that marriage continues through many lifetimes, hence Vishnu and Lakshmi remain married through their many incarnations.

(pronounced pah-ruh-soo-RAH-muh), a young man who freed the Hindu priests from a class of warriors known as the Kshatriyas.

Vishnu's most popular and well-known avatars were Rama (pronounced RAH-muh) and **Krishna** (pronounced KRISH-nuh), the great **heroes** of the epics the *Ramayana* and *Mahabharata*. Rama, the seventh avatar, saved humans from the demon king Ravana (pronounced RAH-vuh-nuh), while Krishna rid the world of many demons and took part in a long struggle against the forces of evil. The ninth avatar of Vishnu was the Buddha (pronounced BOO-duh), the religious leader whose beliefs weakened the opponents of the gods and who founded the Buddhist faith. Vishnu's tenth avatar, Kalki (pronounced KAHL-kee), has not yet arrived on earth. He will come one day, mounted on a white horse, to oversee the final destruction of the wicked, restore purity, renew creation, and bring forth a new era of harmony and order.

## Vishnu in Context

Vishnu's rise in popularity over the centuries reflects the changing nature of Hinduism. In the Vedas, a collection of ancient sacred texts, Vishnu is only a minor god. Early myths also portray Vishnu as a messenger between humans and the gods. Over time, the character of Vishnu combined the traits of a number of heroes and gods, and by the time the *Mahabharata* and the *Ramayana* were written, Vishnu was seen as one of the most important and popular Hindu deities.

## Key Themes and Symbols

Vishnu's main duty in nearly all myths related to his many forms is the protection of humankind. This is shown when he aided Manu before the flood, and when he fought off demons as both Rama and Krishna. Another theme found throughout the myths of Vishnu is death and rebirth: Vishnu is born into the world in various forms over the ages, and after he accomplishes his goal he disappears from the human world until he is once again needed.

## Vishnu in Art, Literature, and Everyday Life

Vishnu is one of the most popular gods in Hindu art and culture, and is represented in many different forms. Most often, he is depicted as having blue skin and four arms, each holding an item: a conch shell, a club or mace, a lotus flower, and a disc-shaped weapon called a chakram. Vishnu is also often depicted in the form of Krishna, as he appears in much of the *Mahabharata*. In the form of Hinduism known as Vaishnavism, the most popular type of Hinduism practiced today, Vishnu is seen as the one supreme god.

## Read, Write, Think, Discuss

Vishnu has ten well-known avatars that figure prominently in Hindu myth. Why do you think Hindus view these ten avatars as aspects of the same god, Vishnu, instead of ten different gods? Using your library, the Internet, or other available resources, research one other major world religion that combines multiple forms within a single deity. What are the functions of the different forms of the deity? Why do you think religions use this symbolism?

**SEE ALSO** Animals in Mythology; Brahma; Buddhism and Mythology; Devils and Demons; Floods; Hinduism and Mythology; Indra; *Mahabharata, The*; *Ramayana, The*; Shiva

# Vulcan

*See* **Hephaestus.**

# W

## Wakan Tanka

### Character Overview

In **Native American mythology**, Wakan Tanka (great mystery) is the supreme being and creator of the Lakota Sioux. Sometimes called Great Spirit, he is similar to the supreme beings found in the myths of many other North American peoples.

**Nationality/Culture**
American Indian

**Pronunciation**
WAH-kuhn tahn-kuh

**Alternate Names**
Great Spirit, Wakanda

**Appears In**
American Indian oral mythology

**Lineage**
None

### Major Myths

According to Lakota myth, before creation Wakan Tanka existed in a great emptiness called Han (darkness). Feeling lonely, he decided to create companions for himself. First, Great Spirit focused his energy into a powerful force and formed Inyan (rock), the first god. Next, he used Inyan to create Maka (earth), and then mated with that god to produce Skan (sky). Skan brought forth Wi (the sun) from Inyan, Maka, and himself. These four gods were separate and powerful, but they were all part of Wakan Tanka.

The first four gods produced four companions—Moon, Wind, Falling Star, and **Thunderbird**—to help with the process of creation. In turn, these companions created various gods and spirits, including Whirlwind, Four Winds, Buffalo, Two-Legged Creatures (humans and bears), Sicun (thought), Nagi (spirit of death), Niya (breath of life), and Nagila (shadow). All of these beings were aspects of Wakan Tanka. Together, they created and oversee everything that exists.

## Wakan Tanka in Context

The idea of Wakan Tanka reflects a common view among American Indian tribes that the natural world is part of a spirit being, or is infused with spirit. Wakan Tanka is not just a specific, defined being, like the various gods in **Greek mythology**, but is a spirit force that can be found in all things, from **corn** to canyons to cockroaches. In modern times, due to the influence of Christian missionaries, Wakan Tanka is often compared to the all-powerful God of Christianity, Judaism, and Islam. Some dismiss this comparison as simplistic, but some American Indians have incorporated Christian beliefs, such as the appearance of Jesus, into their existing mythology of Wakan Tanka.

## Key Themes and Symbols

The main theme of the myths of Wakan Tanka is the interconnected nature of the world. Wakan Tanka is present in all things as a sacred energy, and the original gods—from whom all other things in the world originate—were made from part of Wakan Tanka. This also suggests unity and harmony with the natural world, as opposed to viewing some natural events, such as storms or **floods**, as hostile or evil.

## Wakan Tanka in Art, Literature, and Everyday Life

Wakan Tanka remains a central part of American Indian belief, particularly among the Lakota people. The Great Spirit was popularized by the book *Black Elk Speaks* (1932) by John G. Neihardt, and is also mentioned in the popular book *Bury My Heart at Wounded Knee: An Indian History of the American West* (1970). Like many American Indian deities, however, Wakan Tanka has not yet penetrated mainstream popular culture in a significant way.

## Read, Write, Think, Discuss

In mainstream American culture, Wakan Tanka—the Great Spirit—is perhaps best known from *Black Elk Speaks* (1932), an autobiographical account of Black Elk, an Oglala Sioux medicine man, written from conversations between himself and author John G. Neihardt, a poet and amateur ethnographer. The book documents important events in the history of the Sioux people, such as the battle at Little Bighorn and the massacre at Wounded Knee, both witnessed by

Black Elk. It also contains a wealth of information about Sioux beliefs and myths.

**SEE ALSO** Creation Stories; Native American Mythology

# Witches and Wizards

**Nationality/Culture**
Various

**Alternate Names**
Sorceresses, Warlocks

**Appears In**
Various myths around the world

**Lineage**
Varies

## Character Overview

Witches and wizards are people thought to possess magical powers or to command supernatural forces. They appear in the myths and folktales of many cultures. The word "witch" usually refers to a female, though male witches exist in some traditions. Men who possess the powers associated with witchcraft are often known as wizards or warlocks.

In many myths and legends, witches are evil, dishonest, or dangerous. Some cultures do not consider them fully human. If not evil by nature, witches may be possessed by demons or wicked spirits determined to harm humans. Yet ordinary men and women may learn magic for the purpose of hurting others. Such people are sometimes called sorcerers and sorceresses rather than wizards and witches. African tradition distinguishes between good magicians, or medicine men, and bad magicians, or sorcerers. Both types are distinct from the nonhuman witch.

Not all witches and wizards are evil. Some myths and folktales feature good spirits or magicians who help people. These are said to practice "white magic" rather than the "black magic" of the evil witches and wizards. *The Wonderful Wizard of Oz,* the modern children's book that became a famous movie, features both kinds of witches. It is easy to tell them apart—the wicked witch is an old hag dressed in black, while the good witch is a beautiful, soft-spoken woman dressed like a princess.

The magicians that appear in myths and folktales, however, are not always clearly labeled. They may be unpredictable and of uncertain character—neither completely good nor completely evil. Their treatment of humans may depend on how they are treated. Often people meet old women, not realizing that they are dealing with witches. In such cases, the witch may reward kindness and punish rudeness.

**Legendary Witches and Wizards** Witches take many forms. The traditional image in European and American folklore is that of a wrinkled old woman, perhaps wearing a black robe and a cone-shaped hat. These witches communicate with evil spirits called familiars, which often take the form of a black cat. According to legend, Japanese witches have owls as familiars, and African witches have monkeys.

Flight is often associated with witchcraft. In American folktales, witches usually travel through the night skies on enchanted broomsticks. In some parts of Africa, witches are said to fly on bats. African witches often take the form of animals and eat human flesh. In the mythology of some cultures, witches can change into animals to prey upon their victims.

The tradition of witchcraft is ancient. The book of Samuel in the Old Testament of the Bible contains an account of a sorceress called the Witch of Endor. Saul, the first king of Israel, banished magicians from his kingdom but finally asked for advice from the Witch of Endor, who had "a familiar spirit." Assured that she would not be punished for practicing magic, the witch called up the spirit of Samuel, a dead prophet of the Israelites. The spirit predicted Saul's defeat in the battle that was to take place the next day.

In the ***Odyssey***, an epic of ancient Greece, the hero **Odysseus** (pronounced oh-DIS-ee-uhs) and his men met a witch named **Circe** (pronounced SUR-see). The daughter of a god and an ocean nymph, Circe had the power to turn people into animals and monsters. Her island home was populated with lions, bears, and wolves—all had once been human, but were transformed by her magic. Although she turned some of Odysseus's men into pigs, the hero used a special herb that protected him from her magic.

Witchcraft and magic played an important role in the **Arthurian legends** of Britain. **Merlin**, a powerful wizard, guided and influenced King **Arthur** throughout his life. A witch named Morgan Le Fay also appeared in the legends and took care of Arthur after he was wounded in battle.

Slavic folklore of eastern Europe and western Russia has a witch called Baba Yaga (pronounced BAH-buh yuh-GAH), a thin old woman whose nickname means "bony legs." Baba Yaga lives alone in a hut deep in the forest. The hut stands on the legs of a chicken and is surrounded by a fence decorated with skulls. Visitors who wish to enter must recite a magic formula. Although Baba Yaga sometimes helps the hero or heroine of a story, she is generally a dangerous figure who must be outwitted.

One Baba Yaga story concerns a prince named Ivan who needed a very fast horse to rescue his wife from the clutches of a monster. Ivan learned that Baba Yaga had some special horses and asked her for the use of one. The witch said that he must first guard her horses for three nights. She was sure that Ivan would fail at the task because she ordered the horses to gallop away each night. However, Ivan had shown kindness to various animals and insects, and they gathered the horses together for him. Finally Ivan seized one of the horses and rode off to save his wife. Baba Yaga chased him, but he outran her.

Witches and sorcerers occur frequently in American Indian myths. Unlike shamans and healers, they are fearsome and destructive beings. The Navajo of the American Southwest have stories about the *adilgashii*, witches who travel at night in the skins of coyotes or other animals and who use poison made from the ground bones of babies to harm the living. In English, the *adilgashii* are called skinwalkers.

The Tlingit of the Pacific Northwest believe that a man with an unfaithful wife becomes a witch by drinking from a dead shaman's skull. This first witch then creates other witches, both male and female. They acquire dark powers by lurking in graveyards and handling the dead. In a theme repeated in stories from many cultures, the Tlingit witches make dolls out of the hair, clothing, or food of those they want to harm. By placing these dolls in graves to rot with corpses, the witches cause their victims to become sick. A witch can reverse the spell and cure the victim by rinsing the doll in salt water.

## Witches and Wizards in Context

Many cultures around the world include legends or myths about witches and wizards. The way a culture addresses the idea of magic is reflected in these myths. For example, in Christian cultures, magic is almost always considered to be an act of the Devil. In Christian stories, then, witches are evil beings who seek only to cause harm. It is worth noting that many beneficial magical events are described in Christian stories, but these are nearly always referred to as "miracles" instead of magic.

During the Middle Ages in Europe, the belief in witches was widespread. Witches were said to be worshippers of the Devil. Thousands of women and some men were tortured and executed after being accused of witchcraft. The English who settled in North America brought along a fear of witches. A witch hunt in Salem, Massachusetts,

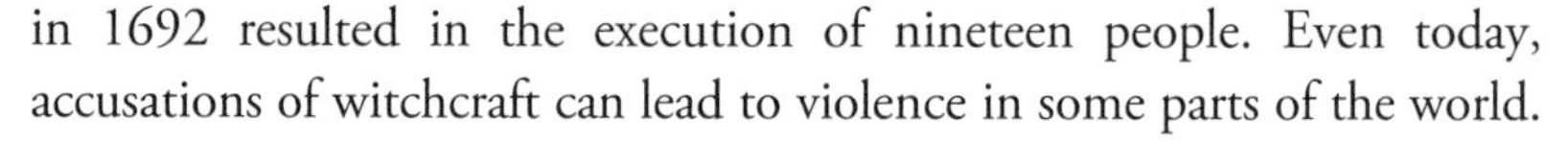

in 1692 resulted in the execution of nineteen people. Even today, accusations of witchcraft can lead to violence in some parts of the world.

In many belief systems, such as Hinduism, magic is seen as something that can be good or bad. In these cultures, wizards and witches might be considered helpful characters or even **heroes**. Very often there are magicians whose sole purpose is to combat evil magic or protect someone from its effects. The wizard Merlin, found in Romano-British legends, uses magic for reasons that are presented as positive or helpful in most cases. In modern times, witches and wizards are viewed rather positively, with many films, television shows, and video games featuring such characters as heroes. This may reflect the feeling that magic and other supernatural forces are taken less seriously because, due to advances in science, they are no longer believed to be the causes of tragic events.

*In Arthurian legend the wizard Merlin is tricked by the enchantress Nimüe into sharing all his secrets. Nimüe then imprisons him behind invisible walls.* © LADY LEVER ART GALLERY, NATIONAL MUSEUMS LIVERPOOL/THE BRIDGEMAN ART LIBRARY.

## Key Themes and Symbols

The central theme in stories about witches and wizards is the ability to control people, objects, and events in supernatural ways. This includes everything from making objects disappear to secretly causing a person's illness. In most stories, this control is motivated by a desire for great riches and power, or a desire for revenge. Sometimes the motivation is love, in both good and bad ways. Circe turned the beautiful nymph Scylla (pronounced SIL-uh) into a monster when a man chose her over Circe.

One of the symbols most commonly associated with witchcraft in European cultures is the broomstick. This is an object traditionally linked to women and their domestic duties, and therefore reflects the view that women were considered to be more attuned to the supernatural. Another common symbol across many cultures is the stick or wand used by a witch or wizard; this is often a tree branch or something made of wood or bone, and symbolizes the importance of nature in channeling magic.

### Witches and Wizards in Art, Literature, and Everyday Life

Throughout history, witches and wizards have never failed to capture the imagination of writers and artists. Artists have traditionally pictured witches as hideous hags, though some characters—such as Circe—are depicted as beautiful and seductive. Authors such as Edmund Spenser, William Shakespeare, and Sir Thomas Malory included wizards and witches as key characters in some of their most important works. In modern times, L. Frank Baum, Stephen King, and J. R. R. Tolkien have created similar memorable characters. Many television shows have been based on the notion of witches and wizards existing in secret as a part of mainstream society. Some notable examples include *Bewitched*; *Sabrina, the Teenage Witch*; and *Wizards of Waverly Place*.

### Read, Write, Think, Discuss

Stories about witches and wizards continue to fascinate the public and to inspire writers. In addition to providing an otherworldly atmosphere, such stories often reveal truths about ordinary human existence. In the Harry Potter series of modern fantasy books, British writer J. K. Rowling describes an entire society involved with magic. The reader follows Harry, an ordinary boy, as he studies at the Hogwarts School for Witchcraft and Wizardry. Between adventures laced with **dragons**, magic potions, and flying broomsticks, Rowling shows how Harry learns about values such as friendship, loyalty, and courage. The first book in the seven-book series is *Harry Potter and the Sorcerer's Stone* (also known as *Harry Potter and the Philosopher's Stone*).

**SEE ALSO** Circe; Devils and Demons; Merlin

# Woman Who Fell from the Sky

**Nationality/Culture**
American Indian/Iroquois and Huron

**Alternate Names**
Sky Woman, Ataensic

**Appears In**
Iroquois and Huron oral creation myths

**Lineage**
None

### Character Overview

In the mythology of the Iroquois and Huron of North America, the Woman Who Fell from the Sky is an ancient ancestor. Also known as

Sky Woman or Ataensic, she plays a central role in the creation of the earth and all living things. She is also a figure of fertility who provides the first **corn** to people.

## Major Myths

According to legend, the Woman Who Fell From the Sky lived in a world above the sky. One day she became pregnant and fell out of the sky. Some stories say that she fell while chasing a bear, while others say that the tree of life was uprooted and she tumbled through the hole left behind. As the woman fell, ducks flew beneath her to slow her descent. She landed in a vast watery place, with no land in sight. Turtle arose from the water and let her rest on his back. Meanwhile, Muskrat dove beneath the water and brought up mud to form the earth. Soon after, the woman gave birth to twin sons—one good and one evil—who created all the natural features of the earth and sky. According to some stories, she gave birth to a daughter, and that woman was the mother of the **twins**.

The good twin shaped the sky and created the **sun**. He also made the moon, stars, mountains, and many plants and animals. The evil twin set out to destroy his brother's creations. He created darkness to drive the sun from the sky, and made monsters, storms, and various kinds of dangerous beasts. When creation was finished, the brothers fought. The good twin won and banished his evil brother from the earth. Some stories say that the evil twin became ruler of the **underworld**, or land of the dead, and still tries to spread evil in the world. After the Woman Who Fell from the Sky died, her good son planted a seed in her body that grew into the first corn as a gift to the people.

## The Woman Who Fell from the Sky in Context

The myth of The Woman Who Fell from the Sky reflects important elements of Iroquois beliefs. First, the myth reflects a belief in a celestial realm that resembles the world on the ground. Second, it suggests the importance of rain and corn to the Iroquois people. The character can be seen as a symbol for rain, which sustains life and is normally the only thing that falls from the sky. Corn grows from her body like a baby grows inside its mother, reflecting the belief that women are the source of fertility and growth.

## Key Themes and Symbols

The Woman Who Fell from the Sky is a myth dealing primarily with fertility, or the ability to grow and sustain life. The woman is already pregnant at the beginning of the tale; the fact that she has twins adds to her representation as an instrument of fertility. Her twins then go on to create the rest of the world, which makes her the source of all life. When she dies, her body remains a source of fertility, and the first corn grows from it.

## The Woman Who Fell from the Sky in Art, Literature, and Everyday Life

The Woman Who Fell from the Sky remains an important part of the creation myths of several American Indian tribes. Joy Harjo, a poet and member of the Muscogee tribe, explores myth, creation, and everyday life in her collection of poems titled *The Woman Who Fell from the Sky.* John Bierhorst's *The Woman Who Fell from the Sky: The Iroquois Story of Creation* is a marvelous retelling of the creation myth, enhanced by Robert Andrew Parker's watercolor and pastel illustrations.

## Read, Write, Think, Discuss

Native American myths contain abundant references to powerful women. Using your library, the Internet, or other available resources, research two or three myths of powerful women and the cultures that produced them. What are some of the characteristics of these women? What are some of the cultural beliefs among Native Americans that might have led to their portrayal of women as powerful?

**SEE ALSO** Creation Stories; Native American Mythology; Twins

# XYZ

## Xian

**Nationality/Culture**
Chinese/Taoist

**Pronunciation**
shee-EN

**Alternate Names**
Hsien

**Appears In**
*The Eight Immortals Depart and Travel to the East*

**Lineage**
Varies

### Character Overview

In the Taoist mythology of China, the Xian (or Hsien) are enlightened beings who at one time lived as humans on earth, but eventually became immortal, or able to live forever. Some of the Xian were real individuals mentioned in historical records; others appear only in myths and legends. Early Chinese texts refer to various numbers of Xian, but the most famous of these, the Eight Immortals, were first identified during the Yuan Dynasty (1271–1368).

The Eight Immortals are said to travel the universe together in a state of perfect health and happiness. They perform various wonders and miracles and serve as models for those seeking the *tao* (pronounced DOW), or way—the path to an ideal state of being and existence. In Chinese art, these Eight Immortals often appear as a group, each depicted with his or her own characteristic clothing and possessions.

**The Stories of the Eight Immortals** The stories about the Xian explain how each achieved immortality in a different way. The first to reach this state was Li Tieguai (pronounced LEE tee-eh-GWYE, meaning "Li of the Iron Crutch"), a hermit who went forty years without food or sleep. According to some stories, Li Tieguai acquired both immortality and his crutch from the Queen Mother of the West, who saw him limping and begging. Other legends say that Laozi (pronounced low-DZOO), the founder of Taoism, came down from **heaven** to teach Li Tieguai the wisdom of the gods. One day Li sent his spirit to Laozi. When he returned, he found that a follower had burned his body, believing him to be dead. So Li entered the body of a deformed beggar who had died, gaining both immortality and a new identity.

Several different tales tell of the life of Zhong-Liquan (pronounced DJORNG-lee-choo-AHN), an army officer and state official. Some stories say that after losing a battle he went into the mountains, became a hermit, and learned the secret of immortality from the Flowers of the East. Other tales say that he was a priest or a beggar and that he discovered a jade box containing the magic potion of eternal life.

The most famous of the Xian was Lu Dongbin (pronounced LOO dorng-BEEN), a prince who traveled throughout China slaying **dragons** with a magic sword. One day he met Zhong-Liquan at an inn, and later that night he dreamed that his royal life would end in disgrace. When he awoke, he turned his back on worldly things and followed Zhong-Liquan into the mountains to seek the tao and gain immortality.

The grandnephew of a great statesman and poet, Han Xiang (pronounced HARN shee-YEN) became a follower of Lu Dongbin. While climbing a sacred peach tree one day, he fell from the branches and achieved immortality before he reached the ground. Some stories say he died as a result of the fall and was then transformed into an immortal.

Cao Guojiu (pronounced TSOW gwor-JEE-yoo) was the brother of an empress. Disgusted by the corruption at the royal court, he went into the mountains to seek the tao. He met a boatman on the way and showed him a golden tablet that would admit the holder to the royal court. The boatman—Lu Dongbin in disguise—was not impressed, but he took Cao Guojiu as a disciple and taught him the tao and the secret of immortality.

The immortal Zhang Guolao (pronounced DJARNG gwor-LOW) was also a hermit. Famous for his skills in magic, he traveled around on a white mule that he could fold up like a sheet of paper and put into a carrying bag. Many stories say that Zhang Guolao achieved immortality simply by never dying, or by appearing alive again after people saw him die.

The immortal Lan Caihe (pronounced LARN TSWEE-HUH) sometimes appears as a man and other times as a woman. One day while gathering medicinal herbs, Lan Caihe met a beggar and helped tend the sores on his body. The beggar was Li Tieguai in disguise, and he rewarded this kindness by granting Lan Caihe immortality. Lan Caihe traveled around the country in a tattered blue dress, urging people to seek the tao.

The eighth Xian, He Xiangu (HUH SHEE-yen-GOO), is the only one who is definitely a woman. As a young girl, He Xiangu dreamed that a spirit told her to grind up and eat some mother-of-pearl. She did this and became immortal. Thereafter, she floated from mountain to mountain gathering herbs and fruit.

## Xian in Context

The story of the Xian reflects the importance of the idea of immortality in Chinese culture. This notion runs through both Taoism and Buddhism; physical death is often seen as the last stage leading to eternal life. The myth of the Xian, like Buddhist teachings, suggests to believers that immortality is something that can be achieved by anyone. This reflects a view that the godlike figures of Chinese myth are not only closely connected to typical humans, but in many cases represent advanced stages of what it means to be human.

## Key Themes and Symbols

The most important theme that runs through all the tales of the Xian is the search for immortality. Some search diligently for it, while others stumble upon it. In most cases, however, immortality is described as a reward or something that is earned. Usually this is earned through acts of cleansing or purifying, or by giving up worldly things. Several items in the myths of the Xian are ancient Chinese symbols of immortality, such as peaches, jade, and mother-of-pearl.

## Xian in Art, Literature, and Everyday Life

The Eight Immortals are identified in Chinese art primarily by their clothes and the things they carry. Li Tieguai is depicted as a disabled beggar with an iron crutch. Zhong-Liquan is usually portrayed as a bearded old man holding a fan made of feathers. Lu Dongbin is usually shown carrying a sword, while Han Xiang is shown carrying a basket of flowers. Cao Guojiu appears wearing official robes and carrying his golden tablet. Zhang Guolao is shown with a peach—a symbol of immortality—and a feather from the legendary **phoenix**. Lan Caihe is usually shown with a flute or a basket of fruit. Artists generally portrayed He Xiangu as a beautiful woman wearing a lotus flower in her hair or on her clothing. The Eight Immortals remain a popular artistic subject in modern times, and several Chinese films have been made about their lives.

### Read, Write, Think, Discuss

*The Secrets of the Immortal Nicholas Flamel* (2007) by Michael Scott is a novel about twin California teens who discover they are at the center of a prophecy about saving—or destroying—the world. One takes a job at a bookstore owned by an alchemist who has discovered the secret of immortality. When the book containing the secret is stolen, the **twins** must learn to use their untapped magical powers to get it back.

SEE ALSO Chinese Mythology

# Xipe Totec

**Nationality/Culture**
Aztec

**Pronunciation**
SHE-pay TOH-tek

**Alternate Names**
None

**Appears In**
Aztec oral mythology

**Lineage**
Son of Coatlicue

## Character Overview

Xipe Totec (pronounced SHE-pay TOH-tek), which means "Our Lord the Flayed One," was an Aztec god of agriculture and the changing of the seasons. Xipe Totec was also associated with disease, death, and rebirth. He was often the recipient of human sacrifices, with priests removing the skin of the victims as part of a special ritual in his honor.

## Major Myths

Like many other important Aztec gods, Xipe Totec was said to be the child of the goddess **Coatlicue** (pronounced koh-aht-LEE-kway). He was worshipped as the provider of food for the Aztec people. According to myth, he wore a human skin over his golden body, and peeled off the skin to feed the people. He also looked after goldsmiths, and presided over the changing of the seasons. Unlike his brothers **Huitzilopochtli** (pronounced wee-tsee-loh-POCH-tlee) and **Quetzalcoatl** (pronounced keht-sahl-koh-AHT-l), Xipe Totec is not the subject of documented

### Human Sacrifice Across Cultures

Human sacrifice has deep roots in world cultures and religions. Just about every world region—from the Americas to Europe to China to India—had societies that practiced human sacrifice. Many religions, including Christianity, have references to human sacrifice in their legends and texts. The purpose of human sacrifice was to offer a gift or atonement to the gods or God in order to placate them, seek protection from harm, or ask for something, such as good crops or more rain. Humans, especially certain categories of humans, such as a firstborn son or daughter, were considered the highest form of sacrifice, hence the most acceptable to the deities. Over time, the sacrifice of humans gave way to substituting animals, or to purely symbolic sacrificial rituals.

myths. However, as the god of the seasons and crop growth, sacrifices to Xipe Totec were plentiful and unusual. Victims, generally slaves, were completely skinned, and a priest would then wear the skin as a ceremonial suit during fertility rituals in honor of the god.

## Xipe Totec in Context

The peeling of Xipe Totec's skin in order to feed the people is a reflection of two important facets of Aztec life. First, it reflects the notion that human **sacrifice** is essential to keep the natural world functioning; the Aztecs believed that blood was the basic fuel needed to power the **sun**. Second, the peeling of Xipe Totec's skin parallels the growth of maize (corn) seeds, which break free of their outer covering as they sprout. Maize was an important part of the Aztec diet and was often referenced in myth.

## Key Themes and Symbols

The central theme in the myth of Xipe Totec is rebirth. Just as spring symbolizes a new cycle of life, Xipe Totec sheds his old, dead skin—much like a snake—and offers it to sustain life. This also represents the Aztec idea that death is necessary to sustain life or to create new life. The color gold is closely associated with Xipe Totec, since he is the protector of goldsmiths and the provider of golden maize. Both are considered treasures, each in its own way.

*This piece of gold jewelry has a representation of the pre-Columbian god Xipe Totec on it.* © OAXACA MUSEUM, MEXICO/BILDARCHIV STEFFENS/HENRI STIERLIN/THE BRIDGEMAN ART LIBRARY.

## Xipe Totec in Art, Literature, and Everyday Life

In Aztec art, Xipe Totec was usually depicted as a golden figure wearing a suit of human skin over most of his body, often with parts of the skin suit—such as the hands—hanging loose to expose his true body underneath. Many statues of the god have been discovered, but he is less often seen in modern art and literature than other Aztec gods.

## Read, Write, Think, Discuss

For the Aztecs, human sacrifice was not viewed as an act of violence so much as an act of giving life to the gods, and in cultures around the world, human and animal sacrifice is associated with religious beliefs and rituals. In modern times, however, acts such as the skinning of another person are more likely to be associated with murderers and Nazi death camps. How do you think this affects the modern view of Aztec gods such as Xipe Totec? Do you think this also creates a negative bias toward the Aztec culture in modern culture? Is such a bias justified? Why or why not?

**SEE ALSO** Aztec Mythology

# Yellow Emperor

**Nationality/Culture**
Chinese/Taoist

**Alternate Names**
Huang-Di

**Appears In**
The *Shiji*

**Lineage**
Son of Shao-dian

## Character Overview

In **Chinese mythology**, Huang-Di (pronounced hoo-arng-DEE), also known as the Yellow Emperor, was the most ancient of five legendary Chinese emperors, as well as a key figure in Taoism, one of China's main religions and philosophies. He was also a hero credited with civilizing the earth, teaching people many skills, and inventing numerous useful items, including the wheel, armor and weapons, ships, writing, the compass, and coined money. According to tradition, the Yellow Emperor began ruling in 2697 BCE. His long reign was said to be a golden age, and he was honored as a generous and wise ruler. Before Huang-Di came to the throne, order and government were unknown in the world. He introduced systems of government and law to humankind, and he also invented music and the arts.

## Major Myths

Legend says that the Yellow Emperor had four faces that gazed out in four directions, allowing him to see all that happened in the world. In

*The Yellow Emperor.* © MARY EVANS PICTURE LIBRARY/THE IMAGE WORKS.

addition, he could communicate directly with the gods through his prayers and sacrifices. When he traveled around his empire, he rode in an ivory chariot pulled by **dragons** and an elephant, accompanied by a procession of tigers, wolves, snakes, and flocks of the fabled **phoenix** birds.

During Huang-Di's reign, only one god challenged his authority. The rebel god was aided by the emperor's son Fei Lian (pronounced FAY lee-EN), lord of the wind. They sent fog and rain to drown the royal armies, but the emperor's daughter Ba (drought) dried up the rain and helped defeat the rebels.

After ruling for many years, Huang-Di became tired and weak. He allowed officials to make decisions for him and went to live in a simple hut in the courtyard of his palace. Through fasting, prayer, and meditation, he discovered the *tao* (pronounced DOW), or way—the path to an ideal state of being and existence. The Yellow Emperor continued to rule for many additional years, attempting to bring a state of perfection to his realm. Upon his death he rose into the heavens and became an immortal, or a being who could live forever.

## Yellow Emperor in Context

The Yellow Emperor is regarded as an actual historical figure in Chinese culture. It is common for real historical figures to acquire layers of myth over the centuries, building upon or exaggerating their accomplishments. However, because of the sweeping nature of the Yellow Emperor's achievements—he is believed to have invented traditional Chinese music, medicine, and the calendar, among other things—some have argued that the reverse has occurred: the Yellow Emperor was a purely mythic figure who was given an "historical" identity. This may have occurred as a way for some groups to claim that they are ancestors of the Yellow Emperor, and therefore hold special rights to rule.

## Key Themes and Symbols

The word *huang* means "yellow" as well as "radiant," which connects the Yellow Emperor to the **sun** as the center part of the universe. The myth of the Yellow Emperor focuses on the theme of progress and advancement. The Yellow Emperor civilizes many diverse peoples and teaches them the basics of civilization, such as medicine and music. The emperor himself then retreats in an effort to achieve his own personal advancement through Taoism. He ultimately achieves this, which leads to his immortality.

## Yellow Emperor in Art, Literature, and Everyday Life

The Yellow Emperor is a popular part of the cultural history of China. He has been the subject of many television shows that expand upon the legends of his life. The Yellow Emperor is also mentioned in a short story by Jorge Luis Borges titled "The Fauna of Mirrors," and in the 2002 video game *Emperor: Rise of the Middle Kingdom.*

## Read, Write, Think, Discuss

For events that are said to have happened in the distant past, there may never be a way of knowing how much of what is believed is factual and how much is legend. In your opinion, would it matter if legendary events could be proven to be either factual or fictional? Why or why not?

**SEE ALSO** Chinese Mythology; Heroes; Xian

# Yggdrasill

**Nationality/Culture**
Norse

**Pronunciation**
IG-druh-sil

**Alternate Names**
None

**Appears In**
The Eddas

## Myth Overview

In **Norse mythology**, a mighty axis, or pole, ran through the universe in which the gods, **giants**, and **heroes** enacted their stormy dramas. That axis, around which all life revolved, was the World Tree, a giant ash tree called Yggdrasill (pronounced IG-druh-sil). The myths paint a complex picture of how the universe was structured around Yggdrasill. Sometimes the World Tree is described as running through nine realms, from the shadowy depths of the **underworld**, or land of the dead, up to the heavenly abode of the gods. At other times, the trunk of Yggdrasill is said to anchor Midgard, the world of humans, while the tree's three great roots reach down into Jotunheim (pronounced YAW-toon-heym), the land of the frost giants; Niflheim (pronounced NIV-uhl-heym), the land of mist; and Asgard (pronounced AHS-gahrd), the home of the gods.

Although the World Tree offered an avenue of passage from one realm to the next, the distances and dangers involved in such travel were great. The only creature that could run up and down Yggdrasill easily was a squirrel, which carried insulting messages back and forth between a fierce eagle perched in the tree's topmost branch and a dragon that gnawed at its root. Yggdrasill existed in a state of delicate balance, being endlessly destroyed and renewed.

The World Tree was closely linked to sources of hidden or magical knowledge. Its name, which means "**Odin**'s horse," refers to Odin hanging himself from the tree for nine days and nights to learn secret mysteries. Near one root rose a spring whose waters provided wisdom. Odin was said to have traded an eye to drink this water. Another root sheltered a spring tended by the Norns, three women who determined the fate of all humans.

## Yggdrasill in Context

The Norse people of Scandinavia built their mythological beliefs upon the foundation of the natural world. Even the realms that they considered supernatural were connected by natural elements, such as the rainbow that acts as a bridge for the gods to enter their home at Asgard. It is not surprising that the different worlds of Norse mythology are all connected by a gigantic version of something found in nature—an ash tree. As with the rainbow bridge to Asgard, the belief in Yggdrasill may have been based on simple observations of the natural world; it has been suggested that high-altitude cirrus clouds may have appeared, to an imaginative Norse eye, like branches of a gigantic tree in the far distance. It is more likely, however, that people throughout the world use natural forms to express the symbolic and meaningful elements of myths.

## Key Themes and Symbols

The World Tree Yggdrasill symbolizes the interconnection of the visible world and the worlds of Norse myth. The tree also represents life as an eternal and fundamental part of the world. After the destruction of the gods at **Ragnarok** (pronounced RAHG-nuh-rok), the only humans that survive are those who seek shelter in the branches of Yggdrasill. In Norse culture, the ash tree was associated with protection from evil.

## Yggdrasill in Art, Literature, and Everyday Life

Although images of Yggdrasill are common in traditional Norse art, they are often decorative or symbolic and are not meant to depict the actual tree in its full glory. Indeed, considering the grand scale of the World Tree, few artists have attempted such a thing. Robert Frost refers to the

*Yggdrasil, the world tree of Norse mythology, with Jotunheim, the land of the frost giants at the bottom; Midgard, the world of humans, in the middle; and Asgard, the land of the gods, at the top.* © TOPHAM/THE IMAGE WORKS.

tree in his poem "A Never Naught Song." Yggdrasill has also appeared in science fiction and fantasy literature, such as the themed short-story collection *Rainbow Mars* (1999) by Larry Niven, and the *Hyperion*

*Cantos* series of novels by Dan Simmons, where it takes the form of a gigantic living spaceship, or treeship.

### Read, Write, Think, Discuss

Yggdrasill is a source of shelter and protection for the last humans at Ragnarok. In modern times, environmental activists sometimes live among the branches of large, old trees—not for their own protection, but to prevent the trees from being cut down. Do you think this is an effective way to draw attention to the uncertain fate of old-growth trees? Why or why not?

**SEE ALSO** Norse Mythology

# Ymir

**Nationality/Culture**
Norse

**Pronunciation**
EE-mir

**Alternate Names**
Aurgelmir

**Appears In**
The Eddas

**Lineage**
Born of ice and fire

### Character Overview

An ancient frost giant of **Norse mythology**, Ymir was formed at the beginning of creation from rivers of ice that flowed from Niflheim (pronounced NIV-uhl-heym), the land of mist, into Ginnungagap (pronounced GIN-oon-gah-GAHP), the yawning emptiness. Ymir emerged from the ice as it melted from the heat of the **fire** kingdom that lay near these two regions.

As the evil Ymir slept, other frost **giants** formed from the sweat of his body. The first male and female emerged from his left armpit, and another man came from his legs. Ymir drank milk from an ancient cow, which in turn licked blocks of ice and released a man called Buri. Buri's grandsons were the gods **Odin** (pronounced OH-din), Vili (pronounced VEE-lee), and Ve (pronounced VEH). These three gods eventually attacked Ymir while he slept and killed him. As Ymir's blood gushed from his body, it caused a flood that drowned all the frost giants except Bergelmir (pronounced BEHR-gel-meer) and his wife. They escaped in a ship and founded a new race of beings.

Odin and his brothers used Ymir's body to form the world. They took his flesh to make earth; his bones became mountains; his teeth turned into stones and boulders; and his hair became trees and

*The Norse gods used the body of Ymir, a frost giant, to form the world.* © MARY EVANS PICTURE LIBRARY/THE IMAGE WORKS.

vegetation. The gods made the sky from Ymir's skull and threw his brains into the air to form clouds. Dwarves emerged out of hills and rocks and helped to hold up the sky. Finally, Odin and his brothers used Ymir's eyebrows to make a great wall to surround and protect Midgard, the world of humans.

## Ymir in Context

The myth of Ymir is a Nordic example of the centrality of **sacrifice**—often violent—in many creation myths throughout the world. According to the Norse myth, all life arose from the violent sacrifice of Ymir. Other Norse gods also bore the scars of violent sacrifices they endured for the good of the larger community: Odin sacrificed an eye in order to gain knowledge of the future and the pain humans would have to endure; and **Tyr** sacrificed his hand in order to secure the giant wolf **Fenrir**.

## Key Themes and Symbols

One of the most important themes in the myth of Ymir is the idea of creation through death. It is only when Ymir is killed by Odin and his brothers that the world as humans know it is created. Ymir's blood drowns the old giants, while his hair becomes the vegetation of the land. This also suggests the cycle of death and rebirth that is seen throughout nature every year, but on a much grander scale. Frost is used to symbolize barrenness and hostility, just like the hostile winters the Norse people faced.

## Ymir in Art, Literature, and Everyday Life

Though his body was used to create the world, Ymir is not one of the more popular figures from Norse mythology. In modern times, Ymir is used as the inspiration for a character of the same name in the Marvel Comics Universe; the Marvel version of Ymir is a giant made completely of ice who seeks to destroy all other forms of life on Earth. This character also appeared in the 2006 video game *Marvel: Ultimate Alliance*. The giant's name was used for one of the planet Saturn's many moons. Ymir was also used as the name of the alien monster in the classic science fiction film *20 Million Miles to Earth* (1957), though he did not resemble the Norse frost giant.

## Read, Write, Think, Discuss

The idea of all life originating from a primordial sacrifice is found throughout the world. Using your library, the Internet, or other available resources, research origin myths from different continents that have sacrifice as an important element of world creation. Do these myths have anything in common? Do the cultures they come from have anything in common? Why do you think sacrifice is such an important element in creation myths?

**SEE ALSO** Creation Stories; Dwarfs and Elves; Floods; Giants; Norse Mythology; Odin

# Yu Huang

*See* **Jade Emperor.**

# Zeus

**Nationality/Culture**
Greek

**Pronunciation**
ZOOS

**Alternate Names**
Jupiter (Roman)

**Appears In**
Hesiod's *Theogony*, Ovid's *Metamorphoses*

**Lineage**
Son of Cronus and Rhea

## Character Overview

Zeus was the most important deity, or god, of ancient Greece. He was the leader of the gods and the all-powerful overseer of earthly events and human destiny. His role in mythology was complex and filled with contradictions. Zeus was the god of law and social order, yet he came to power through violent revolution. A protector of marriage and the household, he was repeatedly unfaithful to his own wife, **Hera** (pronounced HAIR-uh), and fathered children by a variety of women.

## Major Myths

In a myth that some modern scholars believe reflects the triumph of the Greek gods over more ancient deities, Hesiod told how Zeus became the supreme god. Before the gods existed, the **Titans** ruled the universe. Their chief was **Cronus** (pronounced KROH-nuhs). He and his wife Rhea (pronounced REE-uh) had five children, but because Cronus had been warned that one of his children would overthrow him, he devoured each child as soon as it was born. Zeus was the sixth. Rhea was determined to save this child, so she deceived Cronus by giving him a blanket-wrapped stone to swallow and secretly sent the infant to safety on the island of Crete (pronounced KREET). There, **nymphs** (female nature deities) tended the baby Zeus, while Cretan warriors sang and clashed their swords so that Cronus would not hear his crying.

When he grew up, Zeus was ready to overthrow his cruel father and avenge the siblings that Cronus had swallowed. He befriended Metis (pronounced MEE-tis), who was either a Titaness or an ocean nymph. Metis devised a potion to make Cronus vomit out the children he had swallowed, and either she or Zeus gave it to Cronus to drink. Cronus spat forth Zeus's sisters, Hestia (pronounced HESS-tee-uh), **Demeter** (pronounced di-MEE-ter), and Hera, and his brothers, **Hades** (pronounced HAY-deez) and **Poseidon** (pronounced poh-SYE-dun). Last of all, Cronus vomited up the stone he had swallowed in place of Zeus. Tradition says that the stone was later set in a place of honor at **Delphi** (pronounced DEL-fye). It was called the *omphalos*, or the navel of the world.

Zeus, Hades, and Poseidon battled the Titans in a conflict that lasted ten years. Zeus also had the help of the hundred-armed **giants** and the **Cyclopes** (pronounced sigh-KLOH-peez), one-eyed giants imprisoned in Tartarus (pronounced TAR-tur-uhs), a deep pit of the **underworld** or land of the dead. Released by Zeus, the Cyclopes forged a thunderbolt for him to use as a weapon. In the end, the Titans were overthrown, and Zeus sent all those who had opposed him to Tartarus. Only Titans who had not fought against Zeus, such as **Atlas** (pronounced AT-luhs), were spared.

Zeus and his brothers divided the world. Zeus controlled the sky, Hades the underworld, and Poseidon the sea—although Zeus had ultimate control over his brothers. The gods and their sisters took up residence on Mount Olympus (pronounced oh-LIM-puhs), which is why they and their offspring are called the Olympian deities.

**The Loves of Zeus** Zeus fathered children with a series of partners: nymphs, Titanesses, goddesses, and mortal women. The offspring of these unions included deities, demigods (half human, half god), and **heroes**.

Accounts of Zeus's loves and children vary somewhat, but Metis is usually listed as his first partner or wife. When she became pregnant, Zeus learned that her child would be a powerful god who would one day replace him. Like his father Cronus before him, Zeus was determined to preserve his power, but he did not wait to swallow the infant—he swallowed Metis. Their child, **Athena** (pronounced uh-THEE-nuh), emerged full-grown from Zeus's head.

Next, Zeus turned to the Titaness Themis (pronounced THEEM-is), who bore him two sets of daughters known as the **Fates** and the Hours. The ocean nymph Eurynome (pronounced yoo-RIN-uh-mee) also had daughters by Zeus, including the **Graces**. His next wife or partner was his sister, the goddess Demeter (marriages between brother and sister deities occur in the mythologies of many ancient cultures). Their child, **Persephone** (pronounced per-SEF-uh-nee), later became the wife of Hades.

Zeus's union with the Titaness Mnemosyne (pronounced nee-MOSS-uh-nee) produced the nine goddesses known as the **Muses**. Leto (pronounced LEE-toh) bore Zeus's **twins Apollo** (pronounced uh-POL-oh) and **Artemis** (pronounced AHR-tuh-miss). Maia (pronounced MAY-uh), the daughter of Atlas, bore him **Hermes** (pronounced HUR-meez). Eventually, Zeus married Hera, his last wife and the mother of three more Olympian deities: **Ares** (pronounced AIR-eez), Hebe (pronounced HEE-bee), and **Hephaestus** (pronounced hi-FES-tuhs).

Yet Zeus continued to have love affairs, many of them with mortal women. He sometimes mated with them in disguise or in animal form. After he visited the princess **Danaë** (pronounced DAN-uh-ee) as a shower of gold, she bore the hero **Perseus** (pronounced PUR-see-uhs). To Europa (pronounced yoo-ROH-puh), another princess, he appeared as a white bull. He came to Leda in the form of a swan. The children of their union were **Helen** of Troy, her sister Clytemnestra (pronounced klye-tem-NES-truh), and the brothers **Castor and Pollux** (pronounced PAHL-uhks). His most famous half-human son was **Heracles** (pronounced HAIR-uh-kleez), born to Alcmena (pronounced alk-MEE-nuh), to whom he came disguised as her own husband.

Zeus's relations with other women angered Hera, and she despised all the children he fathered by these women. Hera particularly hated Heracles and frequently tried to harm him. Once, when she had gone too far, Zeus hanged her in the heavens with a heavy block pulling her feet down, and he threw Hephaestus out of Olympus for trying to help her.

Surviving Hera's attacks, Heracles aided Zeus and the other Olympians in a battle for survival. They were challenged by a race of giants, which **Gaia** (pronounced GAY-uh), the earth, had produced to bring an end to their rule. Zeus defeated the giants as well as various other threats to his supremacy, including a conspiracy among Hera, Athena, and Poseidon.

**The Roman Jupiter** The Romans, who adopted many elements of Greek culture and mythology, came to identify their own sky god, Jupiter, with Zeus. Associated with weather and agriculture in early Roman myths, Jupiter was the god of storms, thunder, lightning, the sowing of seeds, and the harvesting of grapes. As Roman civilization developed, Jupiter became known as Optimus Maximus, which means "best and greatest." He was viewed as the supreme god and the protector of the Roman state. As Rome became a military power, Jupiter took on such titles as "supreme commander," "unconquerable," and "triumphant."

Although Jupiter acquired many of the characteristics and myths associated with Zeus, his marriage to the goddess Juno (pronounced JOO-noh) was more harmonious than that of Zeus and Hera. Moreover, Jupiter shared some of his power with Juno and the goddess Minerva (pronounced mi-NUR-vuh), the Roman version of Athena. The three deities were believed to preside jointly over both divine and earthly affairs.

## Zeus in Context

As a mythological figure, Zeus changed over the centuries. Originally a sky god, he was believed to bring clouds, rain, thunder, and lightning. His cults were associated with mountain peaks where clouds gathered. As **Greek mythology** developed, the figure of Zeus grew larger until he became the dominant force in the Greek pantheon, or collection of recognized gods and goddesses. Later, as Jupiter (pronounced JOO-pi-tur), he was the chief god of Rome.

Some of the earliest accounts of Zeus appear in the writings of Homer and Hesiod. Homer called Zeus "the father of gods and men," but the term "father" referred more to Zeus's position of authority than to actual parenthood. Zeus did father some of the gods, but many others were his brothers, sisters, nephews, or nieces. Although he ruled many aspects of earthly affairs and human life, Zeus was not a creator god. Other mythological powers brought the earth and human beings into existence. Zeus enforced the laws that governed them.

*Zeus was the supreme ruler of the Greek gods.* SCALA/ART RESOURCE, NY.

## Key Themes and Symbols

One of the central themes found in the myths of Zeus is interference in the affairs of humans. Like many of the Olympian gods, Zeus did not seem content to interact with only other gods and nymphs. He took time and effort to punish specific individuals, such as Phineus (pronounced

FIN-ee-us), a seer whom Zeus blinded for revealing too many of the gods' secrets to humans, or Salmoneus (pronounced sal-MOH-nee-uhs), who impersonated Zeus and was struck dead with a thunderbolt for his mockery. He also provided rewards to others, such as the seer Tiresias (pronounced ty-REE-see-uhs), who took Zeus's side in an argument the god was having with Hera; Tiresias was blinded by an angry Hera, but Zeus gave him the power to see the future.

Another theme common in the myths of Zeus is physical transformation. Very often it was Zeus who transformed himself, such as when he became a shower of gold to reach Danaë, or when he mated with Leda in the form of a swan. However, he often transformed others into animals and objects—usually as punishment, but sometimes for their own safety. Pandareos (pronounced pan-DAHR-ee-ohs) was transformed into stone for stealing a statue of a dog from one of Zeus's temples; Periphas (pronounced PEHR-uh-fas) was a king of Attica whom Zeus changed into an eagle when he died as a reward for living a just life.

## Zeus in Art, Literature, and Everyday Life

Ancient artists generally depicted Zeus as a dignified, bearded man of middle age. Often, he was shown holding, or preparing to hurl, a thunderbolt, which took the form of a winged spear or a cylinder with pointed ends. One of the most remarkable images ever created of Zeus was a statue that stood in his temple at Olympia in Greece. The statue was lost long ago, but a description of it survives. The forty-foot-tall statue showed the god seated, with golden lions at his side. The head and upper body were made of precious ivory, and the lower body was draped in gold—truly a glorious and awe-inspiring representation of "the greatest god of all."

In modern times, Zeus is still the best known of the Olympian gods. He has appeared as a character in numerous television shows and films. Notable examples include *Jason and the Argonauts* (1963), *Clash of the Titans* (1981), and the Disney animated film *Hercules* (1997). He has also appeared in video games, such as *Zeus: Master of Olympus.*

## Read, Write, Think, Discuss

In ancient Greek mythology, Zeus was believed to interact with humans frequently, though not always in his godlike form. In modern times, people generally do not support the idea that a god (or God) regularly appears in physical form on Earth to interact with humans. What do you think this indicates about modern believers when compared to the ancient Greeks? Is there a difference in the way these two groups relate to the realms of the gods?

**SEE ALSO** Athena; Atlas; Castor and Pollux; Cronus; Cyclopes; Danaë; Demeter; Gaia; Graces; Greek Mythology; Hades; Helen of Troy; Hephaestus; Hera; Heracles; Muses; Persephone; Poseidon; Roman Mythology; Titans

# *Where to Learn More*


## African

Altman, Linda Jacobs. *African Mythology.* Berkeley Heights, NJ: Enslow Publishers, 2003.

Ardagh, Philip, and Georgia Peters. *African Myths & Legends.* Chicago: World Book, 2002.

Giles, Bridget. *Myths of West Africa.* Austin, TX: Raintree Steck-Vaughn, 2002.

Husain, Shahrukh, and Bee Willey. *African Myths.* 1st ed. North Mankato, MN: Cherrytree Books, 2007.

Lilly, Melinda. *Spider and His Son Find Wisdom: An Akan Tale.* Vero Beach, FL: Rourke Press, 1998.

Lilly, Melinda. *Warrior Son of a Warrior Son: A Masai Tale.* Vero Beach, FL: Rourke Press, 1998.

Lilly, Melinda. *Zimani's Drum: A Malawian Tale.* Vero Beach, FL: Rourke Press, 1998.

Schomp, Virginia. *The Ancient Africans.* New York: Marshall Cavendish Benchmark, 2008.

Seed, Jenny. *The Bushman's Dream: African Tales of the Creation.* 1st American ed. Scarsdale, NY: Bradbury Press, 1975.

## Anglo-Saxon/Celtic

Ardagh, Philip, and G. Barton Chapple. *Celtic Myths & Legends.* Chicago: World Book, 2002.

Crossley-Holland, Kevin, and Peter Malone. *The World of King Arthur and His Court: People, Places, Legend, and Lore.* New York: Dutton Children's Books, 2004.

Hicks, Penelope, and James McLean. *Beowulf.* New York: Kingfisher, 2007.

Lister, Robin, Alan Baker, and Sir Thomas Malory. *The Story of King Arthur.* Boston: Kingfisher, 2005.

Martell, Hazel Mary. *The Celts.* 1st American ed. New York: Peter Bedrick, 2001.

Morris, Gerald. *The Lioness & Her Knight.* Boston: Houghton Mifflin, 2005.

Whittock, Martyn J. *Beliefs and Myths of Viking Britain.* Oxford: Heinemann, 1996.

Williams, Marcia, ed. *Chaucer's Canterbury Tales.* London: Walker, 2008.

### Asian/Pacific

Behnke, Alison. *Angkor Wat.* Minneapolis: Twenty-First Century Books, 2008.

Carpenter, Frances. *Tales of a Korean Grandmother.* Boston: Tuttle Pub., 1973.

Coburn, Jewell Reinhart. *Encircled Kingdom: Legends and Folktales of Laos.* Rev. ed. Thousand Oaks, CA: Burn, Hart, 1994.

Coulson, Kathy Morrissey, Paula Cookson Melhorn, and Hmong Women's Project (Fitchburg, MA). *Living in Two Worlds: The Hmong Women's Project.* Ashburnham, MA: K. M. Coulson and P. C. Melhorn, 2000.

Dalal, Anita. *Myths of Oceania.* Austin, TX: Raintree Steck-Vaughn, 2002.

Green, Jen. *Myths of China and Japan.* Austin, TX: New York: Raintree Steck-Vaughn Publishers, 2002.

Htin Aung, U., G. Trager, and Pau Oo Thet. *A Kingdom Lost for a Drop of Honey, and Other Burmese Folktales.* New York: Parents' Magazine Press, 1968.

Kanawa, Kiri Te. *Land of the Long White Cloud: Maori Myths, Tales, and Legends.* 1st U.S. ed. New York: Arcade Pub., 1989.

Sakairi, Masao, Shooko Kojima, and Matthew Galgani. *Vietnamese Fables of Frogs and Toads.* Berkeley, CA: Heian International, 2006.

Sakairi, Masao, Shooko Kojima, and Matthew Galgani. *Vietnamese Tales of Rabbits and Watermelons.* Berkeley, CA: Heian International, 2006.

### Egyptian

Ardagh, Philip, and Danuta Mayer. *Ancient Egyptian Myths & Legends.* Chicago: World Book, 2002.

Broyles, Janell. *Egyptian Mythology.* 1st ed. New York: Rosen Pub. Group, 2006.

Cline, Eric H., and Jill Rubalcaba. *The Ancient Egyptian World.* California ed. New York: Oxford University Press, 2005.

Gleason, Katherine. *Ancient Egyptian Culture.* New York: Newbridge Educational Pub., 2006.

Kramer, Ann. *Egyptian Myth: A Treasury of Legends, Art, and History.* Armonk, NY: Sharpe Focus, 2008.

Kudalis, Eric. *The Royal Mummies: Remains from Ancient Egypt.* Mankato, MN: Capstone High-Interest Books, 2003.

McCall, Henrietta. *Gods & Goddesses in the Daily Life of the Ancient Egyptians.* Columbus, OH: Peter Bedrick Books, 2002.

Mitchnik, Helen. *Egyptian and Sudanese Folk-Tales.* New York: Oxford University Press, 1978.

Schomp, Virginia. *The Ancient Egyptians.* New York: Marshall Cavendish Benchmark, 2008.

Wyly, Michael J. *Death and the Underworld.* San Diego, CA: Lucent Books, 2002.

## Greek/Roman

Bingham, Jane. *Classical Myth: A Treasury of Greek and Roman Legends, Art, and History.* Armonk, NY: M. E. Sharpe, 2008.

Hepplewhite, Peter, and Mark Bergin. *The Adventures of Perseus.* Minneapolis, MN: Picture Window Books, 2005.

Lister, Robin, Alan Baker, and Homer. *The Odyssey.* Reformatted ed. Boston: Kingfisher, 2004.

McCarty, Nick, Victor G. Ambrus, and Homer. *The Iliad.* Reformatted ed. Boston: Kingfisher, 2004.

Mellor, Ronald, and Marni McGee. *The Ancient Roman World.* New York: Oxford University Press, 2005.

Roberts, Russell. *Athena.* Hockessin, DE: Mitchell Lane Publishers, 2008.

Roberts, Russell. *Dionysus.* Hockessin, DE: Mitchell Lane Publishers, 2008.

Roberts, Russell. *Zeus.* Hockessin, DE: Mitchell Lane Publishers, 2008.

Schomp, Virginia. *The Ancient Romans.* New York: Marshall Cavendish Benchmark, 2008.

Spires, Elizabeth, and Mordicai Gerstein. *I Am Arachne: Fifteen Greek and Roman Myths.* New York: Frances Foster Books, 2001.

Whiting, Jim. *The Life and Times of Hippocrates.* Hockessin, DE: Mitchell Lane Publishers, 2007.

## Hindu

Choudhury, Bani Roy, and Valmiki. *The Story of Ramayan: The Epic Tale of India.* New Delhi: Hemkunt Press; Pomona, CA: Distributed in North America by Auromere, 1970.

Dalal-Clayton, Diksha, and Marilyn Heeger. *The Adventures of Young Krishna: The Blue God of India.* New York: Oxford University Press, 1992.

Ganeri, Anita. *The* Ramayana *and Hinduism*. Mankato, MN: Smart Apple Media, 2003.

Ganeri, Anita, and Carole Gray. *Hindu Stories.* Minneapolis: Picture Window Books, 2006.

Ganeri, Anita, and Tracy Fennell. *Buddhist Stories.* Minneapolis: Picture Window Books, 2006.

Husain, Shahrukh, and Bee Willey. *Indian Myths.* London: Evans, 2007.

Kipling, Rudyard. *The Jungle Book.* New York: Sterling Pub., 2008.

Parker, Vic, and Philip Ardagh. *Traditional Tales from India.* Thameside Press; North Mankato, MN: Distributed in the United States by Smart Apple Media, 2001.

Sharma, Bulbul. *The* Ramayana *for Children*. Penguin Global, 2004.

Staples, Suzanne Fisher. *Shiva's Fire.* 1st ed. New York: Farrar Straus Giroux, 2000.

## Judeo-Christian

Geras, Adele. *My Grandmother's Stories: A Collection of Jewish Folk Tales.* New York: Alfred A. Knopf, 2003.

Kimmel, Eric A., and John Winch. *Brother Wolf, Sister Sparrow: Stories about Saints and Animals.* 1st ed. New York: Holiday House, 2003.

Schwartz, Howard, and Barbara Rush. *The Diamond Tree: Jewish Tales from Around the World.* 1st Harper Trophy ed. New York: HarperTrophy, 1998.

Schwartz, Howard, and Stephen Fieser. *Invisible Kingdoms: Jewish Tales of Angels, Spirits, and Demons.* 1st ed. New York: HarperCollins Publishers, 2002.

Self, David, and Nick Harris. *Stories from the Christian World.* Englewood Cliffs, NJ: Silver Burdett Press, 1988.

Senker, Cath. *Everyday Life in the Bible Lands.* North Mankato, MN: Smart Apple Media, 2006.

Taback, Simms. *Kibitzers and Fools: Tales My Zayda (Grandfather) Told Me.* New York: Puffin, 2008.

## Native American

Ardagh, Philip, and Syrah Arnold. *South American Myths & Legends.* Chicago: World Book, 2002.

Berk, Ari, and Carolyn Dunn Anderson. *Coyote Speaks: Wonders of the Native American World.* New York: Abrams Books for Young Readers, 2008.

Brown, Virginia Pounds, Laurella Owens, and Nathan H. Glick. *Southern Indian Myths and Legends.* Birmingham, AL: Beechwood Books, 1985.

Curry, Jane Louise. *The Wonderful Sky Boat and Other Native American Tales from the Southeast.* New York: Margaret K. McElderry, 2001.

Monroe, Jean Guard, and Ray A. Williamson. *They Dance in the Sky: Native American Star Myths.* Award ed. Boston: Houghton Mifflin, 1993.

Parker, Victoria. *Traditional Tales from South America.* North Mankato, MN: Thameside Press. Distributed in the United States by Smart Apple Media, 2001.

Philip, Neil. *The Great Mystery: Myths of Native America.* New York: Clarion Books, 2001.

Pijoan, Teresa. *White Wolf Woman: Native American Transformation Myths.* 1st ed. Little Rock, AR: August House Publishers, 1992.

Ramen, Fred. *Native American Mythology.* 1st ed. New York: Rosen Central, 2008.

Schomp, Virginia. *The Native Americans.* New York: Marshall Cavendish Benchmark, 2008.

Vogel, Carole G. *Weather Legends: Native American Lore and the Science of Weather.* Brookfield, CT: Millbrook Press, 2001.

### Near Eastern/Islamic

Ganeri, Anita. *Islamic Stories.* 1st American ed. Minneapolis, MN: Picture Window Books, 2006.

Grimal, Pierre. *Stories from Babylon and Persia.* Cleveland, OH: World Pub, 1964.

Ibrahim, Abdullahi A. *Enuma Elish.* Austin, TX: Steck-Vaughn Co., 1994.

Jabbari, Ahmad. *Amoo Norooz and Other Persian Folk Stories.* Costa Mesa, CA: Mazda Publishers, 2000.

León, Vicki. *Outrageous Women of Ancient Times.* New York: Wiley, 1998.

Marston, Elsa. *Figs and Fate: Stories about Growing Up in the Arab World Today.* 1st ed. New York: George Braziller, 2005.

Marston, Elsa. *Santa Claus in Baghdad and Other Stories about Teens in the Arab World.* Bloomington: Indiana University Press, 2008.

McCaughrean, Geraldine. *Gilgamesh the Hero.* Oxford: Oxford University Press, 2002.

Podany, Amanda H., and Marni McGee. *The Ancient Near Eastern World.* New York: Oxford University Press, 2005.

Schomp, Virginia. *The Ancient Mesopotamians.* New York: Marshall Cavendish Benchmark, 2008.

Walker, Barbara K. *Turkish Folk-Tales.* Oxford: Oxford University Press, 1993.

### Norse/Northern European

Andersen, H. C., Diana Frank, Jeffrey Frank, Vilhelm Pedersen, and Lorenz Frolich. *The Stories of Hans Christian Andersen: A New Translation from the Danish.* Durham: Duke University Press, 2005.

Ardagh, Philip, and Stephen May. *Norse Myths & Legends.* Chicago: World Book, 2002.

Branford, Henrietta, and Dave Bowyer. *The Theft of Thor's Hammer.* Crystal Lake, IL: Rigby Interactive Library, 1996.

D'Aulaire, Ingri, and Edgar Parin. *D'Aulaires' Book of Norse Myths.* New York: New York Review of Books, 2005.

Evan, Cheryl, and Anne Millard. *Usborne Illustrated Guide to Norse Myths and Legends.* London: Usborne, 2003.

Jones, Gwyn, and Joan Kiddell-Monroe. *Scandinavian Legends and Folk-Tales.* New ed. Oxford: Oxford University Press, 1992.

Osborne, Mary Pope. *Favorite Norse Myths.* New York: Scholastic, 2001.

Porterfield, Jason. *Scandinavian Mythology.* New York: Rosen Central, 2008.

### Web Sites

*American Folklore*. http://www.americanfolklore.net/ (accessed on June 11, 2008).

*The British Museum: Mesopotamia*. http://www.mesopotamia.co.uk/menu.html (accessed on June 11, 2008).

*The Camelot Project at the University of Rochester*. http://www.lib.rochester.edu/CAMELOT/cphome.stm (accessed on June 11, 2008).

*Common Elements in Creation Myths*. http://www.cs.williams.edu/~lindsey/myths (accessed on June 11, 2008).

*Egyptian Museum Official Site*. http://www.egyptianmuseum.gov.eg/ (accessed on June 11, 2008).

*Internet History Sourcebooks Project*. http://www.fordham.edu/halsall/ (accessed on June 11, 2008). Last updated on December 10, 2006.

*Iron Age Celts*. http://www.bbc.co.uk/wales/celts/ (accessed on June 11, 2008).

*Kidipede: History for Kids*. http://www.historyforkids.org/ (accessed on June 11, 2008).

*Mythography*. http://www.loggia.com/myth/myth.html (accessed on June 11, 2008). Last updated on April 17, 2008.

*National Geographic*. http://www.nationalgeographic.com/ (accessed on June 11, 2008).

*NOVA Online: The Vikings*. http://www.pbs.org/wgbh/nova/vikings/ (accessed on June 11, 2008).

*Perseus Project*. http://www.perseus.tufts.edu/ (accessed on June 11, 2008).

*Sanskrit Documents.* http://sanskritdocuments.org/ (accessed on June 11, 2008). Last updated on February 2, 2008.

*United Nations Educational, Scientific and Cultural Organization.* http://portal.unesco.org/ (accessed on June 11, 2008).

*World Myths & Legends in Art.* http://www.artsmia.org/world-myths/artbyculture/index.html (accessed on June 11, 2008).

# *Index*

*Italic* type indicates volume number; **boldface** type indicates main entries and their page numbers; (ill.) indicates photos and illustrations.

## A

## B

## D

## E

## F

## H

J

K

## M

N

## O

## P

## Q

## R

## S

## V

W

X

BOCA RATON PUBLIC LIBRARY, FLORIDA
3 3656 0483293 4